Issue | 150

RADICAL
HISTORY *Review*

Revolutionary Papers: Anticolonial Periodicals from the Global South
*Issue Editors: Mahvish Ahmad, Koni Benson, and Hana Morgenstern,
with Alex Lichtenstein*

Revolutionary Papers

The Counterinstitutions, Counterpolitics, and Countercultures of Anticolonial Periodicals

Mahvish Ahmad, Koni Benson, and Hana Morgenstern

In the early 1970s, an eighteen-year-old poet and writer joined the Communist Party of Pakistan (CPP) and was tasked with a simple but crucial responsibility: to diligently pick up fifteen to twenty copies of the party's monthly publication and ensure that they were delivered to a regular roster of readers.[1] Banned in 1954 as part of a global wave of anticommunism, the CPP had no access to formal printing presses and distribution networks for its newly established organ, *surkh parcham* (*Red Flag*). In response, the party set up a bare-bones underground infrastructure. Party members penned *surkh parcham*, converted this to stencil, covered it with ink, and hand-printed multiple mimeographs. The CPP cadre, including the young poet-writer, would replace formal distribution networks to circumvent policies of censorship. Often constituting the cadre's first act of disciplined, political work, distribution went hand in hand with reading *surkh parcham* and sometimes writing and editing the organ. In the case of Ahmad Salim, the young poet-writer, *surkh parcham* became a defining political and intellectual turning point, inaugurating a multidecade commitment to collectively building progressive politics and culture in Pakistan, a place characterized by imperially funded state repression and institutional neglect.

We begin this special issue on left, anticolonial periodicals of the global south with Ahmad Salim and his politicization through *surkh parcham* because his life history represents what journals do to people and what people can do with

Radical History Review
Issue 150 (October 2024)   DOI 10.1215/01636545-11257369

journals. *Surkh parcham* indexed Ahmad Salim's lifelong foray into left culture and politics, teaching him discipline through political work, intellectual production, and cultural expression. He became a regular contributor and joined the editorial board. He eventually spent his life contributing to the survival and flourishing of progressive culture and politics in Pakistan. Wearing many hats—including those of a political worker, editor, poet, historian, translator, journalist, researcher, teacher, folklorist, and archivist—Salim authored over 150 writings focusing on a dizzying array of topics, including multiple collections of Punjabi poetry, books on the left and oppressed nations in Pakistani history, and in-depth studies of labor, children, education, and religious minorities.[2] He joined forces with many figures and networks, including the Urdu literary giant and communist Faiz Ahmad Faiz[3] (whose work he translated into Punjabi), and as a member of other political parties on the left.[4] Often, this was done at a cost to his own livelihood and comfort; his love of history, literature, and politics meant he spent much time in poverty and in jail. Journals remained a central motif of his life. In Pakistan, a vibrant culture of periodicals found innovative ways to circumvent censorship, and Salim established, contributed to, or edited many of them.[5] In 2001, he established arguably the largest independent archive of progressive materials in Pakistan, the South Asian Research and Resource Center (SARRC), which today houses rare periodicals and other print ephemera central to the reproduction of progressive culture and movements in Pakistan (fig. 1).[6] A key collaborator in our multiyear, transnational investigation into left, anticolonial journals of the global south, Salim passed away as we were preparing this issue for *Radical History Review*. We dedicate this issue to him.

.   .   .   .   .

The Revolutionary Papers project has spent the last five years engaging in conversations, collaborations, and coproductions to unpack the role of the periodical in making left, anticolonial, and anti-imperial politics and cultures in the global south. This issue is a culmination of a larger project. As a transnational research and teaching initiative, Revolutionary Papers has included research and input from editors, archivists, and movement organizers like Ahmad Salim, as well as nearly a hundred university-based researchers. This issue of *Radical History Review*, also entitled "Revolutionary Papers," is just one arm of a larger set of activities. These include online workshops (2020) and a major international conference (2022) hosted at Community House in Cape Town, a site of historic anti-apartheid struggles and contemporary grassroots movements (figs 2–3).

It includes collaborations with archives of progressive and radical materials, most significantly a yearlong project with Ahmad Salim's forty-thousand-item collection. Throughout 2023, we coedited a research-based blog series on the archival remnants of African and Black diaspora anticolonial movement materials in a contemporary site of opinion, analysis, and new writing of the African left, *Africa Is a*

Figure 1. A screenshot from a video introducing Ahmad Salim and the South Asian Research and Resource Center, SARRC. Here, Salim holds *surkh parcham* in his hands, flicking through it and talking about it. Visit his website at www.sarrc.org.pk.

Country.[7] And over the past five years, we have developed a digital platform at revolutionarypapers.org that hosts a growing repository of digital teaching tools on periodicals from Palestine, Pakistan, Tunisia, South Africa, Cuba, India, and elsewhere.[8] Our first two teaching tools were based on journals collected and conserved by Ahmad Salim.[9] With this issue, we launch a fresh crop of tools out of Kenya, Palestine, Namibia, Oman, Chile, and the broader Third World, embodied in the famous transnational publication published out of Beirut, *Lotus*.

In this issue of *Radical History Review*, we deepen our research and teaching project through a focus on a wide array of periodicals that circulated throughout the global south in the twentieth and into the twenty-first centuries. The issue begins with six feature essays in a section entitled "Engaging Revolutionary Periodicals." This section challenges us to expand our studies of the periodical and left anticolonialism more broadly, as well as what constitutes the geographies of the global south. Through essays from China, Cuba, South Africa, Ka Pae 'Āina o Hawai'i (the Hawaiian archipelago), Ethiopia, and the broader Black Atlantic, each study makes key intellectual and political interventions in our understanding of the revolutionary and the place of the periodical in the past and present. The second half of the issue is dedicated to seven teaching tools, most developed exclusively for this special issue, introduced by an essay on periodicals as political pedagogy by our key collaborator, the literary scholar, political organizer, and artist Sara Kazmi. This section, entitled "Periodicals as Digital Pedagogy: Archival Tools for Political Education," is coedited by Kazmi and Hana Morgenstern. The issue combines scholarship, education, and organizing in a deliberate effort to mirror an approach we have found central to revolutionary politics, cultures, and papers. We strive to reproduce, in other words,

Figure 2. *Quiet Dog, Bite Hard! Clandestine Networks of Revolutionary Papers*,
a traveling exhibition by Phokeng Setai at the conference "Revolutionary Papers:
Counter-institutions, Politics, and Culture in Periodicals of the Global South,"
Community House, Cape Town, South Africa, April 28–30, 2022. Photo: Ruvan
Boshoff.

Figure 3. Revolutionary Papers Conference 2022. Teaching Tool on the
Revolutionary Papers website: https://revolutionarypapers.org/teaching-tool
/revolutionary-papers-conference/.

the antipartitionist ethics that formed journals like *surkh parcham* and people like
Ahmad Salim.[10]

In this essay, we lay the conceptual and political groundwork for the larger
project which informs this special issue. We begin by introducing our expansive definition of revolutionary periodicals of the global south. The next section argues that
these materials offer an alternate method for studying and practicing left anticolonialism (Toward the Journal as Method). We propose an analytical approach to periodicals that allows us to unpack the place of the journal in building left, anticolonial institutions, politics, and cultures. Finally, we discuss how the essays in this issue have
engaged with this approach (Countering Power: Building Left Institutions, Politics,
and Cultures), deepening and complicating our understanding of radical periodicals.

Revolutionary Periodicals of the Global South

Like the rest of our project, this issue encompasses periodicals and related movement materials, which includes newspapers, magazines, pamphlets, handbills, and other serialized public communiqués. What holds our terms together is that these materials were published on paper, usually in a serialized format, meaning they include handbills and communiqués that came out more than once, like mimeographs published during the 1989 prodemocracy movement in Tiananmen Square (Li, this issue) or the Palestinian *bayanat* that circulated regularly during the First Intifada (Hastings, this issue). Occasionally we include movement materials and print that do not fall into the periodical's precise remit in that they were issued only once, as in the case of *US Imperialism in Ethiopia*, a pamphlet transcribed by hand in the late 1960s critical to Ethiopian anti-imperial thought (Alemu, this issue).

We understand these periodicals as revolutionary insofar as they emerged with a structural critique of regimes of power and sought in one way or another to uproot those structures and regimes. Their purpose was to revolutionize societies and cultures. The political formations behind these ideas and the visions of revolution pursued exist on a continuum. They include the publications of parties and organizations actively interested in overthrowing existing colonial governments as well as community and civic organizations aimed at mobilizing for alternative social and cultural life. They also include diasporic journals aimed at supporting movements abroad or radical political and cultural projects in the West. And finally, they include cultural journals aimed at revolutionizing art, language, and literary form.

Many of the periodicals under consideration were associated with communist, socialist, or national liberation parties, anticolonial or anti-imperial movements, or related organizations like student or labor unions. Although we limit our study to antiauthoritarian publications, some journals were hierarchical or beholden to specific party lines. A vanguardist structure was, after all, one of the forms taken by left, anticolonial organizations. Other publications fall more broadly into universalist or nonaligned internationalisms and anticolonial projects, including those run by artists, thinkers, and organizers. The plurality of proposals on how to manifest revolutionary politics and culture reflects the rich conversations and disagreements that took place across these journals. Indeed, intense debate took place within and across journals on the content and contours of revolution. For example, political formations marginal to larger national liberation movements would use periodicals as a space to analyze how colonial, imperial, capitalist, patriarchal, casteist, or other hegemonic logics and practices survived even in spaces professing to be revolutionary.

Yet, while an understanding of the revolutionary differed across and even within periodicals, they largely shared what we understand as an antipartitionist approach, or a refusal to segregate politics and economics from culture and the arts. Instead, art, literature, education, protest, critical economic analysis, and political organizing were often seen as interconnected and mutually reinforcing elements necessary for the attainment of consciousness and liberation. This is reflected in news articles, essays, literature, and artworks that were printed on neighboring pages, forming interesting continuums and conversations. Many radicals, like the Palestinian Ghassan Kanafani, Neville Alexander in South Africa, and Ahmad Salim in Pakistan, mirrored this approach by acting simultaneously as editors, critics, organizers, poets, archivists, or scholars. If decolonization requires pulling the existing colonial structure up by the roots and replacing it with liberatory ideas and practices, then this requires work across political, cultural, and social arenas.

We deploy the term *global south* as an imprecise yet critical outgrowth of the idea or project of the "Third World" so central to the imaginary of many of these publications.[11] Framed by anticolonial and postcolonial movements, the Third World highlights the regional visions, solidarities and tricontinentalisms linking the decolonizing countries of Africa, Asia, and Latin America, especially in the first three decades following World War II (fig 4). Most periodicals showcased in our project and in this special issue are associated with this latter period of anticolonial struggle, known as the heyday of decolonization. Global south diaspora and minoritized communities are another major site of radical journals, especially those fighting for decolonization, including Indigenous communities in settler colonial contexts like North America and Australia. Finally, from the postindependence period onward, the global south encompasses the failure of the democratic and socialist ambitions of anticolonial movements in neocolonial states and the continuation of imperial and colonial dynamics, especially through the adoption of capitalist logics and neoliberal policies. This includes extractive and exploitative global capital, military occupation, extreme inequality, majoritarianism, authoritarianism, climate catastrophe, global crises of democracy, and crises of displaced persons and refugees. Within this issue, periodicals associated with this period include those tied to Palestinian liberation during and after the first Intifada, the anti-apartheid movement in South Africa, antiauthoritarian struggles in Kenya, the prodemocracy movement in China, Indigenous movements for decolonization in Ka Pae ʻĀina o Hawaiʻi, and popular front politics in Cuba. What becomes clear as we read within and across these journals is that, like the revolutionary, what constitutes anticolonial geographies of liberation shifts depending on context, history, and political orientation. The global south is both material and imagined, connected through similar forms of material subjugation and defined through political discourse and struggle.

Toward the Journal as Method

Periodicals of the global south offer us a new method for critiquing and overturning colonialism and intervening in how anticolonialism is studied and practiced in the twenty-first century. We believe that far too many scholars study these materials while distancing their work from contemporary political questions and movements. As we write, we find the starkest example of this in the tepid responses to the genocidal onslaught by the Israeli state on Palestinians in Gaza by many who have built

Figure 4. *Tricontinental* Bulletin no. 66, September 1971. Published
by the Organization of Solidarity with the People of Asia, Africa, and
Latin America (OSPAAAL). This edition included articles on Mexico's
Second Tlateloco, a deadly attack on students in Mexico City on June 10,
1971, resembling the 1968 Tlatelolco military massacre aimed at students
of the National Autonomous University of Mexico; a letter written from
Angela Davis from Marin County Jail on June 14, 1971 to Mexican political
prisoners; an article on a Principled Solution from Vietnam by Huynh Van
Ba; an article on the violent realities of oil for the people of Venezuela by
Eduardo Galeano; "Palestine: People's Revolution, an interview with
Yasser Arafat," by Osvaldo Ortego; an article about radical priests in
Colombia, "Cristianism and Marxism" by Josem Mayo; and a final
section for "appeals and messages." Courtesy of The Freedom Archives.

careers publicly critiquing racism and colonialism. The disconnect between practicing "radical" scholarship and practicing radical politics is indicative of many of the
problems outlined below. Against this disconnect, Revolutionary Papers calls on
scholars to harness these movement histories in order to reflect and act on the injustices and issues of our times.

Like others who study colonialism and anticolonialism, we seek to foreground the periodical as an important archive. Yet we also take issue with how periodicals and anticolonial archives more generally are approached as repositories from which we lift articles and insights that are then integrated into scholarship. In far too many cases, archival materials are delinked from their radical politics, fetishized and commodified as part of a new interest in anticolonial print and art.[12] In contrast, we believe that journals offer us an alternative form for theorizing and practicing anticolonialism. Thus we propose to view the journal as method rather than (merely) as source.

We are not the first to offer a site like the journal as a method. In recent decades, many scholars have proposed the framing of disparate objects and locations—the ocean, the body, Asia, Malaysia, China, intersectionality, or utopia—as frameworks for new methodologies. What these scholars have in common is a concern with "the way one thinks, not what one thinks about."[13] Their purpose is "programmatic and oppositional, in that each study proposes an alternative methodological approach while also critically interrogating an existing set of analytical practices."[14] Our own method centers on the notion that anticolonial journals functioned as revolutionary, counterhegemonic tools of worldmaking. In the midst of repression and ruin, journals fostered provisional *counterinstitutions* through the labor of political and cultural workers. They became the means for the circulation of *counterpolitical* ideas that emerged from collective and dynamic conversations between multiple people and movements. And they offered opportunities for experimentation with new *countercultural* forms necessary for the creation of resistant and liberatory social consciousness (fig. 5).

In contrast to these counterhegemonic methods, the study of anticolonialism and postcolonialism is largely approached through a fixation on the Western episteme, individual thinkers (as opposed to collective labor), established fields and disciplinary (rather than antidisciplinary) orientations, and static canons versus thought in action. From the 1980s onward, postcolonial studies have been especially influenced by these modalities. Though the field is shifting significantly, it has traditionally been dominated by the project of unearthing the imperial and colonial logics that underpin existing disciplines and institutions,[15] part of a decades-old preoccupation with displacing "the truth-claims of Eurocentric discourses" and "interven[ing] in and interrupt[ing] the Western discourses on modernity."[16] Though critically important, postcolonial studies focus on the West has paradoxically elided history's most important critics of colonialism, namely the political, social, and cultural movements that established decolonization and ousted colonial powers. Individuals and institutions that continue to distance themselves from one of the most important, anticolonial struggles of the twenty-first century—the Palestinian national liberation movement—amplify this decontextualized orientation. In more extreme cases, they repress solidarity with the Palestinian struggle.

The problem of method manifests itself equally in academic canonization, which plucks great authors, works, figures, and ideas out of the crowd and elevates them into disciplinary recognition. Scholars have rightfully sought to expand the Eurocentric canon, by focusing on the works of seminal thinkers like Frantz Fanon, W. E. B. Du Bois, Aimé Césaire, Mahatma Gandhi, or Ngũgĩ wa Thiong'o.[17] Yet canonization has defined postcolonial and decolonial studies around the work of these individuals, who are sometimes referred to as the "big men" of anticolonial history.[18] A move to pluralize this field, then, inadvertently falls back on an individuated search for expertise and mastery. Another result of canonical framing is that the field of postcolonial literature and decolonial social and political theory is largely dominated by the oeuvre of individual authors, while histories of cultural and literary movements fall to the margins. This approach not only overlooks but indeed negates the counterhegemonic logics of decolonization, in which ideas and art were not the products of individual genius but of collective social processes. It also elides the centrality of antidisciplinarity in anticolonial movements. The consequence of all of this is, of course, that we read thinkers out of joint with the movements and debates from which they emerged, erasing collective labor and conversations.

In historical studies, critics of people's history have claimed that accounts "from below" can be uncritical, oversimplified, and romantic approaches to the working classes or that they have imposed a homogenous radical vision onto the "masses."[19] Marxist historiography has come under critique for similar reasons. Yet, inspired by historians challenging power in history writing,[20] we argue that a critical reading of both the product and the production of movements and the materials they produced can offer a deep and layered sense of social process necessary for social history. A careful reading of these materials and the power dynamics they were immersed in, in fact, offers us (often inconvenient) complexity about both the history at hand and our approach to engaging it, rather than oversimplified correctives. As Howard Zinn reminds us in the preface to *A People's History of the Third World*, "a people's history does more than add to the catalogue of what we already know."[21]

It is our hope that the anticolonial journal can offer some tools for addressing these critiques. For us, the shift in method involves the understanding that periodicals provide a view into the counterhegemonic processes central to decolonization that individual texts cannot. Indeed, it is precisely the provisional and conversational nature of this form that lends the periodical its oppositional capacities.

To begin with, in its plurality of authors and workers, the journal reminds us that anticolonialism is a process that requires a laboring collective. The production, circulation, and reading of anticolonial journals involved a wide range of people who made the journal happen and were transformed in the process. Everything that made it onto its pages was the product of a process, a set of relations, and labor that included editors, writers, translators, printers, distributors, artists, and readers.[22] These networks extended to the counterpublics that were influenced and produced by periodicals and in turn influenced and produced a periodical's publication and editorial decisions. Centering collective work and infrastructure highlights the periodical as a social and reproductive space, which we elaborate on when discussing the notion of the counterinstitutional below. As Merve Fejzula argues, "we must incorporate 'movement chores' into intellectual history's purview."[23] In a powerful essay reconstructing gendered labor in the making of the 1956 Congress of Black Writers and Artists, Fejzula shows how these chores were often feminized, taking place in "reproductive settings like the home and cafés" in ways that reveal the immense, invisible labor that made anticolonial intellection, including literatures and arts, possible.[24]

Likewise, when we view anticolonial thought through the lens of collective process the journal emerges as a self-theorizing text. The periodical's many authors and workers theorized power and social change through many media and across time. And yet we often treat these journals as primary sources, producing a division between who does politics and who does theory. By approaching the journal as a method rather than a source, we interrupt the binary between primary and secondary and insist that these journals—and the people that made them—were makers and writers of history and producers of anticolonial theory. To recognize the vibrant counterpolitical concepts that circulated in periodicals as "social theory" requires breaking with an attachment to theory as an object of individual authorship and as a tract of writing that takes place at a distance from political struggle. It requires opening up to ideas circulating quickly, embedded in the heat of struggle.

The notion of collective authorship also has consequences for how anticolonialism is researched and taught. In social and political theory, it means paying less attention to Fanon the individual and more to the movements that surrounded him and the debates in which he was enmeshed. It requires that we turn back toward what David Scott calls the "problem spaces"[25] of anticolonialism, a discursive space made up of an "ensemble of questions and answers around which a horizon of identifiable stakes (conceptual as well as ideological-political stakes) hangs."[26] We might look at social rather than individual thought as the place where questions were asked, unsettled, and worked out through processes of dialogue and disagreement.

The journal's local and time-bound nature also reminds us that these questions were geared toward specific political, historical, and cultural contexts. We are reminded that most anticolonial intellectuals were busy trying to understand how phenomena like race, colonialism, empire, and capital manifested in their locales. These were not universal terms but forces that showed up differently across time and space and intersected with emplaced, precolonial forms of hierarchy (like caste). These questions were often worked through in literature or art that combined local elements such as folklore with transnational anticolonial forms such as

Figure 5. *Staffrider* magazine, vol. 2, no. July/August 1979, in
Nombuso Mathibela "Transient Literatures and Maps," *Africa is a
Country*, special series on Revolutionary Papers, June 30, 2023, https://
africasacountry.com/2023/06/transient-literatures-and-maps.

surrealism. The worldmaking constituted through thought and imagination were
key elements in the countercultures fostered by periodicals in the midst of
decolonization.

In offering the journal as a method for doing anticolonialism differently, we
are building on other interventions centering anticolonial movements and periodicals in recent years.[27] This includes work that highlights the journal as an infrastructure and aesthetic forum necessary for publishing outside the colony and the Western metropole.[28] The consequences of these multiple interventions on the way we
approach anticolonialism are immense, and each brings attention to certain tacit
assumptions embedded in existing approaches. One of the more direct ways that
we mirror this method of practicing anticolonialism differently is through our digital
teaching tools. These have been designed to address journals as a present-day

method to practicing anticolonialism and not just as a source for the past. Just as anticolonial periodicals intended to communicate, educate, agitate, and connect so too does Revolutionary Papers experiment with forms of alternative pedagogy for a wider and deeper engagement with movement materials. In "The Periodical as Political Educator: Anticolonial Print and Digital Humanities in the Classroom and Beyond," section coeditor Sara Kazmi reflects on this topic in the movements that produced the periodicals and through the Revolutionary Papers teaching tool initiative today. These tools are designed as interactive digital presentations for scholars, students, organizers, and activists to engage and learn directly from and with anticolonial and left periodicals, understanding them in their wider context. At the same time, the digital pages offer alternative history and pedagogical guides for educators and organizers to revisit key questions around history, politics, and culture in the present. Kazmi demonstrates how teaching tools offer an alternative curriculum that can connect anticolonial knowledges with political struggle. As an experiment in anticolonial pedagogy in the present, our digital teaching tools are one attempt to excavate earlier imaginaries of decolonization that can shape present resistance to neoliberal knowledge and potentially inform contemporary political organizing.

Countering Power: Building Left Institutions, Politics, and Cultures

To fully realize the journal as method, periodicals must be approached in an expansive manner. We propose the hermeneutic of the counterinstitutional, the counterpolitical, and the countercultural to facilitate this. What constitutes the counterhegemonic is not static across time and space or even contemporaneous journals in the same site. These journals force us to be sensitive to the plurality of lefts and anticolonialisms imagined in response to power, even as they reveal a surprising consistency in ideas of the revolutionary across the global south. The counterinstitutional helps tease out how periodicals acted as alternatives to colonial and neocolonial institutions, or as vehicles of recovery in the aftermath of destruction, serving as and catalyzing new infrastructures, organizations, and networks. The counterpolitical narrows in on how the periodical facilitated critiques and alternatives, often underground, through the articulation of translated and novel political vocabularies and ideas. The countercultural shows how periodicals fostered local literary and art scenes outside the colonial sphere and the Western metropole, challenging and reconstituting the aesthetic and literary parameters of anticolonial and postcolonial cultural production.

Building Counterinstitutions

Periodicals were one of the tools anticolonial movements used to build new worlds during the ruins and erasure of colonialism, imperialism, and authoritarianism. They functioned as radical alternatives to political or cultural institutions that either did not exist, had been repressed or destroyed, or were only active in the context of an existing colonial or authoritarian apparatus. As low-cost, flexible publishing venues, periodicals circulated easily, nurturing local and regional culture through the publication of new thinkers and the transmission of ideas and information. Many periodicals constituted alternative organizations in themselves, communities of left critique and action. And many played an incubation role for new organizations and movements and local and international networks, scenes, readerships and counterpublics.

For us, then, the counterinstitutional encompasses the social and material histories of periodicals and requires us to approach the journal through a materialist lens, attentive to the concrete practices that made the journal and that the journal helped create. We read for histories of collective, institution and network formation, both those documented in the pages of the journal (such as weekly or monthly reports from intellectual or political clubs or reports on conferences in different parts of the world) and the social histories of production, circulation, and sparks journals nurtured. We consider the journal as an archive of cultural infrastructure and movement-building history and a catalyst and tool of organizational formation. Here we unpack and appreciate how counterinstitutional practices were constituted through the writing, production, distribution, and reading of these papers. Specifically, we highlight anticolonial publication practices as collective endeavors, vehicles for transnational and transtemporal alliance building, organizing, education, and mobilizing tools, and as catalysts and platforms of new publics producing political, literary, and cultural scenes.

First, the making of periodicals was a social and relational process, binding many people together in the formation of new organizations, work sites, networks, and tendencies. These were curated spaces that connected political organizers, writers, editors, translators, distributors, artists, readers, printers, and more in the work of putting editions together. If we look at the backstage work, the tables of contents, ads, announcements, and attributions, the people that came together in the process of producing and disseminating these papers, and the conversations and links created by them, we can map the evolution of broader cultural and political collectives and movements that constituted the conditions of possibility for the journals.

The range of democratic practice within editorial collectives varies widely. For instance, in a teaching tool prepared for the larger Revolutionary Papers project, Sam Longford shows how *Dawn*, the official organ of Umkhonto weSizwe (MK), the armed wing of the African National Congress (ANC), functioned as a device to discipline the cadre.[29] Yet a significant number of anticolonial left periodicals were intended as collaborative spaces to think, imagine, and strategize. As Katerina Gonzalez Seligmann notes, the creation of the cultural magazine *Tropiques* by Suzanne and Aimé Césaire and their friends in Martinique in the 1940s emerged from what they articulated as the need for a "bureau de pensée" (thought office) and a "centre de réflexion" (center for reflection).[30] In parallel, Koni Benson, Asher Gamedze, and Nashilongweshipwe Mushaandja, in a digital teaching tool prepared for this special issue, highlight that the *Namibian Review* was governed by a constitution that envisioned a collective, anti-imperialist, anticolonial, and antiracist "platform" to "serve as the instrument and conscience of national unity," a space for "political dialogue," and for the "broadest possible united front against foreign domination."[31]

Second, periodicals helped forge cross-border and transtemporal relationships in and through the production and circulation of materials, as they constituted political communities and formed links that countered the limits of existing colonial spatial impositions and historical imaginations. As transnational bridges and key tools of alliance building, these publications were key to forging local and internationalist solidarity. Deemed scaffolds, mouthpieces, or organs, these vehicles of communication and connection enabled alternative networks and social formations beyond the localized and international divide and rule at the heart of coloniality.

The broader project of socialist internationalism abounds with examples of movement-related solidarity publications that reimagined and built anti-imperial, anticolonial, and antiracist networks as Afro-Asian, Pan-African, Pan-Arab, or African diaspora. This was the mission of the *Tricontinental*, founded in 1967 by the Organization of Solidarity of the Peoples of Africa, Asia, and Latin America (OSPAAAL) following the first Tricontinental conference. This well-known periodical, published in Havana, covered topics from national liberation movements to the capitalist exploitation of natural resources, imperial policies, and international solidarity between leftist political movements across Africa, Asia, and Latin America. For instance, the literary and cultural journal *Lotus: Afro-Asian Writings*, published in Arabic, English, and French from 1968 to 1991, was established by the Afro-Asian Writers Association in 1958 with the goal of supporting solidarity of the nonaligned movement at its seminal Bandung conference in 1955. In a teaching tool prepared for this special issue, Sara Marzagora and Rafeef Ziadah present *Lotus* as part of infrastructures of solidarity forged between different movements, connecting networks of writers, authors, and exhibits to create, theorize, and build relations across anticolonial struggles.[32]

Beyond the coverage of anticolonial movements elsewhere, many papers held space when particular politics could not take organized political form, enabling transnational alliances and connections of places across time. Tony Wood shows us this in his essay "Fighting Fascism on Empire's Doorstep: *Mediodía* and Popular Front Politics in 1930s Cuba." According to Wood, the 1930s left Cuban magazine *Mediodía* saw itself as a "cause of Cuban democracy and of a new national independence." It thus took a Popular Front strategy in its editorial approach to build public consensus against fascism at a time when most communist parties were illegal and had to operate clandestinely. A "Popular Front culture" in Cuba, argues Wood, "developed predominantly through the articulation of a leftist internationalism." Limited press freedom meant that urgent questions about imperialism, sovereignty, racial inequality, and social justice could not be debated openly. By highlighting the systemic nature of the common enemies in reportage on events in Nanjing or Barcelona, in the Spanish Civil War, or in Chinese resistance to Japanese occupation, *Mediodía* enabled the development of antifascist counterpolitics. These 1930s collective writings and juxtapositions of local and international struggles were important precursors for building alternative links and imaginations, which Wood argues laid the groundwork for the surge of internationalism two decades later in the Cuban Revolution. A similar new mapping of milestones in the revolutionary history of Kenya emerges in the teaching tool of the Ukombozi Library by Njoki Wamai, Wairimu Gathimba, and Kimani Waweru, prepared for this issue. Here, dissident journals uncover an alternative history of regimes and resistances that challenge conventional disconnections between the colonial and postcolonial periods.

Third, the periodical can be understood as an organizer, mobilizer, and political educator. This is brought into sharp focus in Noor Nieftagodien's essay for this issue, "*Congress Militant*: Revolutionary Paper as Political Organizer." In his study of *Inqaba ya Basebenzi* and *Congress Militant* (1981–90), the journal and paper of the Marxist Workers' Tendency of the ANC, Nieftagodien argues that these papers functioned as socialist tools of political organizing aimed at transforming the ANC into a mass anti-apartheid organization of the working class. He notes that the Tendency's ideas about the role of its paper was derived from Lenin's explanation of the purposes of *Iskra*, the official organ of the Russian Democratic Labour Party (1900–1905): a "newspaper is not only a collective propagandist and a collective agitator, it is also a collective organizer." A paper "may be compared to the scaffolding erected around a building under construction; it marks the contours of the structure and facilitates communication between the builders, permitting them to distribute the work and to view the common results achieved by their organized labor."[33] As a historian who was a youth activist in the 1980s with groups that joined the Tendency, Nieftagodien shows how "the entire cycle of producing the paper—from writing to editing and dissemination—was integrally woven into the structure and the activities of the organization."

Fourth, some serialized materials became an outlet for widespread public opinion, organizing and self-fashioning, establishing what Promise Li describes as a kind of public square. In his essay for this issue, "From Mimeographs to Self-organization: Beijing Workers' Writings in the 1989 Tiananmen Movement," Li studies the creation and circulation of daily handbills by the Workers' Autonomous Federation (WAF) in Beijing as an example of how democratic political spaces can be forged through periodicals. Li argues that these writings—small leaflets containing workers' writings, public letters, calls for direct action, manifestos, and poetry circulated and posted on Beijing walls daily throughout April to June 1989—

represent efforts to create "an inchoate civil society" under authoritarian conditions, "stimulating everyday citizens' capacity for political self-activity." The handbills developed into agitational leaflets with clear demands, and in form and content they served as a public square, a space created by WAF outside the bounds of the Chinese state. Li tracks this development "from mimeographs to self-organization," which is but one manifestation of the kinds of sparks revolutionary papers intended to ignite. After all, *iskra* means "spark" in many Slavic languages and became a common name for many movement self-publications, including *Cheche Magazine* (*Spark* in Kiswahili), the radical, socialist student magazine at the University of Dar es Salaam, which was banned in the late 1960s.[34]

    We are introduced to another serial form that opened new vistas of public space in Thayer Hastings's teaching tool prepared for this issue on the *bayanat*, or communiqués, posted on walls to organize, shape, and sustain public participation during the First Intifada, the Palestinian popular uprising against repressive Israeli military rule (1987 to the early 1990s). The communiqués were a locus through which protests, general strikes, and other community gatherings were coordinated, as well as a forum for news and political critique about the military occupation and the resistance. Hastings argues that a public was defined and animated through circulating, concealing, reading, and implementing calls to action articulated in the *bayanat*. Through its function as a flexible notice board, the *bayanat* enabled a reclaiming of public and political space from the occupation, in turn reflecting and strengthening the self-conception of Palestinian civil society as a counterinstitutional move.

Articulating Counterpolitics

As we can see in the example of WAF's handbills and the Palestinian *bayanat*, the importance of periodicals lay not only in their unique organizational capacities but also in specific resources they offered in relation to the development of public discourses and ideas. Expanding who had access to the "means of publication" on a regular, affordable basis, newspapers, handbills, and/or magazines were platforms for anticolonial, antiauthoritarian intellection and discourse. These scenes were precarious. The publications often operated without the patronage of state and elites, under violent colonial and authoritarian conditions, and in politically urgent times. The primary aim of their ideas was not "only to interpret the world" but to "change it."[35] As a result, counterpolitical concepts had specific foci and took on distinct shapes on the pages of periodicals. Ideas had to circulate in a way that allowed them to escape capture and destruction by empire, states, elites, and majorities, while simultaneously fueling the collective formation of oppositional political consciousness that could be mobilized against power. It was critical, then, to locate print forms that did not require support from established publishing houses, media outfits, or academic institutions, as well as print that was low cost and papers easy to carry and smuggle.[36]

The print form of the anticolonial periodical as a collection of genres—whether they be news journalism, essays, letters to the editor, records of debates, or short stories—more easily mirrors the pace of political events than any monograph could. With multiple and dialogic authorships and reports on conferences and events, periodicals reflected social debate and the development of ideas as accumulated through multiple perspectives, opinions, and responses, developing and shifting across time. Indeed, to recognize the vibrant counterpolitical concepts that circulated in periodicals as "social theory" requires a break with an attachment to theory as an object of individual authorship, as writing that takes place at a distance from political struggle.[37] It requires an opening up to ideas circulating quickly, embedded in the heat of struggle.

Reading across periodicals in such a manner can reveal how many became forums for the development of unique conceptual vocabularies on a collective scale. In this regard, the subject and method of revolutionary politics constitute one area of focus. A second, recurrent focus in radical papers dealt with conceptualizing the spatial and temporal scale of revolutionary politics in various sites across the global south. A number of periodicals thus became forums for new vocabularies meant to facilitate links between universalist visions of socialist, anticolonial worlds and the contingencies of particular struggles. Should a movement to radically overturn an existing colonial order come from the factory floor or the rural hinterlands, through the worker or the landless peasant, for instance? Should they wait for capitalism's internal contradictions to manifest themselves in a crisis, or force this crisis to come about immediately through armed uprising? Though these debates are in one way quite canonical in major Marxist writings, periodicals offer us insight into a plurality of attempts to expand and apply the scale of revolution across various contexts in the decolonizing world. For instance, in a teaching tool for this issue, Marral Shamshiri shows how *Sawt-al-Thawra* (*Voice of the Revolution*)—a weekly bulletin published by the Popular Front for the Liberation of Oman and the Arabian Gulf (PFLOAG)—placed the Dhofar Revolution within the global constellation of revolutionary Third World, leftist, and anticolonial networks including the Palestinian and Iranian Left, national liberation movements from Cuba to Vietnam, global women's liberation, and the New Left.

Three kinds of vocabularies recur in journals that attempted to do this work of connection. First, within and across radical papers, writers translated or transliterated global revolutionary vocabularies across languages. Terms like *capitalism*, *imperialism*, *colonialism*, *feminism*, *feudalism*, *socialism*, and *communism*—all terms of European provenance—were worked out in disparate southern contexts in many languages. This working out included not merely a linguistic translation but a political one. Periodicals operated as paper platforms where radicals could critically reflect on a particular term's ability to tie local conditions to broader structures of power while simultaneously retaining an explanatory force that unmasked the specific operations of power on southern ground.

For instance, Amsale Alemu traces how a plurality of Ethiopian radical prints—specifically "journals, stand-alone pamphlets, and reprinted issues created and distributed among organizations based in Addis Ababa, North America, and Europe"—occasioned an intergenerational and geographically dispersed working through of how US imperialism materializes in an Ethiopian context. In "Clandestine Issues: Tracing US Imperialism across Ethiopian Revolutionary Papers," Alemu argues that this "was a necessary step to clarify and link the Ethiopian revolutionary struggle to anticolonialism" around the world. Alemu argues that Ethiopian revolutionary thought, which during the 1974 Ethiopian Revolution avowed Marxist-Leninism, "required an anticolonial argument, precisely to make the case for the world-historical problematic of what they alleged was Ethiopian feudo-capitalism." Alemu goes on to show how a plurality of prints helped generate the "problem space of this anticolonial argument." The very materiality of the papers reviewed is what made possible the mobilization of US imperialism as a key analytic in Ethiopian revolutionary politics, prior to the 1974 revolution. It is precisely because it was printed inside and outside Ethiopia that the analysis of US imperialism could eventually be deepened.

Second, periodicals became the means through which individuals and movements mobilized terms from non-European linguistic worlds, turning these terms themselves into forums and tools for occasioning revolutionary connections. Sometimes, non-European terms have traveled to become part of a global revolutionary lexicon. We see this today; as we witness the largest global protests in solidarity with Palestine in history, *Intifada* in slogans like "There is only one solution! Intifada, revolution!" has emerged out of a particular anticolonial and Arab-speaking context to signify universalist resistance against settler colonialism, apartheid, racism, and imperialism everywhere. This is alongside its widespread invocation as a term for uprising, rebellion, and the "shaking off" of all sorts of oppressive structures across the Arab-speaking world. At other times, non-European terms have been mobilized to ensure that local imaginaries are plugged into global revolutionary politics.

For instance, in an essay entitled "'Ka Aina No Ka Poe o Hawaii': Kokua Hawaii's *Huli* Newspaper, 1971–73" for this special issue, Aaron Katzeman and Drew Kahuʻāina Broderick study *Huli*, a semiregular newspaper issued by the grassroots political organization Kōkua Hawaiʻi. They show how *huli*, both the concept and the periodical, was mobilized to encourage a commitment to "shared struggle across racial, ethnic, and cultural backgrounds in opposition to intensifying capital investment and US military entrenchment in Ka Pae ʻĀina o Hawaiʻi, the Hawaiian archipelago, following US 'statehood.'" *Huli*, which denotes a "desire to 'overturn,' or 'the need to transform the current political and economic system to construct a new order, not merely soften up the existing one,'" according to the "prominent Hawaiian sovereignty leader, anti-imperialist activist, poet, and political science scholar Haunani-Kay Trask," is mobilized in this periodical as a conceptual medium to connect the nascent Hawaiian sovereignty movement to the anticolonial, liberatory politics of the Third World in the 1970s. Katzeman and Broderick challenge in particular a nativist, identitarian, and exclusionary idea of what constitutes the histories of Hawai'i's sovereignty movement, showing instead that the desire to transform was deeply interlinked with class struggle across racial and ethnic lines.

Finally, figures and places travel through periodicals to signify particular imperial and colonial conditions as well as possible imaginations for shapes that resistance could take. So we see recurrent invocations of Patrice Lumumba, Ho Chi Minh, Che Guevara, Mao Zedong, Vietnam, Ethiopia, South Africa, and Palestine as shorthand for imperial violence and anti-imperial resistance (fig. 6). A portrait of Ho Chi Minh, for instance, adorns the cover of the Mazdoor Kissan Party Circular, an organ of Pakistan's Workers and Peasants Party, as the party invokes transnational peasant movements. In their teaching tool on APSI magazine, included in this issue, Pablo Álvarez and Francisco Rodriguez show how journalists invoked dictatorships in Argentina and Brazil to indirectly talk about Pinochet in Chile, and used the 1987 First Palestinian Intifada to speak surreptitiously about conditions of protest and repression in Chile. Similarly, Corinne Sandwith, who presented on the newspaper of the Communist Party of South Africa at the 2022 Revolutionary Papers conference in Cape Town, analyzed how "Ethiopia" became a trope in political cartoons published by the paper, providing a kind of visual pedagogy in counterpolitical modes of debate and participation. She stressed the affective labor performed by the newspaper through these visual depictions, alongside its detailed documentation of atrocity and its practice of "truth-telling against the lies of the state," sharing contrasting representations of Mussolini and Zulu warriors to illustrate her point. Time and time again, periodicals invoked revolutionary figures, places, and events as symbolic shorthand for shared repressions and visions for liberation politics. It would require another project to unpack, for instance, the work that any one of these invoked; for instance an entire book could be written just on the shared and divergent meanings of Ho Chi Minh and Vietnam across southern radical papers.

Practicing Countercultures

Periodicals fostered local literary and art scenes as alternatives to the colonial sphere and the Western metropole, challenging and reconstituting the aesthetic and literary parameters of anticolonial and postcolonial cultural production. The framework of countercultural formation highlights how journals provided a forum for new anticolonial aesthetics, art practices, and print forms. It reflects on how the latter took shape through circulations between local, regional, and international channels and how they contributed to literacy and political education.

While the journal could certainly not replace the vast institutional resources of states or empires, in many colonial contexts it offered valuable tools for the reconstitution of culture. In his essay on national culture, Fanon provides us with evidence of the immense obstacles involved in the creation of culture during and after colonization.[38] Where can the artist identify art materials and practices in the rubble of languages, traditions, philosophies, and denigration of entire worlds? What is the literary subject of an African writer who has been schooled in English and French and exclusively within the Western canon? Just a few years later, similar questions were raised by the Palestinian writer and organizer Ghassan Kanafani. Among other things, he asks how colonized Palestinian writers and writing might develop in light of the colonial destruction of urban centers, where readings and gatherings, cafés, literary presses, bookshops, intellectual and literary clubs, and cultural organizations would otherwise form the core of a country's productive cultural scene.[39] As Katerina Gonzales-Seligmann notes, literary development requires a publishing industry, gathering places, organizations, literary journals, and a wide array of "institutions that provide literary training [or mentorship], facilitate and promote the circulation of literary texts, and consecrate literary value, including commercial, non-commercial and academic or state-supported cultural projects."[40] These reflections speak to the broader question of how to form an anticolonial cultural and "literary infrastructure," in light of erasure.[41]

In Palestine and across the global south, periodicals came in to address this gap. Indeed, the importance of the press in establishing Palestinian counterpublics and national culture both before and after the Nakba has been established irrefutably.[42] Refqa Abu-Remaileh and Ibrahim Mahfouz Abdou argue that the literature that established modern Palestinian identity before 1948 can in itself be understood as a literature of periodicals (*adab maqalat*) as opposed to one of books, and the same could likely be argued for some post–1948 scenes.[43] As Hana Morgenstern and Maha Nassar both discuss, the Palestinian newspaper *al-Ittihad* and the journal *al-Jadid* launched a literary and cultural movement that played an outsized role in the revival of the literary scene and the formation of an anticolonial Palestinian cultural and political movement.[44] Through short stories, poetry, and new aesthetic experiments, *al-Jadid* imagined solidarity between Palestinians and anti-Zionist Jews; documented the lives of Palestinians living under Israeli military occupation and their experiences of the Palestinian Nakba; produced political critique while evading the political censors; promoted education, literacy, and a left public imaginary; and mobilized Palestinian national gatherings around illegal poetry festivals.[45] Fanon's queries in *On National Literature* also speak to a deeper question about anticolonial worldmaking: namely, how to imagine a new world in the midst of the old, to dismantle the master's house when one has only ever known the master's tools. Here, too, the journal was key as a forum in which to debate aesthetics and forms and experiment with them. This included writing literature in service of social, political, and psychic processes of decolonization. These processes include the integration of precolonial models into contemporary forms, the rehearsal of liberated relations in stories or songs, the creation of new regional imaginaries, or the social realist documentation of colonial histories and anticolonial struggles.

African and Caribbean journals such as *Tropiques* were instrumental in framing, arguing for, and giving a forum for experimentation with Negritude, surrealism, and other anticolonial styles.[46] They revived precolonial African cultural elements for contemporary imaginaries and broke Western aesthetics and binaries toward an anticolonial poetics. The North African journal *Souffles-Anfas* became a venue for multilingual regional writing.[47]

It is clear that the journal's dialogic form, combining literature, art, and aesthetic theory and circulating conversations across regions and countries, was critical to the fertilizations that made all this possible. Seligmann, for example, uses the idea of "location writing" to show how magazines actively imagined new pan-Caribbean identities across space and time.[48] Likewise, in a teaching tool on *Savera* magazine for this issue, Areej Akhtar, Javaria Ahmad, and Sana Farrukh Khan discuss the articulation and literary practice of "critical realism" as part of the work of the India Progressive Writers' Association. As Akhtar, Ahmad and Khan note, critical realism indexed "self-reflexive literature that compelled its readers to look 'inward' at natal institutions of class, gender, language, ethnicity, and religion that contributed to social inequalities rather than simply looking 'outward' at colonial wrongdoings." This form was closely linked to international trends including socialist and social realisms, as well as the project of Arab commitment literature found in journals such as *al-Jadid* (Palestine), *al-Tariq* (Lebanon), and *al-Adab* (Lebanon) in the Arab world.[49]

Indeed, culture broadly conceived may have played the greatest role in the elusive yet vital aim of (re)shaping consciousness pursued equally across communist and anticolonial movements. This was a milieu in which the writer was venerated as "the engineer of the human soul." Spanning poetry, art, critique, and learning, the journal was uniquely situated to address multiple aspects of consciousness such as awareness, relationality, identity, imagination, and analysis. Yet as Mae A. Miller-Likhethe suggests in this issue, the consciousness of the audience and the readership is largely absent from the scholarly record. In "Black Internationalism, Print Culture, and Political Education in Claude McKay's *Banjo*," Miller-Likhethe asks us to interrogate "the history of the audience" and the process of consciousness formation inherent in readership, which are largely "missing" from our conception of Black radical and anticolonial traditions. The article posits modes of diasporic readership through Claude McKay's semi-autobiographical novel *Banjo* (1929). By reading the character's engagement with Black periodicals such as *Negro World* and *La Race Nègre,* Miller-Likhethe opens a speculative door into the consciousness-shaping power of periodicals, giving form to anticolonial imaginaries past and future. She reminds us that we cannot assume to know the full effects of these periodicals in the shaping of political consciousness. More crucially, Miller-Likhethe offers us an innovative methodological route into charting how these periodicals were received and how they created awareness in the broader political battle against

Figure 6. The December 1980 issue of the Popular Front for the Liberation of Palestine (PFLP) English-language publication, the *PFLP Bulletin*, Number 45. On Revolutionary Papers site, see: https://revolutionarypapers.org/person-organisation/danah-abdullah/.

racism and colonialism. She opens the door, in other words, for another phase in our Revolutionary Papers project: the study of how periodicals shaped our imaginations of a world after empire.

Conclusion
We began this essay with Ahmad Salim and wish to end it with his story. Salim was buried in Lahore at the end of 2023, his funeral attended by poets, writers, and political workers similarly committed to the protection and reproduction of progressive politics and culture in Pakistan. In the months that have followed, memorial events have been held across the world, remembering the work of an old comrade and writer-poet, radicalized as a young man and committed throughout his life to the making of a more just and capacious world through the production and protection

of the word, written, spoken, and performed. At Revolutionary Papers, we will honor his memory by continuing to work with his collection and the people in whose trust he has left it, foremost Dr. Humaira Ashfaq, a scholar of progressive Urdu literature. Neither all the papers Salim conserved nor all the periodicals that we have come across in our broader work reflect liberatory and egalitarian ideas of anticolonial worlds (the revolutionary pursuing vanguardist—even hierarchical visions of the world—persists even in these journals). They nevertheless offer us profound insights into thousands of political and cultural experimentations pursued by cultural and political workers around the world faced with the overwhelming violence of colonialism, racism, empire, capitalism, patriarchy, and authoritarianism.

In this essay, we have pointed to the journal as an alternative method to studying and doing anticolonialism. The journal, we have argued, forces us to consider anticolonialism as a process always in formation and conversation rather than a finished product, the result of collective labor rather than individuated thought, and antidisciplinary in its antisegregationist approach to the creation of knowledges and the arts rather than committed to the reproduction of siloed disciplines. This is not to say that the journal did not have its limitations. For instance, it assumed that people could read and write, itself a sign of privilege. Though there are several examples of how journals circulated even among those who were technically illiterate (Nieftagodien tells stories of how political workers preparing the *Congress Militant* transcribed stories from those who could not write and read them back to those who could not read; in work elsewhere, Kazmi reflects on how writings in the Mazdoor Kissan Party circular traveled as performances through street theater) the form of the periodical is nevertheless as exclusive as it is inclusive, potentially productive of other kinds of hierarchies.[50] Nevertheless, the journal has the potential to stretch how we think about lefts and anticolonialisms in the past, present, and future. It also has the potential to challenge how we enact anticolonial thought and politics today. As part of this essay and this issue of *RHR*, we show how we at Revolutionary Papers have experimented with reproducing the ethos of the journal through the creation of digital teaching tools aimed at mobilizing these periodicals as interventions into how we think about the past and the present.

By laying out the hermeneutic of the counterinstitutional, the counterpolitical, and the countercultural, we have offered an approach to the journal that treats it not merely as a source from which to cull information but as a product of broader movements and productive of bigger collectives. Through the lens of the counterinstitutional, we have argued that it is possible to map how the periodical's flexible and circulatory power made possible the creation of alternative institutions and infrastructures to those of the (nation) state, often in the aftermath of colonial and imperial destruction. Through the optic of the counterpolitical, we show how one can draw out noncanonical concepts that seek to critique and provide alternatives to colonialism, capitalism, and authoritarian power. And finally, through the prism of the countercultural, we have shown that journals provided fertile grounds for the experimentation in new aesthetic and political forms of cultural expression often necessary for the creation of political consciousness that could counter colonialism and other forms of violent power.

　　This article is an offering for others who wish to engage the staggering archive of southern socialisms and anticolonialisms that we have collectively inherited. We hope that it can be the beginning of a conversation that critically honors the legacies—however checkered at times—left behind by Ahmad Salim and the many others who have tried to create a world free of colonialism.

Mahvish Ahmad works on the material legacies of anticolonial and left movements, archival practices and fugitive organizing in sites of disappearance, and techniques of imperial and sovereign violence. She is a coconvenor of Revolutionary Papers, Archives of the Disappeared (with Mezna Qato, Yael Navaro, and Hana Morgenstern), and *Tanqeed* (with Madiha Tahir), and a trustee of the South Asian Research and Resource Centre (founded by Ahmad Salim). She is assistant professor in human rights and politics and a codirector of LSE Human Rights at the London School of Economics. Contact: m.ahmad14@lse.ac.uk.

Koni Benson is a historian, organizer, and educator. She is a senior lecturer in the Department of Historical Studies at the University of the Western Cape. Her research focuses on the mobilization, demobilization, and remobilization of struggle history in southern Africa's past and present. She draws on critical and creative approaches to people's history projects, anticolonial archiving practices, popular education, and feminist collaborative research praxis to coproduce histories of struggles for the commons with social movement archives and with student, activist, and cultural collectives in southern Africa. She is a coconvener of the Revolutionary Papers and author of *Crossroads: I Live Where I Like* (illustrated by the Trantraal Brothers and Ashley Marais, foreword by Robin D. G. Kelley, 2021). Contact: kbenson@uwc.ac.za.

Hana Morgenstern is associate professor in postcolonial and Middle Eastern literature at Cambridge University and Fellow at Newnham College. Dr. Morgenstern is a scholar of Middle Eastern literature and cultural histories of the Left, with a specialization in Palestine and Israel, including Arab Jewish, Hebrew, Palestinian, and Arabic literary cultures. Her upcoming book, *Cultural Co-resistance in Palestine/Israel: Anticolonial Literature, Translation and Magazines* (2025), reconstructs a history of anticolonial Palestinian and Jewish literary and cultural collaborations from the 1940s to the present day. Morgenstern is cofounder and coinvestigator of Revolutionary Papers and cofounder of Archives of the Disappeared, an interdisciplinary research initiative for the study of communities, social movements, spaces, literatures, and cultures that have been destroyed through acts of political repression and mass violence. Contact: cm894@cam.ac.uk.

Notes

There are no primary authors. This paper is the result of a collaborative research and writing process between all three authors, listed here alphabetically.

1.　Salim, *Meri dharti, mere log*; Ahmad, Rashid, and Salim, "On Progressive Papers in Pakistan."
2.　Some examples of his publications include his books *Jab aankh se na tapka: Saif Khalid* (*When It Did Not Drip from the Eyes: Saif Khalid*), *Bhagat Singh, Bhutto aur Kashmir* (*Bhagat Singh, Bhutto and Kashmir*); *Pakistan ke siyaasi qatl* (*The Political Assassinations*

of Pakistan), *Meri dharti, mere log* (*My Land, My People*), *Jeeve Punjab tehrik kidhar nun?* (*Whither 'Long Live Punjab' Movement?*), and *Tooti, banti assamblian* (*Dissolution of Assemblies in Pakistan*). He is the author of multiple books of Punjabi poetry and literature, starting from his first compilation of Punjabi poetry, *Noor munarey*, in 1966. Examples of his translations include *Raat ki baat*, a translation into Punjabi of Faiz Ahmad Faiz's Urdu poetry; *Jo Bijal Nain Aakhia*, a Punjabi translation of Sheikh Ayaz's poems; and *Eik udaas kitab*, a translation of Amrita Pritam's compilations on the poets and writers of the world who laid down their lives in the struggle for democracy.

3. They first worked together at Abdul Haroon College and later at the National Council of Arts Folklore Research Centre. Salim, *Meri dharti, mere log*.

4. He was an active member of the National Awami Party, which combined the urban left with marginalized nations on the peripheries of Pakistani power.

5. For more on how the cultural sphere remained a key site for the reproduction of left politics, see Toor, *State of Islam*; and Ali, *Surkh Salam*.

6. He cofounded SARRC with two friends, Leanord D'Souza and Nosheen D'Souza, but remained the only initial founder involved throughout the establishment and running of SARRC.

7. There are thirteen articles published as part of this special series on Revolutionary Papers in *Africa is a Country* special series. For the introductory article, see Ahmad, Benson, and Morgenstern, "The Media of the Useable Past."

8. Revolutionary Papers, "Teaching Tools," https://revolutionarypapers.org/teaching-tool/.

9. These were a banned pamphlet called *Jabal* and the organ of the Mazdoor Kissan Party or Workers and Peasants Party, both out of counterhegemonic and left movements in 1970s Pakistan.

10. Salim's antipartitionist ethics was most strikingly on display through his Punjabi literary pursuits. Along with other radical scholars, poets, and writers of Punjab, partitioned in 1947, Salim pursued antipartitionist literary collaborations across the India-Pakistan border.

11. Like other broad geographical terms, *global south* is an imprecise indicator for vast territories and populations. We recognize the multiple global Norths in the global South and vice versa. We also use it to signify the areas and peoples active in resisting colonialism and imperialism.

12. A good example of this is the large-scale buying up of Arab modernist art, much of it anticolonial, by the Museum of Modern Art in New York, an institution which has also come under harsh criticism by a collective called the International Imagination of Anti-National Anti-Imperialist Feelings (IIAAF) which is committed to radical politics and art in the present. See Strike MoMA Working Group of IIAAF, "Strike MoMA: A Reader."

13. MacKinnon, "Intersectionality as Method: A Note," 1019.

14. Rojas, "Method as Method," 211.

15. Bhambra and Holmwood, *Colonialism and Modern Social Theory*; Connell, "Decolonizing Sociology"; Go, *Postcolonial Thought and Social Theory*; Shilliam, *Decolonizing Politics*; Marwah et. al., "Empire and Its Afterlives"; Pitts, "Political Theory of Empire and Imperialism."

16. Parry, "The Institutionalization of Postcolonial Studies," 67.

17. Getachew and Mantena, "Anticolonialism and the Decolonization of Political Theory"; Shilliam "Decolonizing Politics"; Alatas and Sinha, "Sociological Theory Beyond the Canon"; Onwuzuruigbo, "Indigenising Eurocentric Sociology"; Patel, "The ISA Handbook of Diverse Sociological Traditions"; Morris, "The Scholar Denied."

18. This selection tends to get further narrowed to works that are translated and available in European languages.

19. Minkley and Rousseau, "'This Narrow Language'"; Rousseau, "'Unpalatable Truths'"; Lissoni, "From Protest to Challenge," 149–151; Hyslop, "E. P. Thompson in South Africa"; Magubane, "Whose Memory—Whose History?"; Rassool, "Rethinking Documentary History."

20. Choudry and Vally, *History's Schools;* Durrani, *Never Be Silent*; Depelchin, *Silences in African History*; Prashad, *The Darker Nations*; Hillebrecht, "Hendrik Witbooi and Samuel Maharero"; Kelley, *Freedom Dreams*; Trouillot, *Silencing the Past*; Lissoni, Nieftagodien, and Ally, "'Life after Thirty;'" Namhila, "Archives of Anti-Colonial Resistance."

21. Zinn, series preface, x.

22. We also think it is necessary to forge these relations with archivists and the archival collections that often hold these periodicals. We have no space to unpack this argument here but have written about it elsewhere. See Benson, "Feminist Activist Archives"; and Ahmad, "On Political Friendship and Archival Labour."

23. Fejzula, "Gendered Labour," 424.

24. Fejzula, "Gendered Labour," 423. In fact, recent interventions by Fejzula and Sohrabi offer a route to bringing into visibility essential re/productive labour that is erased when anticolonialism is primarily categorized as an instance of individually authored intellection. See Fejzula, "Gendered Labour"; and Sohrabi, "Writing Revolution as If Women Mattered." See also Armstrong, *Bury the Corpse of Colonialism*; and Boyce Davies, *Left of Marx*.

25. Scott, *Conscripts of Modernity*, 3.

26. Scott, *Conscripts of Modernity*, 4.

27. See for example a number of recent works that center anticolonial movements and/or theoretical and cultural frameworks, including Gulick, *Literature, Law, and Rhetorical Performance in the Anticolonial Atlantic*; Rhodes, "Power to the People: The Black Panther and the Pre-Digital Age of Radical Media;" Salem, *Anticolonial Afterlives in Egypt*; Tinson, *Liberator Magazine and Black Activism in the 1960s*; Gopal, *Insurgent Empire*; Gandhi, *Affective Communities*; Di-Capua, *No Exit.*

28. Almohsen, "Arab Critical Culture and Its (Palestinian) Discontents;" Bulson, *Little Magazine, World Form*; Gamedze and Naidoo, "The Mustfall Mo(ve)ments and Publica[c]tion;" Halim, "Afro-Asian Third-Worldism into Global South;" Harrison, *Transcolonial Maghreb*; Hirji, *Cheche*; Kendall, *Literature, Journalism, and the Avant-Garde*; Morgenstern, "Beating Hearts"; Nassar, *Brothers Apart*; Seligmann, *Writing the Caribbean in Magazine Time*; Steiber, "The Haitian Literary Magazine;" Tinson, *Liberator Magazine and Black Activism in the 1960s*.

29. Longford, "*Dawn*."

30. Seligmann, "The Void, the Distance, Elsewhere," 6; Césaire, Ménil and Leiner, *Tropiques*, v.

31. Abrahams, "Editorial: Introducing the Namibian Review," 3.

32. Desai and Ziadah, "*Lotus* and Its Afterlives."

33. Lenin, "Declaration of the Editorial Board of *Iskra*."

34. Hirji, *Cheche.*

35. Marx and Engels, *Marx/Engels Selected Works*, 1: 13–15.

36. See Ahmad, "Movement Texts as Anti-colonial Theory."

37. This attachment to finding anticolonial authors reflects an attachment to anticolonial authority and mastery. Such an attachment works to erase the multiple collectives, dialogic processes, and (re)productive labor necessary for anticolonial intellection, which was never the product of an individualized and atomized mind. See Singh, *Unthinking Mastery*; Elam, *World Literature*; and Fejzula, "Gendered Labour."

38. Fanon, *The Wretched of the Earth*, 206.

39. Kanafani, *Adab Al-Muqawama Fi Falastin al-Muhtala* [*Literature of Resistance in Occupied Palestine*].

40. Seligmann, "The Void, the Distance, Elsewhere," 1.

41. Seligmann, "The Void, the Distance, Elsewhere," 1.

42. See for example, Kabha, "The Arabic Palestinian Press between the Two World Wars."

43. Abdou and Abu-Remaileh, "A Literary *Nahda* Interrupted."

44. Morgenstern, "An Archive of Literary Reconstruction after the Palestinian Nakba"; Nassar, "The Marginal as Central."

45. Morgenstern, "Beating Hearts."

46. Wilder, *Freedom Time*.

47. Harrison, *Transcolonial Maghreb*.

48. Seligmann, *Writing the Caribbean in Magazine Time*.

49. Di-Capua, *No Exit*.

50. For instance, in a contribution at our Revolutionary Papers 2022 conference, Ciraj Rassool argued that periodicals like *Anti-CAD Bulletin* and *Torch* published by the Non-European Unity Movement in South Africa reproduced the hierarchies of the school. Rassool, "Schooling the Nation through Words."

References

Abdou, Ibrahim Mahfouz, and Refqa Abu-Remaileh. "A Literary *Nahda* Interrupted: Pre-Nakba Palestinian Literature as *Adab Maqalat*." *Journal of Palestine Studies* 51, no. 3 (2022): 23–43.

Abrahams, Kenneth. "Editorial: Introducing the Namibian Review." *Namibian Review: A Journal of Southwest African Affairs*, no. 1 (1976): 1–6.

Ahmad, Mahvish. "Movement Texts as Anti-colonial Theory." *Sociology* 57, no. 1 (2023): 54–71.

Ahmad, Mahvish. "On Political Friendship and Archival Labour." Archive Stories. https://archive-stories.com/On-Political-Friendship-and-Archival-Labour (accessed February 29, 2024).

Ahmad, Mahvish, Koni Benson, and Hana Morgenstern. "The Media of the Useable Past." *Africa Is a Country*. https://africasacountry.com/2023/02/the-media-of-the-useable-past (accessed February 28, 2024).

Ahmad, Mahvish, Hashim bin Rashid, and Ahmad Salim. "On Progressive Papers in Pakistan." In *Towards Peoples' Histories in Pakistan*, edited by Kamran Asdar Ali and Asad Ali, 59–78. London: Bloomsbury Academic, 2023.

Alatas, Syed Farid, and Vineeta Sinha. *Sociological Theory beyond the Canon*. London: Palgrave Macmillan, 2017.

Ali, Kamran Asdar. *Surkh Salam: Communist Politics and Class Activism in Pakistan, 1947–1972*. Oxford: Oxford University Press, 2015.

Almohsen, Adey. "Arab Critical Culture and Its (Palestinian) Discontents after the Second World War." *Arab Studies Journal* 29, no. 1 (2021): 56–83.

Armstrong, Elisabeth. *Bury the Corpse of Colonialism: The Revolutionary Feminist Conference of 1949.* Oakland: University of California Press, 2023.

Benson, Koni. 2018. "Feminist Activist Archives: Towards a Living History of the Gender Education Training Network (GETNET)." *Education as Change* 22, no. 2 (2018). https://doi.org/10.25159/1947-9417/3704.

Benson, Koni, Mahvish Ahmad, and Hana Morgenstern, eds. *Africa Is a Country.* Revolutionary Papers, special series, 2023. https://revolutionarypapers.org/series/africa-is-a-country/.

Bhambra, Gurminder K., and John Holmwood. *Colonialism and Modern Social Theory.* Cambridge, MA: Polity, 2021.

Boyce Davies, Carole. *Left of Marx: The Political Life of Black Communist Claudia Jones.* Durham, NC: Duke University Press, 2008.

Bulson, Eric. *Little Magazine, World Form.* New York: Columbia University Press, 2016.

Césaire, Aimé, René Ménil, and Jacqueline Leiner. *Tropiques, 1941–1945: Collection complète.* Paris: Jean-Michel Place, 1978.

Choudry, Aziz, and Salim Vally, eds. *History's Schools: Past Struggles and Present Realities.* London: Routledge, 2018.

Connell, Raewyn. "Decolonizing Sociology." *Contemporary Sociology* 47, no. 4 (2018): 399–407.

Depelchin, Jacques. *Silences in African History: Between the Syndromes of Discovery and Abolition.* Dar es Salaam: Mkuku na Nyota Publishers, 2004.

Desai, Chandni, and Rafeef Ziadah. "*Lotus* and Its Afterlives: Memory, Pedagogy and Anticolonial Solidarity." *Curriculum Inquiry* 52, no. 3 (2022): 289–301.

Di-Capua, Yoav. *No Exit: Arab Existentialism, Jean-Paul Sartre, and Decolonization.* Chicago: University of Chicago Press, 2018.

Durrani, Shiraz. *Never Be Silent: Publishing and Imperialism in Kenya, 1884–1963.* London: Vita Books, 2006.

Elam, J. Daniel. *World Literature for the Wretched of the Earth.* New York: Fordham University Press, 2020.

Fanon, Frantz. *The Wretched of the Earth.* Translated by Constance Farrington. New York: Grove Press, 1966.

Fejzula, Merve. "Gendered Labour, Negritude, and the Black Public Sphere." *Historical Research* 95, no. 269 (2022): 423–46. https://doi.org/10.1093/hisres/htac008.

Gamedze, Asher, and Leigh-Ann Naidoo. "The Mustfall Mo(ve)ments and Publica[c]tion: Reflections on Collective Knowledge Production in South Africa." In *The University and Social Justice,* edited by Aziz Choudry and Salim Vally, 190–206. London: Pluto Press, 2020.

Gandhi, Leela. *Affective Communities: Anticolonial Thought, Fin-de-Siècle Radicalism, and the Politics of Friendship.* Durham, NC: Duke University Press, 2006.

Getachew, Adom, and Karuna Mantena. "Anticolonialism and the Decolonization of Political Theory." *Critical Times* 4, no. 3 (2021): 359–88. https://doi.org/10.1215/26410478-9355193.

Gopal, Priyamvada. *Insurgent Empire: Anticolonial Resistance and British Dissent.* London: Verso, 2019.

Gulick, Anne W. *Literature, Law, and Rhetorical Performance in the Anticolonial Atlantic.* Columbus: Ohio State University Press, 2016.

Halim, Hala. "Afro-Asian Third-Worldism into Global South: The Case of Lotus Journal." *Global South Studies* (2017). https://globalsouthstudies.as.virginia.edu/key-moments/afro-asian-third-worldism-global-south-case-lotus-journal.

Harrison, Olivia. *Transcolonial Maghreb: Imagining Palestine in the Era of Decolonization.* Stanford, CA: Stanford University Press, 2015.

Hillebrecht, Werner. "Hendrik Witbooi and Samuel Maharero: The Ambiguity of Heroes." In *Re-viewing Resistance in Namibian History*, edited by Jeremy Silvester, 38–55. Windhoek: University of Namibia Press, 2015.

Hirji, Karim, ed. *Cheche: Reminiscences of a Radical Magazine*. Tanzania: Mkuki na Nyota Publishers, 2010.

Hyslop, Jonathan. "E. P. Thompson in South Africa." *International Review of Social History* 61, no. 1 (2016): 95–116.

Kabha, Mustafa. "The Arabic Palestinian Press between the Two World Wars." In *The Press in the Middle East and North Africa, 1850–1950*, edited by Anthony Gorman and Didier Monciaud, 99–126. Edinburgh: Edinburgh University Press, 2018.

Kanafani, Ghassan. *Adab Al-Muqawama Fi Falastin al-Muhtala* (*Literature of Resistance in Occupied Palestine, 1948–1966*). Reprint; Cyprus: Rimal, 1966.

Kelley, Robin. *Freedom Dreams: The Black Radical Imagination*. Boston: Beacon Press, 2002.

Lenin, Vladimir. "Declaration of the Editorial Board of *Iskra*." September 1900. *Marxist Internet Archive.* (accessed April 4, 2022). https://www.marxists.org/archive/lenin/works/1900/sep/iskra.htm.

Lissoni, Arianna. "From Protest to Challenge: A Documentary History of African Politics in South Africa, 1882–1990. Volume 6: Challenge and Victory, 1980–1990." *African Historical Review* 45, no. 2 (2013): 149–51. https://doi.org.10.1080/17532523.2013.857099.

Lissoni, Arianna, Noor Nieftagodien, and Shireen Ally. "Introduction: 'Life after Thirty'—A Critical Celebration." In "Life after Thirty: The History Workshop," special issue, *African Studies* 69, no. 1 (2010): 1–12.

Longford, Sam. "*Dawn*: Sites of Struggle, Contested Historical Narratives and the Making of the Disciplined Cadre." Revolutionary Papers, updated April 24, 2022. https://revolutionary papers.org/teaching-tool/dawn/.

MacKinnon, Catharine A. "Intersectionality as Method: A Note." *Signs* 38, no. 4 (2013): 1019–30. https://doi.org/10.1086/669570.

Magubane, Bernhard Makhosezwe. "Whose Memory—Whose History? The Illusion of Liberal and Radical Historical Debate." In *History Making and Present Day Politics: The Meaning of Collective Memory in South Africa*, edited by Hans Erik Stolten, 251–279. Uppsala: Nordiska Afrikainstitutet, 2007.

Marwah, Inder S., Jennifer Pitts, Timothy Bowers Vasko, Onur Ulas Ince, and Robert Nichols. "Empire and Its Afterlives." *Contemporary Political Theory* 19, no. 2 (2020): 274–305.

Marx, Karl, and Friedrich Engels. *Marx/Engels Selected Works*, vol. 1. Moscow: Progress Publishers, 1969.

Minkley, Gary, and Nicky Rousseau. "'This Narrow Language': People's History and the University: Reflections from the University of the Western Cape." *South African Historical Journal* 34, no. 1 (1996): 175–95.

Morgenstern, Hana. "An Archive of Literary Reconstruction after the Nakba." *Middle East Report*, no. 291 (Summer 2019).

Morgenstern, Hana. "Beating Hearts: Arab Marxism, Anti-colonialism and Literatures of Coexistence in Palestine/Israel, 1944–60." In *The Arab Lefts: Histories and Legacies, 1950s–1970s*, edited by Laure Guirguis, 39–56. Edinburgh: Edinburgh University Press, 2020.

Morris, Aldon. *The Scholar Denied: W. E. B. Du Bois and the Birth of Modern Sociology*. Reprint ed. Oakland: University of California Press, 2017.

Namhila Ndeshi, Ellen. "Archives of Anti-Colonial Resistance and the Liberation Struggle (AACRLS): An Integrated Programme to Fill the Colonial Gaps in the Archival Record of Namibia." *Journal for Studies in Humanities and Social Sciences* 4, nos. 1–2 (2015): 168–97.

Nassar, Maha. *Brothers Apart: Palestinian Citizens of Israel and the Arab World*. Stanford, CA: Stanford University Press, 2017.

Nassar, Maha. "The Marginal as Central: *Al-Jadid* and the Development of a Palestinian Public Sphere, 1953–1970." *Middle East Journal of Culture and Communication* 3, no. 3 (2010): 333–51.

Onwuzuruigbo, Ifeanyi. "Indigenising Eurocentric Sociology: The 'Captive Mind' and Five Decades of Sociology in Nigeria." *Current Sociology* 66, no. 6 (2018): 831–48. https://doi.org/10.1177/0011392117704242.

Parry, Benita. "The Institutionalization of Postcolonial Studies." In *The Cambridge Companion to Postcolonial Literary Studies*, edited by Neil Lazarus, 66–82. Cambridge: Cambridge University Press, 2004.

Patel, Sujata, ed. *The ISA Handbook of Diverse Sociological Traditions*. Los Angeles: SAGE, 2009.

Pitts, Jennifer. "Political Theory of Empire and Imperialism." *Annual Review of Political Science*, no. 13 (2010): 211–35.

Prashad, Vijay. *The Darker Nations: A People's History of the Third World*. New York: New Press, 2007.

Rassool, Ciraj. "Rethinking Documentary History and South African Political Biography." *South African Review of Sociology* 41, no. 1 (2010): 28–55.

Rassool, Ciraj. "Schooling the Nation through Words: Reading and Writing in the Non-European Unity Movement, 1940s–1950s." Revolutionary Papers Conference: Counter-institutions, Politics, and Culture in Periodicals of the Global South, Community House. Cape Town, South Africa, April 30, 2022.

Rhodes, Jane. "Power to the People: The Black Panther and the Pre-Digital Age of Radical Media." *Funambulist*, no. 22 (2019): 26–30.

Rojas, Carlos. "Method as Method." *Prism* 16, no. 2 (2019): 211–20. https://doi.org/10.1215/25783491-7978475.

Rousseau, Nicky. "'Unpalatable Truths' and 'Popular Hunger': Reflections on Popular History in the 1980s." In *Out of History: Re-imagining South African Pasts*, edited by Jung Ran Forte, Paolo Israel, and Leslie Witz, 53–71. Cape Town: HSRC Press, 2016.

Salem, Sara. *Anticolonial Afterlives in Egypt: The Politics of Hegemony*. Cambridge: Cambridge University Press, 2020.

Salim, Ahmad. *Meri dharti, mere log*. Lahore: Sang-e-Meel, 2023.

Sandwith, Corrine. "*Umsebenzi / Umvikele-thebe*: Reading Ethiopia in Radical South African Newspapers." Revolutionary Papers Conference: Counter-institutions, Politics, and Culture in Periodicals of the Global South, Community House. Cape Town, South Africa, April, 29 2022.

Scott, David. *Conscripts of Modernity: The Tragedy of Colonial Enlightenment*. Durham, NC: Duke University Press, 2004.

Seligmann, Katerina Gonzalez. *Writing the Caribbean in Magazine Time*. New York: Rutgers University Press, 2021.

Seligmann, Katerina Gonzalez. "The Void, the Distance, Elsewhere: Literary Infrastructure and Empire in the Caribbean." *Small Axe* 24, no. 2 (2020): 1–16.

Shilliam, Robbie. *Decolonizing Politics: An Introduction*. Cambridge: Polity, 2021.

Singh, Julietta. *Unthinking Mastery: Dehumanism and Decolonial Entanglements*. Durham, NC: Duke University Press, 2017.

Sohrabi, Naghmeh. "Writing Revolution as If Women Mattered." *Comparative Studies of South Asia, Africa and the Middle East* 42, no. 2 (2022): 546–50. https://doi.org/10.1215/1089201X-9988048.

Stieber, Chelsea. "The Haitian Literary Magazine in Francophone Postcolonial Literary and Cultural Production." In *French Cultural Studies for the Twenty-First Century*, edited by Masha Belenky, Kathryn Kleppinger, and Anne O'Neil-Henry, 21–40. Newark: University of Delaware Press, 2017.

Strike MoMA Working Group of IIAAF. "Strike MoMA: A Reader." *Strike MoMA*. https://www.strikemoma.org/reader (accessed February 28, 2024).

Tinson, Christopher M. *Liberator Magazine and Black Activism in the 1960s*. Chapel Hill: University of North Carolina Press, 2017.

Toor, Saadia. *State of Islam: Culture and Cold War Politics in Pakistan*. London: Pluto Press, 2011.

Trouillot, Michel-Rolph. *Silencing the Past: Power and the Production of History*. Boston: Beacon Press, 1995.

Wilder, Gary. *Freedom Time: Negritude, Decolonization, and the Future of the World*. Durham, NC: Duke University Press, 2015.

Zinn, Howard. Series preface to Prashad, *The Darker Nations*, iv–x.

From Mimeographs to Self-organization

Beijing Workers' Writings in the 1989 Tiananmen Movement

Promise Li

In the spring of 1989 the workers on the streets of Tiananmen produced some of the most advanced writings on mass organizing in the history of the People's Republic of China (PRC). These texts, however, were not published through any academic or institutional outlets at the time. The Workers' Autonomous Federation (WAF), grassroots mass organizations formed by workers and some student protestors that emerged from Beijing and other cities during the movement, coordinated and disseminated new printings nearly every day in May.[1] These appeared as small leaflets circulated on the streets and plastered on walls, from manifestos to workers' public letters. Beijing's censorship regime has traditionally limited avenues for independent Marxist thinking in official outlets, while liberal dissident thought has dominated the rest of the mainstream dissident outlets. In contrast to the mass circulation of liberal dissident writing by the likes of Fang Lizhi and Liu Xiaobo, these materials have received little attention in scholarship.[2] Only a few articles have referenced these texts to examine workers' roles in the protests, and even fewer have carefully analyzed the workers' organizing strategies—best captured in the print ephemera they disseminated during the movement.[3] Under conditions of authoritarianism and state surveillance, the informal circulation of print ephemera has long served as a means to maintain forms of independent politics unavailable through legal public institutions at the time.

Radical History Review
Issue 150 (October 2024)   DOI 10.1215/01636545-11257382
© 2024 by MARHO: The Radical Historians' Organization, Inc.

This essay unpacks how the Beijing WAF's propaganda system served as a counterinstitution that enabled everyday workers to translate immediate demands—from calling for wage stabilization on the shop floor to defending other citizens against soldiers—into broader political programs and organizations. Thus, I build on Zhang Yueran's observation that "the workers' vision of democracy was reflected first and foremost in what they did, not what they proclaimed," by establishing that what the WAF did and what it proclaimed had a symbiotic relationship.[4] The form of these writings and the circumstances of their publication cannot be separated from how the workers organized, informing the means and tactics of workers' struggle.

These writings are important because they represent Chinese workers' autonomous attempts to think and act beyond shop-floor action and in terms of independent politics—an arena from which they have been historically excluded in the PRC. As the WAF organizer Jian Yang reflected, upon the movement's defeat, "the Chinese Communist Party has never given workers any opportunity for truly independent and autonomous participation in politics . . . the authoritarian system has not created the climate or provided the soil for the survival of workers' democracy movements for any length of time."[5] The difficulty of transforming the handbills into sustainable, formal institutions for programmatic discussion between workers and other movements beyond June testifies not only to the intensity of state repression but also to workers' inexperience in democratic politics. On the other hand, the diverse forms of workers' writings, varying from open letters, organizational constitutions, and emergency calls for direct action, demonstrate their willingness to rediscover democratic practice anew by stimulating everyday citizens' capacity for political self-activity. In bridging mass action with a critical attitude toward the party-state's growing bureaucratism as a by-product of market reforms, this self-activity exceeds the boundaries of liberalism.

. . . . .

Handbills and posters have played a central role in the history of protests under the PRC, but those produced by Beijing workers are distinctive in that they articulate a larger program for political democracy grounded on grassroots organizations independent from state organs.[6] Independent publications by grassroots activists outside the Chinese state, called *minkan*, serve as a forum or public square of sorts, as former Tiananmen student protestor and researcher Shao Jiang describes, "a way of networking, a periodic inquisition of the establishment, a source of alternative information, and a way of influencing the society . . . to realize self-conscious practice."[7] But few independent publications and organizations can persist in the PRC's political atmosphere. Some of the genres used by the WAF harken back to Cultural Revolution–era writings, while the *dazibao* (big-character posters) of the democracy movement in the late 1970s functioned as an early precursor for political discourse in civil society independent from official outlets. Unlike previous mobilizations, the Tiananmen workers organized themselves as an independent force *as workers* beyond local grievances on the shop floor, connecting writing to mass mobilization. While party members and even some bureaucrats supported the movement, unlike the Cultural Revolution, the Tiananmen workers received little support from even parts of the state bureaucracy in an organized manner.

By and large, these texts did not simply dictate specific forms of action but evolved alongside workers' organization and the movement's changing objective conditions. Mass action opened up space for more nuanced political interventions through these handbills and posters, as in the efforts to consolidate the WAF constitution toward late May after workers' mobilization against martial law. In addition, early conversations about principles of unity gave direction to workers' outreach in different workplaces in the brief period of lull in early May. This understanding allows us to challenge the conventional understanding that the WAF's political work only seriously emerged after it officially declared its organizational existence and released the majority of its documented propaganda work. In reality, the WAF's organizing groundwork began as early as mid-April, when a handful of workers first gathered in the square to strategize the next steps to raise workers' demands in a nascent student movement.

While scholars such as Zhang rightly correct the commonplace that the workers simply tailed the students' demands with no political intervention of their own, this essay further argues that the broad counterinstitutional space that the workers modeled offered a vision of political democracy grounded on class politics.[8] Raymond Lau, whose article is one of the few that analyzes the workers' agitational texts, identifies a disconnection between the workers' demands and their political practice. He writes that "while [the WAF] still expressed the intention of establishing a working-class organization, it did not put that intention into the group's practice at all."[9] Such a view narrows what counts as working-class politics, failing to see the workers' insistence in organizing beyond economic demands as an expression of class politics aimed at transforming social relations in all their totality. A more accurate way to understand their written productions is Oskar Negt and Alexander Kluge's conception of a "proletarian public sphere," which promotes "the interests of the productive class" as "the driving force" in "creat[ing] a medium of intercourse that relates the particular interests of the productive sector and society as a whole to one another."[10] The fact that bourgeois liberal ideas of freedom coexisted with more radical ones that synthesize Chinese society as a totality of production relations to be transformed does not compromise the uneven birth of this proletarian public sphere. As Negt and Kluge write, "The worker is unable to conceive of the totality of society without finding himself in the bourgeois camp. He has to choose between his own present identity and his historical capacity as a proletarian, revolutionary force that sublates the totality of society in a new mode of production."[11]

This essay explores how the concrete dialectic of evolving propaganda (represented by the prints) and mass action quickens the transformation of an inchoate civil society in illiberal conditions toward proletarian consciousness.

Groundwork

One of the first acts of self-organization at Tiananmen Square, just hours after the death of the former general secretary Hu Yaobang, began with a conversation among some workers gathering at the square.[12] Regardless of Hu's actual political stances, he had been seen by many ordinary citizens as a key symbol of reform against the party bureaucracy. China's market reforms in the 1980s produced social contradictions that alienated various sectors of Chinese society for different reasons: politically minded students supported economic liberalization but bemoaned that it did not bring political liberalization; workers were mainly dissatisfied by the threats to their wages and other forms of social security. Worker-student solidarity had been common in Chinese history, and the distinction between both identities was highly blurred in the democracy movement of the late 1970s. But the market reforms and the rise of Western liberal thought in Chinese academia in the 1980s quickened the disconnection between workers and students. By and large, workers did not show up en masse with the students in brief student protests during the mid-1980s until the mass mobilizations in 1989 (though workers and students often read the same cultural texts throughout the decade).[13]

But Hu's death provided the occasion for students and workers' different reasons for discontent to coalesce into a movement, though tensions between the two persisted from shortly after the earliest days of mobilization until the final week or two before the massacre. A few workers met on the night of April 15 to discuss their grievances and decided to meet again the next evening to coordinate further. Many worked in Beijing-based industrial factories, such as iron and steel. Some were department store and other service employees, along with a few lecturers.[14] On the following night, the construction worker Wang Dengyue brought others from his work unit, and others did the same. Fewer than twenty in number at the time, the workers witnessed the first gathering of student protests on April 17, with thousands of Beijing University students marching with a petition calling out the party bureaucracy's corruption. Glimmers of a dissident movement had long been brewing on campuses even months before Hu's death, but the following days marked the first emergence of an organized workers' movement that intersected with student mobilization. Zhao Hongliang, a department store clerk and former ticket seller for a bus company, recalled that the workers agreed to solicit ideas from other workers in their work units on how to support the students, agreeing to meet again the next evening.[15]

April 18—the second day of the protests—was a pivotal moment for the development of the workers' self-organization. Students began to launch a sit-in at the square. Later that evening, the police began to violently clamp down on the protestors—both students and workers—gathering at Xinhua Gate, and news of police brutality began to spread quickly in the city. The workers came to the conclusion that they broadly supported students' demands for political reform but had their own grievances. As the students began their sit-in on April 18, the workers began putting these demands in writing, leading to the first documented workers' handbill: an open letter addressed to all the people of Beijing. The letter began by criticizing the regime's "bureaucratic-dictatorial forms of control"—an echo of the students' demand against authoritarianism—but connected this system of governance to class-based concerns of "uncontrolled inflation and declining living standards." The letter concluded with a set of demands that affirmed solidarity with the student movement while going beyond it: "We earnestly demand the following: a wage increase, price stabilization, and a publication of the incomes and possessions of government officials and their families. We, the workers of Beijing, and citizens from all walks of life, support the university students and their fight for honesty and justice."[16] At this point, there was little formal organization among the workers, but as Zhao recounts, "the people in our units said we were doing the right thing, and people from other units also supported us. Only in this way could we post a proclamation in the name of a workers' association."[17] This handbill of demands, the first of many to come, emerged from a process of organized deliberation among workers at the square and some in the work units. The initial demands were rudimentary and not particularly radical, but expressed the workers' interest in linking common shop-floor grievances into a set of demands meant to induce a change in state policy.

In particular, the demand for party bureaucrats to publish their holdings directly aims to expose how the state bureaucracy was becoming an accumulating class of its own—challenging the basis of its political power.[18] On the flip side, the workers were demanding recognition in the sphere of politics by positioning themselves as an entity to which the ruling bureaucracy must respond. Demands without political organization would have no real force, and the start of police violence on the evening of April 18 gave the workers impetus to escalate. By then, the students' sit-in had reportedly dwindled to around a few hundred people after the police deployed force, while the workers' group reportedly grew to around seventy to eighty people by the end of the day.[19] The workers' group began giving their first public speeches that day and the next and roused the students while calling for other workers to openly share their views.

The second handbill, first published on April 20, developed from the workers' organic mobilization in response to police brutality.[20] The "Ten Questions for the Chinese Communist Party" doubles down on the first letter's targeting of the property of government officials. This document goes further in its demands to the party bureaucrats, merging specifics about their personal expenses (e.g., questioning who pays for Zhao Ziyang's golfing expenses) with larger political topics: the plan behind China's repayment of foreign loans, the party's self-conception and definition of the revolution, the meaning of "rank" in Deng Xiaoping's conception of social sectors. These demands' growing scale and ambition accompanied the radicalization of workers' actions. In his public speech that day in response to the police violence, Wang encouraged the students to question the very legitimacy of the state's armed forces, declaring that "the people should no longer have any good feelings towards the army."[21]

These two documents and the early workers' protests from April 18 to 20 led this nucleus of workers to a crucial step: publicly calling on other workers and other Beijing citizens to join them, as Zhao recalled, "to raise their views."[22] In the following days, more handbills appeared in the western gallery, some of which the workers posted on the walls. The workers facilitated their own discursive system that remained distinct while still tethered to the broader aims for political democracy led by the students. Their mobilization, starting on April 20, began to gather their first large base of recruits—including one who was later seen as their most prominent leader, a young railway worker named Han Dongfang—developing the foundations for a formal political organization. Zhao directly attributed the group's rapid growth in new members from different work units to its decision to publish open letters in their handbills.[23]

The next week saw an influx of submissions of public letters from everyday workers. The letters covered strategies for how to best advance the movement along with political analysis of the existing state. Workers had little access to mimeographs and printers, largely used by students at their universities. Some began approaching students, who were also pasting *dazibao* and other flyers at the square, for help to mimeograph copies of their writing (mimeograph being the most common printing format used by the workers). Some were able to covertly access mimeographs at their work units, though few were printed there since they were closely surveilled.[24] A flyer dated April 23 encouraged students to "propagate the truth widely through all kinds of channels, including leaflets, propaganda teams . . . so that the people can separate the truth from the lies."[25] It further called on the students to "plan and conduct every step very carefully with great vigilance, including parades, petitions, demonstrations" to "produce pressure." The letter also encouraged the participation of "tertiary education institutes," which had more working-class students, as a concrete step to bridge the gap between workers and students. Another open letter by a worker on April 28, posted at Beijing University, echoed the need for an independent press and called on the students to deepen their analysis beyond "empty cries for democracy." It identified the regime's system of "state ownership" as "ownership by a few elite bureaucrats" in reality, functionally acting as "the biggest capitalists in China" against whom students, peasants, and workers should unite.[26]

Such political analysis was by no means unanimously shared among militant workers on the square, but these handbills represented the seeds of a new infrastructure of independent organization. As the workers' movement grew in size, the student movement also ballooned and forced the state to act. Official Communist Party leaders scrambled to respond to the mass movement growing at the square, culminating in a series of harsh injunctions over party broadcasts and in the official party publication that further incensed the students on April 25 and 26.[27] The party editorial accused protestors of seeking "to confuse people's feelings, throw the entire country into turmoil, and destroy political stability and unity."[28] University administrators pressured Zhou Yongjun, a university member of the Beijing Students' Autonomous Federation and later one of the few key student supporters of the WAF, along with other student leaders, to cancel planned rallies.[29] These efforts failed, and April 27 saw a jointly organized rally by the student and workers' organizations. Workers "helped the students maintain order and push through the police lines," while ensuring supplies for the students.[30]

While the following weeks saw a lull in the movement, this period provided an important glimpse into how the drafting of print ephemera continued to inform a new stage of workers' organizing. After the unofficial formation of the WAF on April 21, the members went to their own and other work units to publicize the workers' organizing and discover more workers interested in strengthening political programs and organizational structure.[31] Some gave practical suggestions that the WAF later incorporated into their handbills, for example, steelworkers gave input on "what programme we should have for the new workers' organization."[32] This interest in a new workers' organization stems from a common dissatisfaction with the official state-run union federation, the All-China Federation of Trade Unions (ACFTU). Thus the workers began to directly approach other workers, not just the union bureaucrats and cadres (some of whom were quietly supportive), on the shop floors during their lunch breaks.[33]

Such organizing discussions informed the drafting of formal organizational documents around May 1, and in turn, these documents and other handbills became organizing tools for worker organizers to start conversations with new workers in the factories (see fig. 1). Between late-April to mid-May, the workers tried to strengthen the connection between the activities on the square and different work units. Zhao recounts:

The people with strong abilities did organizational work, and others went back to their own work units to gather workers' opinions. The information coming back was unanimous: the workers all welcomed us to form our own organization. For example, a worker at the Beijing Boiler Plant said, don't be like the official trade union. Your aims, methods, goals, and regulations should all be made very clear, and you ought to register and not give the government an excuse to suppress you. Once your organization is established, go ahead regardless of what happens. At that time, there were people who came to help us write our declarations, charter, constitution, and other documents.[34]

Figure 1. The manifesto
of the Chinese
Construction Workers'
Autonomous Federation,
May 21, 1989.

These conversations informed the development of new organizational guidelines and declarations, as other workers drafted and discussed five new demands. By May 2, the workers had registered over two thousand members from different work sectors into the skeleton of an organization still to be defined. Throughout early May, the WAF doubled down on these efforts to outreach to different work units, "proceed[ing] with its prime task of publicity and the recruitment of more workers. We met and held discussions with representatives sent to join the WAF from various factories in Beijing. . . . We organized public meetings to discuss many topical issues such as the productivity of the nation, the promotion of export earnings, workers' welfare, human rights, democracy, and freedom."[35] While many workers later rallied under the WAF's banner, some formed their own workers' organizations that appeared in the middle of May—though there is little information about them.

These efforts are ill documented—and unspectacular in comparison to the growing fanfare surrounding the square—and the WAF did not yet officially exist as an organization. But they represent a new level of mass organizing across factories nearly unprecedented in the course of the history of the Communist regime, as they translated economic demands from the shop floor to political ones mobilizing workers into a national political movement. A worker testified that never had "people conceived of organizing something like the WAF in the factories."[36] But the strength of the organization's political work lies not in the strength of its program and constitution—these remained in flux throughout the course of its existence—but in *how* the WAF became a vehicle for workers to rediscover the long-lost art of programmatic politics through the experience of a mass movement. This organizing work in the early weeks of May laid the foundation for the outpouring of print ephemera and the height of the WAF's militant organizing that characterized the final two weeks of the Tiananmen movement after the hunger strike.

Mass Action

While the weeks before the middle of May already laid important foundations for the WAF's mass work, the WAF did not officially declare its organizational existence until the middle of May, when the Tiananmen protests escalated into a mass movement with the students' hunger strike. In early May, student leaders in the square decided to start a hunger strike to continue the movement. Around May 13, the hunger strike led to widespread support from the populace of Beijing, and anger with public officials continued to increase, especially after an unsatisfactory public discussion on May 14 between student representatives and party leaders. As the historian Jeremy Brown notes, "The peaceful uprising of millions of people in Beijing, sparked by sympathy with hunger-striking students, meant that the students' numbers were dwarfed by a mass citizens' movement. In the middle of May, the movement suddenly became much more diverse and inclusive, ranging from factory workers to elderly officials, not to mention the tens of thousands of people from hinterland provinces."[37] And between May 17 and the start of martial law on May 20, the workers' organizing within this citywide movement not only revived but quickly accelerated to new heights. Their core members came from different industrial sectors: construction, education, steel, freight hauling, rail, and so on.[38] The content of the handbills was becoming more nuanced, suggesting either the direct participation of new and more politically advanced members or the influence of the early May outreach. Shen Yinhan (a worker involved in the WAF since April) distributed and circulated the "Letter to the Whole Nation's Compatriots," on May 17, which merged the students' key demands for "science, democracy, freedom, human rights, and rule of law" with workers' demands about wage increases, stabilization of inflation, and others.[39] The analysis here is more precise than in earlier documents. The letter invokes "Marx's *Capital*" as "a method for understanding the character of our oppression," identifying that the remaining portion of surplus value beyond what is needed to sustain workers and maintain the means of production ("wages . . . medical welfare . . . equipment depreciation") is "swallow[ed]" by "civil servants" for their personal expenditures. It advocates for a formal "national investigation committee" to investigate the bureaucrats and calls on workers to "remain closely united with the Beijing WAF" so that "the Democracy Movement can be raised to new heights." More specifically, the letter concludes with a key organizing request, calling on workers to join the WAF in a "workers' march" to the square to support the students on May 22.[40]

The WAF members, already drawing from the expertise of the most politically advanced workers they can find to strengthen their demands and analysis, are reaching some limits. Handbills from Peking University (mostly likely written by the institution's academic workers or students) floated the idea of a general strike as early as April 22 or 23—weeks before the students' hunger strike—but there was little momentum or expertise to execute it up to this point.[41] As they continued to meet publicly en masse, the workers were keen to identify individuals to help them finalize their goal of forming an independent organization with a clear and well-defined constitution. WAF members approached the students to send representatives to support them but were largely rebuffed—with some key exceptions, like Li Jinjin, then a law student who later became the key legal advisor for the WAF. As Li recounts in a recent reflection, he first encountered WAF workers when he witnessed "a few hundred workers [already] congregating to unionize in the east side of the Great Hall . . . hoping for the students to send representatives to support."[42] He volunteered and was led by WAF leaders to the rest of the workers, where he answered questions fielded by workers, such as whether the constitution legally protected the right to strike. He responded that it does not protect this right, but neither does it explicitly forbid it—to which the "workers felt great encouragement."

Immediately after this meeting, Li gathered the workers' thoughts and drafted the "Declaration of the Beijing Workers," which formally articulates a call for "a one-day general strike," quoted in full below:

We recognize that the students' democratic and patriotic movement, which began in April, has become a national movement which directly influenced the interests of the workers.

We recognize that, in the national interest, the students have given their all, and that the lives of the hunger strikers are now in danger.

In order to save the lives of those thousands of students, for the interest of we workers, and for the welfare of the entire nation, we formally declare:

The Politburo must unconditionally accept the two student demands within twenty-four hours. Otherwise, beginning on May 20th at noon, there will be a one-day general strike, after which we will decide further steps.

Furthermore, let the workers of the whole nation know that the workers of Beijing are now organized.

The document was signed by the "preparatory committee" of the WAF and reaffirms the workers' consistent belief that "the interest of we workers [*sic*]" and "the welfare of the entire nation" are inseparable. Class politics illustrates not just economic demands, but also questions how social production as a whole in the nation is organized. The demand for a general strike recognizes that the heart of national politics is in its productive capacities, and thus the most powerful way to restore national welfare is by forcing production to a halt to pressure the authorities. The final, emphatic statement that Chinese workers "are now organized" points to the most important ingredient of this operation: not just the spontaneous activity of everyday workers, but their capacity for organization and emergence in the political arena. Li read this brief declaration to the workers, who unanimously approved the document. In other words, Li's contributions concretized an ongoing process since April, when WAF organizers were shuffling between work units, the western gallery, and the students with the materials they had already published with the intention of gathering more mass input.

The chain of handbills and mass action, which the workers spearheaded when martial law was introduced the following week, marked the high point of the WAF's self-organization. The martial law drastically affected the lives of Beijing's citizens; by this point, the effects of the protests at the square were felt by everyone in the city, as normal modes of life were disrupted by the soldiers' entry. This quickened everyday citizens' mass resistance and their participation in politics. A handbill posted on Beijing streets on the morning of May 21 recorded that "the streets are filled with passersby, leaflets, and knots of people continually forming and reforming. People are exchanging news, discussing the development of events, and expressing their opinions."[43] Lau treats the workers' "agitational-cum-mobilizational calls" in this period as abandoning the task of independently organizing workers and "served merely to mobilize workers and *shimen* to follow the political program of the intellectuals."[44] But in reality, the WAF's handbills developed into agitational leaflets with clear demands that refuse to separate between workers' and mass movements, as evidenced in "The Workers' Manifesto" on May 21 (fig. 2).

The brief manifesto underscores the central role of "the proletariat" as "the central force within the democracy movement. The students are absent in this document as it centers the role of workers in advancing democratic progress, which demands "overthrow[ing] all forms of despotism and domination," because of the workers' "value of knowledge and skills in production."[45] In other words, knowledge of how production is organized—and how to disrupt it (as the workers show in their call for a general strike)—integrally relates to democratic struggle. The workers put this into practice in their calls to action through public notices on May 20 and 21, around the same time as the manifesto's publication. These notices emphasize the WAF as an *organized* and *autonomous* body of workers with a directive "to unite people for the democratization of the country," detailing how the group has just

Figure 2. Workers'
Manifesto (anonymous),
May 21, 1989.

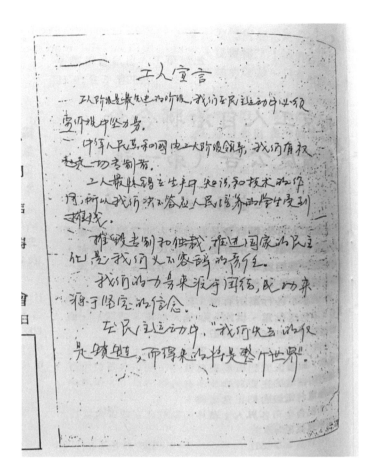

"completed organizing its leadership, setting up a leaders' group, a secretariat, a publicity section, and a liaison and supplies section."[46] They further called for the formation of a Workers' Picket Team and other workers' organizations to maintain order, protect the citizens, ensure protestors' access to supplies, and resist the army's advances in the city. These directives centered the workers' role as a key aspect of a larger mass democratic movement, and the shifting genres and demands of these handbills identified the organization's openness to accommodate their organizing to actual conditions at the time. The second public notice repeatedly underscored the necessity of aligning political tasks to "the present situation," "in the current circumstances," and "given the present state of affairs."[47]

What Lau sees as the WAF's "non-class-specific response to a practical demand" in the early days of martial law relies on a limited horizon of how organizing workers as a class can adapt to circumstances and take on broader forms.[48] Workers began from economic demands that led to spearheading a larger struggle to take ownership of productive industries and mobilize for self-defense across Beijing.

This is precisely a political expression of working-class power rather than an abandonment of class interests. They understood that any movement calling for radical change must expand on, not abstain from, the basic demands for democracy and self-determination against oppression that the liberal students advocated. The tragedy is that there was not enough time and resources for this nucleus of workers to clarify and develop their politics so that an organized political opposition could emerge from this counterinstitution of workers' democracy.

Still, the WAF's call for mass resistance to martial law, as Zhang puts it, enabled everyday people "to concretely build power to control production and manage society."[49] Zhang further describes that

The development of organization led to a radicalization of action. Workers started organizing self-armed quasi-militias, such as "picket corps" and "dare-to-die brigades," to monitor and broadcast the military's whereabouts. These quasi-militias were also responsible for maintaining public order, so as not to provide any pretext for military intervention. In a sense, Beijing became a city self-managed by workers.

The Hong Kong socialist Au Loong-yu further observes that "the de facto strike thrust the entirety of Beijing into partial paralysis, deepening the Party's crisis; transportation workers drove buses to block military vehicles; workers repurposed their factories to produce defensive weapons for protesters; and railway workers refused to carry military personnel."[50] This call to armed resistance and reorganization of the city's productive capacities by workers, as Au suggests, sustained the political consciousness at Tiananmen as an alternative strategy in contrast to the pacifistic students.

Of course, the WAF did not have enough time to cohere a unified political vision for how society should be governed, but its organizing opened up space for everyday people to think in terms of such questions. The temporary success of the civilian resistance against the soldiers further boosted the WAF's visibility and influence. As they began formally registering workers as members en masse, they set up their own public broadcasting system in the western gallery to broadcast the handbills around May 26 and 27. During that week, the WAF's propaganda structure materialized as a physical counterinstitution for mass politics around the square. Lu Jinghua, a self-employed clothing shop worker and organizer who joined the WAF that week and became the key broadcaster, describes how the handbills were printed, read, and distributed in this period:

We had a printing shop to print handbills. A lot of the broadcast statements were printed up as handbills. After we read out a statement, a lot of people would run up and ask for a copy, and we would give them the handbill. One of them takes one copy, and when they return to their factory at least ten people read it, and these ten people tell their families; isn't that a lot of people? So the force of our propaganda was very great. We had liaison personnel for every one of the colleges and universities. We also carried out propaganda at the gates of various factories.[51]

The WAF's propaganda network continued to flower and reached its height in the days leading up to the massacre on June 4, when the mobilization protesting the arrest of a few WAF leaders on May 30 finally convinced the students to allow the WAF's organizational activities within the center of the square. The police abducted three WAF worker-leaders that week, including Shen. The WAF sent out a flurry of handbills mobilizing people to rally at the Beijing Police Bureau for their release on the following day.[52] These notices functioned as both rapid news updates of key events on the ground and calls to action. These were particularly important to provide a sense of coherence and direction for movement participants in the chaos of Beijing's streets. In the first emergency notice, the WAF gave detailed information on the circumstances of Shen's arrest, narrating how "a cyclist was seen being dragged from his bike by two policemen" on May 30. These handbills also functioned as a mirror image of the opaque proceedings of the party bureaucracy. "An Urgent Dispatch" closely details the interaction between WAF leaders negotiating Shen's release and the police to public readers, describing when they arrived at the police bureau, how many were present, what requests Han and Li as WAF representatives made to the police, and how the police responded. The campaign was successful and the workers were released (though they were imprisoned again shortly after the massacre as part of the larger crackdown on the WAF), and the students finally agreed to allow the WAF to move its base from the west side into the square itself to protect workers against further state kidnapping. Lu recounts that at the square, the WAF would receive fifty to sixty statements per day, from workers and peasants or disgruntled cadres, for them to publish as handbills that she read aloud on the broadcast.[53] At its height, the WAF essentially coordinated an independent publication for the broader masses, run by workers themselves, blurring the line between workers' media and an independent platform for the broad movement itself.

Despite the WAF's efforts, the movement was severely repressed. It is perhaps not a coincidence that WAF leaders and many everyday workers were among those killed outside of Tiananmen, and the historian Maurice Meisner observes that "most of those imprisoned and all who were executed were workers or other ordinary citizens."[54] On June 8, a few days after the massacre, the party-state officially singled out and condemned the WAF as one of "the main instigators and organizers in the capital of the counter-revolutionary rebellion."[55] The PRC understood that a nationally coordinated and independent movement of workers would provide the greatest challenge to its legitimacy. More importantly, the workers in Beijing, to the best of their ability, modeled a plan to raise political consciousness through their own propaganda work mixed with mass action. Of course, there were still vast limitations throughout the process. The greatest obstacle is that few workers had political or organizational experience, and in addition, the WAF was not able to build enough support in the work units in the brief time span it had.

Conclusion

It would be inadequate to simply judge the historical contributions of the WAF on the unevenness of the programs and demands on its handbills. These print ephemera show us that Chinese workers were compelled to think and act in terms of programmatic politics that built on—but went beyond—shop-floor grievances and local mobilization independent of the party-state. These workers did not come to these instincts and actions ex nihilo, as the subjective conditions for this moment of radicalization emerged from years of dissatisfaction in the work units and some limited, but crucial, experience in organizing for workplace democracy.[56] What was new from April to June 1989 was that a group of workers, spurred by the student mobilization around them, was moved to channel these grievances from the economic to the political arena. They began to think in terms of independent political programs and organization, as crude and uncertain as they may be. Their programs and constitutions were not static; they tried to respond and develop according to the real developments of the struggle on the ground. This required bridging the need for everyday workers to practice and exercise their power to express themselves politically in these handbills and the need for some centralization and formalization. Unlike the student leaders' entrenched liberalism, the WAF members unevenly but powerfully expressed a political practice that targeted the production and reproduction of class relations, evidenced by their call for a general strike. As a sympathetic participant from the official trade union ACFTU points out, "it is not enough to rely solely on the strength of students . . . in the handbills we printed and distributed, we stated clearly that we must 'arouse the millions of workers and peasants' and only then could we ultimately achieve victory for the Democracy Movement."[57] These workers articulated a horizon of class politics grounded on spurring political democracy and mass action across all sectors of society.

The WAF's political work is an invaluable historical record of workers and other activists in China discovering their subjective role in a long-depoliticized terrain of struggle. As such, their organizing was *revolutionary* in the sense that Marx conceived in the *Theses on Feuerbach*: "The coincidence of the changing of circumstances and of human activity or self-changing can be conceived and rationally understood only as revolutionary practice."[58] The WAF represented an important attempt by Chinese workers to build a political organization beyond their workplace to transform the effective reality of authoritarian capitalist rule. Their print ephemera shows the seeds of a counterinstitution that encouraged mass participation in politics, linking the broad struggle for democracy to the transformation of who controls the productive forces. Such a counterinstitution challenges the PRC's institutional hegemony that stretches from state media broadcasts to the soldiers on the street. The WAF's successes are grounded on its instinct to adequately calibrate its programmatic action to empower broad masses of workers' participation in materially changing the broad movement's ever-shifting realities. Thus the mass movement and the workers' movement grew together dialectically. In this sense, we must consider the ephemeral textual productions by these workers not only as a record of ideas but also in how they were inextricably linked to their conditions of production and circulation—as instruments of struggle.

Promise Li is a socialist activist from Hong Kong and Los Angeles and a member of Tempest and Solidarity (US). He is active in international solidarity with movements from Hong Kong and China, tenant and anti-gentrification organizing in LA Chinatown, and rank-and-file graduate worker labor organizing. His other writings are published in *Spectre*, *Jacobin*, and the *Nation*.

Notes

I wish to thank Janis Yue and Zhang Yueran for their thoughtful comments on earlier drafts of this article.

1. This essay focuses only on workers' organizing in relation to their written productions in Beijing. Thus its conclusions should not be generalized to reflect workers' participation in the movement as a whole. Writings by Beijing workers are most represented among recovered texts by workers in this period.
2. The most extensive collection of Chinese workers' writings during the movement in English is Lu, *A Moment of Truth*. Some other materials are collected in Benton and Hunter, *Wild Lily, Prairie Fire*; and Han, *Cries for Democracy*. For some book-length histories of the broader movement in Beijing, see Calhoun, *Neither Gods nor Emperors*; Zhao, *Power of Tiananmen*; and Brown, *June Fourth*.
3. The main source for the WAF's activities is Walder and Gong, "Workers in the Tiananmen Protests." For other research on the WAF, see Wang, "Deng Xiaoping's Reform"; Black and Munro, *Black Hands of Beijing*; Leung, "Politics of Labour Rebellions"; Zhang, "Forgotten Socialists"; and Zhang, "Workers on Tiananmen Square."
4. Zhang, "Forgotten Socialists."
5. Jian, "Why Were Chinese Workers Not Mobilized Successfully," 139.
6. Examples of independent posters and other media during the democracy movement can be found in Widor, *Documents on the Chinese Democratic Movement*. For an analysis of these texts in the movement, see Chen, *Democracy Wall and the Unofficial Journals*; on workers' mobilization, see Heilmann, "Social Context of Mobilization in China." Calhoun and Wasserstrom, "Legacies of Radicalism," draws connections between the Cultural Revolution and the 1989 movement. The most detailed analysis of nonstate independent political publications in China since the 1950s can be found in Shao, *Citizen Publications in China*. For independent publications in 1989 specifically, see Shao, "*Minkan* of the 1989 Movement."
7. Shao, *Citizen Publications in China*, 31.

8. In *The Power of Tiananmen*, Zhao Dingxin claims that "the major workers' unions formed during the movement were actually established, supervised, and financially supported by the students" (5). On the contrary, while there was no exact boundary between workers and students' movements, they often advocated for different demands and political strategies.

9. Lau, "Role of the Working Class," 344.

10. Negt and Kluge, *Public Sphere and Experience*, 91–92.

11. Negt and Kluge, *Public Sphere and Experience*, 61.

12. Walder and Gong, "Workers in the Tiananmen Protests," 1–2.

13. Shao Jiang, interview by Promise Li, London, July 29, 2023.

14. Walder and Gong, "Workers in the Tiananmen Protests," 16.

15. Liang, "Beijing Workers' Autonomous Federation," 2.

16. "Letter to the People of Beijing," 181.

17. Zhao Hongliang, phone interview by Andrew Walder and Gong Xiaoxia, June 9, 1990.

18. This form of bureaucratic capital, as Au Loong Yu observes in *China's Rise: Strength and Fragility*, "describes the kind of capital owned or controlled by bureaucrats through their monopoly and exercise of state power, from which they profit" (17).

19. Zhao Hongliang, phone interview by Andrew Walder and Gong Xiaoxia, June 9, 1990.

20. Walder and Gong, "Workers in the Tiananmen Protests," 4: "The decision to form an independent union coincided with the outrage elicited by the beating of students at Xinhuamen."

21. Zhao Hongliang, phone interview by Andrew Walder and Gong Xiaoxia, June 9, 1990.

22. Liang, "Beijing Workers' Autonomous Federation," 2. The author's full name is Zhao Hongliang; in *A Moment of Truth*, he is named as Liang Hong.

23. Zhao Hongliang, phone interview by Andrew Walder and Gong Xiaoxia, June 9, 1990.

24. Shao Jiang, interview by Promise Li, London, July 29, 2023.

25. "Open Letter to the Students from a Beijing Worker."

26. "Letter from a Worker to the Students."

27. Brown, *June Fourth*, 55–56.

28. Brown, *June Fourth*, 55–56.

29. Brown, *June Fourth*, 58.

30. Zhao Hongliang, phone interview by Andrew Walder and Gong Xiaoxia, June 9, 1990.

31. Some of these outreach efforts led to autonomous workers' organizations outside the WAF, though these is little documentation. WAF members entered discussions with workers at Capital Steel, who formed a "workers' autonomous union" that was "an independent organization, and did not have a subordinate relationship to [the WAF]." This union turned out its members on their own factory truck at a later rally on May 28 (phone interview with Zhao Hongliang by Andrew Walder and Gong Xiaoxia, June 9, 1990).

32. "From Salesperson to Supplies Team Leader," 31–32.

33. "From Salesperson to Supplies Team Leader," 30.

34. Zhao Hongliang, phone interview by Andrew Walder and Gong Xiaoxia, June 9, 1990.

35. Liang, "Beijing Workers' Autonomous Federation," 4.

36. "'This Is a Movement of the Whole People,'" 101.

37. Brown, *June Fourth*, 73.

38. Walder and Gong, "Workers in the Tiananmen Protests," 16.

39. "Letter to the Whole Nation's Compatriots."

40. Zhao adds that these demands on May 17 expressed the WAF's interest in "form[ing] a union, and we called for people with union work experience to come and help us out, give us a little advice and direction" (Zhao Hongliang, phone interview by Andrew Walder and Gong Xiaoxia, June 9, 1990).

41. Shao Jiang, interview by Promise Li, London, UK; July 29, 2023.

42. Li, "記第一個工人自治組織——北京工自聯" ("Jì dì yī gè gōngrén zìzhì zǔzhī-běijīng gōng zì lián / Remembering the first autonomous workers' organization—Beijing's WAF").

43. "Heroic People," 267.

44. Lau, "Role of the Working Class," 352.

45. "The Workers' Manifesto."

46. "Public Notice (I)."

47. "Public Notice (II)."

48. Lau, "Role of the Working Class," 351.

49. Zhang, "Forgotten Socialists."

50. Au, "Reform or Revolution."

51. Lu Jinghua, phone interview by Andrew Walder and Gong Xiaoxia, June 9, 1990.

52. "Emergency Notice from Beijing WAF (I)"; "Emergency Notice from Beijing WAF (II)"; "Urgent Dispatch."

53. Lu Jinghua, phone interview by Andrew Walder and Gong Xiaoxia, June 9, 1990.

54. Meisner, *Mao's China and After*, 511.

55. "Public Notice (No. 10)," 373.

56. Andreas, *Disenfranchised*. Zhang Yueran's forthcoming dissertation further examines Chinese workers' experiences struggling for workplace democracy in the late 1970s and 1980s and how they informed workers' collective action in 1989.

57. "'This Is a Movement of the Whole People,'" 91.

58. Marx, "Theses on Feuerbach," 108.

References

Andreas, Joel. *Disenfranchised: The Rise and Fall of Industrial Citizenship in China*. Oxford: Oxford University Press, 2019.

Au, Loong Yu. *China's Rise: Strength and Fragility*. London: Merlin Press in association with Resistance Books and IIRE, 2012.

Au, Loong Yu. "Reform or Revolution: The Strengths and Setbacks of the 1989 Pro-Democracy Movement." *Lausan*, June 4, 2022. https://lausancollective.com/2022/reform-or-revolution -the-strengths-and-setbacks-of-the-1989-pro-democracy-movement/.

Benton, Gregor, and Alan Hunter, eds. *Wild Lily, Prairie Fire: China's Road to Democracy, Yan'an to Tian'anmen, 1942–1989*. Princeton, NJ: Princeton University Press, 1995.

Black, George, and Robin Munro. *Black Hands of Beijing: Lives of Defiance in China's Democracy Movement*. New York: Wiley, 1993.

Brown, Jeremy. *June Fourth: The Tiananmen Protests and the Beijing Massacre of 1989*. Cambridge: Cambridge University Press, 2021.

Calhoun, Craig. *Neither Gods nor Emperors: Students and the Struggle for Democracy in China*. Berkeley: University of California Press, 1997.

Calhoun, Craig, and Jeff Wasserstrom. "Legacies of Radicalism: China's Cultural Revolution and the Democracy Movement of 1989." *Thesis Eleven* 57, no. 1 (1999): 33–52.

Chen, Ruoxi. *Democracy Wall and the Unofficial Journals.* Berkeley: Center for Chinese Studies, Institute of East Asian Studies, University of California, 1982.

"Declaration of the Beijing Workers." In Lu, *A Moment of Truth*, 187.

"An Emergency Notice from Beijing WAF (I)." In Lu, *A Moment of Truth*, 206–7.

"An Emergency Notice from Beijing WAF (II)." In Lu, *A Moment of Truth*, 208.

"From Salesperson to Supplies Team Leader: WAF Activist Profile One: Beijing." In Lu, *A Moment of Truth*, 21–40.

Han Minzhu, ed. *Cries for Democracy: Writings and Speeches from the 1989 Chinese Democracy Movement.* Princeton, NJ: Princeton University Press, 1990.

Heilmann, Sebastian. "The Social Context of Mobilization in China: Factions, Work Units, and Activists during the 1976 April Fifth Movement." *China Information* 8, no. 3 (1993): 1–19.

"The Heroic People: A Record of the May 20, 1989, Incident." In Han, *Cries for Democracy*, 267–68.

Lau, Raymond W. K. "The Role of the Working Class in the 1989 Mass Movement in Beijing." *Journal of Communist Studies and Transition Politics* 12, no. 3 (1996): 343–73.

"A Letter from a Worker to the Students." In Lu, *A Moment of Truth*, 216–17.

"Letter to the People of Beijing." In Lu, *A Moment of Truth*, 181.

"Letter to the Whole Nation's Compatriots." In Lu, *A Moment of Truth*, 185–86.

Leung, Trini Wing-yue. "The Politics of Labour Rebellions in China, 1989–1994." PhD diss., University of Hong Kong, 1998.

Li, Jinjin. "Jì dì yī gè gōngrén zìzhì zǔzhī-běijīng gōng zì lián (Remembering the First Autonomous Workers' Organization—Beijing's WAF)." *Independent Chinese PEN Center*, June 16, 1999. https://www.chinesepen.org/blog/archives/43309.

Liang Hong. "Beijing Workers' Autonomous Federation: Origin and Activities." In Lu, *A Moment of Truth*, 1–12.

Lu Ping, ed. *A Moment of Truth: Workers' Participation in China's 1989 Democracy Movement and the Emergence of Independent Unions.* Hong Kong: Hong Kong Trade Union Education Centre, 1990.

Marx, Karl. "Theses on Feuerbach." In *The Marx-Engels Reader*, edited by Robert C. Tucker, 107–9. New York: W. W. Norton, 1972.

Meisner, Maurice. *Mao's China and After: A History of the People's Republic.* New York: Free Press, 1999.

Negt, Oskar, and Alexander Kluge. *Public Sphere and Experience: Toward an Analysis of the Bourgeois and Proletarian Public Sphere.* Minneapolis: University of Minnesota Press, 1993.

"An Open Letter to the Students from a Beijing Worker." In Lu, *A Moment of Truth*, 215–16.

"Public Notice (I)." In Lu, *A Moment of Truth*, 189.

"Public Notice (II)." In Lu, *A Moment of Truth*, 189–90.

"Public Notice (No. 10)." In Han, *Cries for Democracy*, 373–74.

Shao, Jiang. *Citizen Publications in China before the Internet.* New York: Palgrave Macmillan, 2015.

Shao, Jiang. "The *Minkan* of the 1989 Movement." *Taiwan Human Rights Journal* 5, no. 2 (2019): 61–94.

"Ten Questions for the Chinese Communist Party." In Lu, *A Moment of Truth*, 184.

"'This Is a Movement of the Whole People': Interview with Beijing WAF: One." In Lu, *A Moment of Truth*, 97–105.

"An Urgent Dispatch." In Lu, *A Moment of Truth*, 208–9.

Walder, Andrew, and Gong Xiaoxia. "Workers in the Tiananmen Protests: The Politics of the Beijing Workers' Autonomous Federation." *Australian Journal of Chinese Affairs*, no. 29 (1993): 1–29.

Wang, Shaoguang. "Deng Xiaoping's Reform and the Chinese Workers' Participation in the Protest Movement of 1989." In *Research in Political Economy*, vol. 13, edited by Paul Zarembka, 163–97. New York: Elsevier, 1992.

Widor, Claude, ed. *Documents on the Chinese Democratic Movement, 1978–1980: Unofficial Magazines and Wall Posters*. Paris: Éditions de l'École des hautes études en sciences sociales, 1981.

"The Workers' Manifesto." In Lu, *A Moment of Truth*, 188.

Yang, Jian. "Why Were Chinese Workers Not Mobilised Successfully in the 1989 Democracy Movement?" In Lu, *A Moment of Truth*, 137–43.

Zhang, Yueran. "Workers on Tiananmen Square." In *Proletarian China: A Century of Chinese Labor*, edited by Ivan Franceschini and Christian Sorace, 496–504. London: Verso, 2022.

Zhang, Yueran. "The Forgotten Socialists of Tiananmen Square." *Jacobin*, June 4, 2019. https://jacobin.com/2019/06/tiananmen-square-worker-organization-socialist-democracy.

Zhao, Dingxin. *The Power of Tiananmen: State-Society Relations and the 1989 Beijing Student Movement*. Chicago: University of Chicago Press, 2001.

Black Internationalism, Print Culture, and Political Education in Claude McKay's *Banjo*

Mae Miller-Likhethe

The history of the audience is what is missing from the history of Black
Radicalism.
—Robert Hill, "On Collectors"

Over three decades ago, Robert Hill, the celebrated archivist and historian
of the Universal Negro Improvement Association (UNIA) movement, argued that
"the history of the audience is what's missing in the history of black radicalism."[1]
Historians, Hill argued, had been "most concerned to document the rhetoric and
sources of the ideas of the street orators who emerged on Lenox Avenue in Harlem"
with less emphasis on the "history of the audience that presented itself to the intel-
ligentsia . . . [as they] strolled between soapboxes" en route to workplaces, community centers, or dance halls. The combined effect of limited archival preservation
and epistemic priorities and the lack of attention to the reading and listening audience has stifled knowledge of political education and revolutionary movement
building, as relatively little is known about the collective practices through which
ideas were debated and ascribed meaning by ordinary people.

The publication of new political biographies of Black leaders and street orators, grassroots histories of liberation struggles, and the dynamic editorial landscape
of the global Black press have shed new light on the historical geographies of Black
internationalism and the role of print culture in shaping political imaginaries and
communities of resistance.[2] Despite new efforts to trace the spatial practices and

Radical History Review
Issue 150 (October 2024)   DOI 10.1215/01636545-11257395
© 2024 by MARHO: The Radical Historians' Organization, Inc.

patterns of global Black press readership among ordinary people, the specific and heterogeneous processes of interpretation and contestation remain elusive, particularly for interlocutors who—for various reasons including ambivalence, illiteracy, and fear of state repression—did not submit editorials, workers' correspondence, or other commentary for publication and whose debates took place outside official forums at lunch counters, living rooms, church banquets, and other lesser-studied sites of print culture.

Broadly, print culture encompasses the study of books, magazines, periodicals, newspapers, letters, diaries, and other textual sources. To gauge practices of intellectual production "from below" requires accessing "not only intellectual texts produced by social movements but also the dynamics of group belief and conversation by which ideas travel, transform, and take flight."[3] More than discursive analysis, the interdisciplinary field of print culture studies is concerned with "transforming print ecologies" that include material histories of textual production and circulation, the formation of political subjectivities and spaces, the social configuration of editorial networks and communities of readership, and the relationship between printed media, geopolitics, and technology.[4] Recent efforts to decolonize and expand histories of print culture in the twentieth century have explored the role of migrant and maritime workers who covertly distributed newspapers and periodicals across national and imperial borders and decentered cities such as New York and London and elite publishing housing by foregrounding the influences of small regional papers from the Caribbean to the Cape of Good Hope. Such studies bring into view the active knowledge production of readers and editors from peripheral towns and assert the political significance of "tin trunk archives"—collections of scrapbooks, letters, photographs, and clippings documenting communities of resistance from Chicago to Nairobi that are stored under beds and in intimate domestic spaces—as the "necessary counterpart to the fragmentary migrated colonial archive lying on the cold temperature-controlled shelves" and inaccessible to the global majority.[5] Stretching the historical subjects and spaces of knowledge production brings into sharp focus the conditions of (im)mobility that structured subaltern life and, in turn, formations of diasporic racial consciousness through print culture. Yet the specific contours of political education—the substance of debate and struggle to transform attitudes and actions—through the combination of ephemeral encounters and sustained engagements remains difficult to grasp within archival repositories.

"Every historian of the multitude, the dispossessed, the subaltern, and the enslaved," as the cultural theorist Saidiya Hartman explains, "is forced to grapple with the power and authority of the archive and the limits it sets on what can be known, whose perspective matters, and who is endowed with the gravity and authority of historical actor."[6] While some scholars have turned to the "tin trunk" as a source of subaltern counterknowledge, others have adopted speculative and literary modes of analytical redress in instances where such intimate accounts of ordinary life are yet to be shared. To address long histories of epistemic violence, erasure, and dehumanization, scholars of race and empire have "reimagin[ed] the relationship between materiality and memory and creating alternative archival forms that fill the spaces of exclusion."[7] Within this body of work, scholars have developed new methodologies for listening to the "undercurrents of images" for traces of refusal and self-formation, queer approaches that embrace the elusive—that which cannot "quite be explained or filed away according to the usual categories," and transdisciplinary research that blends archival analysis with family histories.[8]

This article turns to Claude McKay's semi-autobiographical novel *Banjo* (1929) as both a cultural artifact produced within a particular historical conjuncture and as a text that simultaneously indexes and works to redress the gaps in archival knowledge and practice in the context of Black internationalism and global histories of print culture (fig. 1). Set in Marseilles, France, *Banjo* follows the daily adventures of a group of transient men—seafarers, dockworkers, and soldiers—from across the African diaspora who, however briefly, have made a home in the French port district. The novel's distinct blend of politics, pleasure, and cultural production were further brought to life by the acclaimed Harlem Renaissance artist Aaron Douglas, who designed the book jacket for the first edition (fig. 1). Douglas depicts a scene of improvised music making—combined with diving, dancing, and deep discussion—along the waterfront against the backdrop of the Marseilles skyline, mirroring McKay's depictions of the city's social and sonic landscapes. As the characters wander between cafes, boardinghouses, and the docks in search of work and pursuing their goal of forming a blues band, they engage in heated debates about Black liberation. Ranging from Black nationalism and communism to discourses of racial uplift and respectability, the ideological positions held by the novel's characters exemplify the multiplicity of diasporic worldviews that circulated throughout the early twentieth century. While scholars have discussed *Banjo* in the context of Black masculinity and homosocial community formation, vernacular musical cultures, and the politics of linguistic translation, I argue that the text also provides a critical exploration of processes of political education and practices of collective readership among transient, working-class subjects from across the Black diaspora.[9]

Through its depiction of the countercultural spaces and complex political subjectivities of ordinary people, *Banjo* offers a blueprint for the engaging informal spaces of debate and political education that emerged around and as a result of revolutionary periodicals, as workers sought to link local concerns to global revolutionary praxis. *Banjo* must be read, in part, as an extension of McKay's political journalism and within his broader efforts to bridge Black nationalist and communist movements throughout the interwar period. The audience depicted in *Banjo* is marked not only by contentious debate but also by the material contradictions of daily life and extraordinary challenges of consciousness-raising among ordinary people across racial, national, and class-based lines, all of which shape and constrain

Figure 1. *Banjo*, first
edition cover, 1929. Art
by Aaron Douglas.

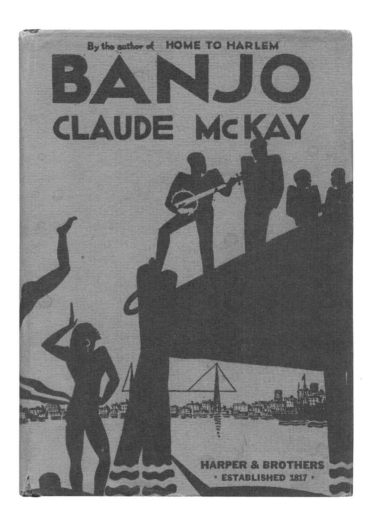

possibilities for political education and collective action. As a foundational Black diasporic literary text of the interwar period, *Banjo* sheds critical light on the politics of
vernacular knowledge production through radical periodicals, while also enriching
understandings of interwar activism and the historical geographies of revolutionary
print culture more broadly.

Black Radicalism, Print Culture, and Political Education

McKay's novel should be understood as a piece of a much broader archival repository developed by Black people themselves. Throughout the nineteenth and twentieth centuries, print cultures of the African diaspora were arguably the most important modality through which communities of resistance were formed and competing
visions of freedom were articulated and contested. Described as "the single greatest
power in the Negro race," the Black press played a foundational role in the

internationalization of liberatory struggles.[10] Black print culture did not simply communicate with the public but rather "reset the terms of public conversation" around race and nationhood and, further, aimed to create publics by carving out material and discursive space for audiences to collectively "debate the boundaries of their common interests."[11] Articles and stories circulated and new geographical imaginaries were forged in the dialogic exchange between readers and editors.[12] Black newspapers and periodicals fomented racial consciousness through the coverage of antiracist and anti-imperial struggles, challenging stereotypes and pathology within mainstream outlets, chronicling daily life in Black communities, and celebrating advances in legal recognition, labor rights, and racial uplift.[13]

The archives of interwar Black print culture are partial and fragmented, due in part to the dearth of remaining original manuscripts and the institutional devaluation of Black social history except as a matter of pathology or security.[14] Despite archival limitations, researchers have published invaluable works that attend to textual analysis and complex meanings as well as to the way that "the page peeled off a letter press, traveled to far-flung towns, landed in the lands of literate people, and then accelerated through the voice of a reader who broadcast to friends and community."[15] Careful studies have explored the historical conjunctures that shaped and constrained the editorial directions of Black internationalists such as Claudia Jones, C. L. R. James, and George Padmore, and demonstrated how the distinct cosmopolitanism of the imperial metropole paradoxically created the conditions for anti-imperialist critique and solidarity through print culture.[16] Moreover, journalists encouraged readers to forge connections between Jim Crow segregation in the United States, imperial expansion throughout Asia and Africa, the imminent rise of fascism in Europe, and the systematic repression of Black workers' movements from South Africa to the South of France.[17]

The issues of the day were debated through informal study groups. For instance, public debates about the paper *Negro World* were integral to Ella Baker's political education in Harlem.[18] In Johannesburg, T. W. Thibedi led communist night schools where he taught miners how to read by candlelight using Bukharin's *ABCs of Communism* and the *Workers' Herald*.[19] Of the communist *Negro Worker*, C. L. R. James declared, "Tens of thousands of black workers in various parts of the world received their first political education from the paper," which "gave information, advice, guidance, ideas about black struggles on every continent."[20] Each of these instances speaks to the capacity of radical print culture as a tool of political education that can galvanize militant action and promote critical literacy for social transformation. Yet political education cannot be reduced to the sum of exposure to revolutionary ideas and experiences of injustice. Rather, the study of political education requires an epistemological shift from "winning over" readers to a dynamic exploration of how—through which kinds of conversations, debate, reflection, relationships, and collaborative study—existing worldviews are transformed.[21]

In some instances, editorials provide a capacious repository of public sentiment, transformative potential, and collective organization. A patron of the *Limón Search-light*, a Costa Rican weekly that regularly reprinted articles from the *Chicago Defender* and *Negro World*, detailed his own dedicated readership and extensive efforts to distribute the paper throughout the region: "It is my habit, 'good or bad,' to send a weekly copy of your Invaluable Weekly to Trinidad, so that my relatives may see what is what in Limón. Again, I send a weekly copy to Colón to a girl friend, who passes it around to her girlfriends. . . . Now and then I would send a copy to Jamaica, to my school friends. And I also keep a weekly copy for my further reference."[22] A South African hospital worker, James Diraath, documented his efforts to circulate the *Negro World* through the Kimberley mining compounds in the 1920s: "Every copy [was] carefully preserved and passed from hand to hand so that as many people as possible may hear the truth" and, as a result, "thousands of our native people here . . . are greatly encouraged by the . . . splendid work of the UNIA."[23] A Nigerian union member proclaimed that the *Negro Worker* "opened our eyes to the true light, we will never turn back and stop reading, even if it means 100 instead of 10 years in jail."[24] The editorials provide an important glimpse into the readers' dedication to actively shaping and stretching the geographies of solidarity through interwar print culture. The passing of periodicals between neighbors, kin, and comrades was an integral aspect of the "cycle of action, reflection, and action through which human beings work to transform their worlds."[25]

Still, the editorials do not shed light on the conversations, commentary, or lines of inquiry that accompanied these embodied modes of circulation. Historians have recuperated traces of political commentary, and terms of informal debate appear in the self-made archives of African American scrapbooks—intricate compilations of articles clipped from the mainstream white press and Black newspapers such as *Crisis*, the official organ of the National Association for the Advancement of Colored People, interspersed with handwritten annotations, oral histories, and contextual analysis.[26] The selection, juxtaposition, and annotation of articles for personal use and possible sharing among neighbors and friends is an indicative measure of dialogic learning and archival construction. The scrapbooks can be understood more broadly as a practice of diasporic "tin trunk" archiving whereby ordinary people compiled letters, diaries, photographs, and ephemera alongside news clippings to produce an intimate counterarchive of community struggle that stretches from lynching in the United States to the repression of the Mau Mau uprising in Kenya. Like scrapbooks, the tin trunk (or suitcase) records prominent throughout colonial West and Southern Africa contributed to the formation of local publics through reading circles and debates while chronicling the processes of self-identification and consciousness formation among ordinary people who challenged—and in some cases internalized—colonial bureaucratic discourses.[27]

Despite efforts to recuperate subaltern, self-authored collections, imperial intelligence archives remain among the most authoritative account of distributional networks and hold some of the most extensive collections of anti-imperial pamphlets and periodicals.[28] Often, suspects from various organizations espousing "pan-Islamism, Garveyism, communism, and worker's activism" were "lumped together with little regard to such differences."[29] This tendency is reflected in a 1919 internal memorandum exchanged between US intelligence officials, which noted that "the negro editors and writers . . . were fully alive to the influence they possess over their readers as well as to the fact that in their hands the negro masses may be made to assume a very dangerous power." According to the report, three papers—the socialist *Messenger*, the communist *Crusader*, and the Black nationalist *Negro World*—all emerged in response to the relative conservativism of existing periodicals such as the NAACP's *Crisis* and the *Amsterdam News*. Despite ideological differences, J. Edgar Hoover expressed concern that the "radical movement in the negro press [had] become remarkably accelerated" and that the result was "increasing defiance and organized alignment with the most destructive forces of our political life today."[30] As the passages demonstrate, the organization and annotation of these documents is more indicative of colonial anxieties about the proliferation of "seditious" materials than any nuanced account of how the materials were being debated or ascribed meaning on the ground.

Finally, scholars have used numerous available quantitative methods ranging from historical analysis of reader surveys to new tools within the digital humanities to trace the attitudes of ordinary readers. Among these, studies have compared newspaper sales and distribution as a measure of how readers used their purchasing power as an expression of ideological and intellectual agreement, analyzed records of library loans from worker education centers to assess which periodicals were most widely read by patrons and to identify networks of readers based on common interests, and examined reader surveys from the nineteenth and twentieth century to determine which political issues were most important to newspaper readers as well as how literature and community theater were mobilized alongside discussions of current events to raise political consciousness.[31] While shedding important light on aggregate trends of readership and engagement with print culture among working-class communities, quantitative studies tell us little about readers' motivations, learning processes, or political transformations.

Indeed, there is schism between the content conveyed within print materials, the specific associative dimensions of lived experiences that mediate readership practices across space and time, and the affective responses that prompt, delay, or stymie subsequent actions—whether the action is further reading, retelling of news, or joining a protest or chapter. From memoirs, editorials and reader correspondences, sales ledgers, and library loans we know that print materials were debated in collective spaces, but glimpses of *how* remain elusive.[32] In response, cultural theorists have adopted speculative and literary approaches to archival analysis in order to recuperate the voices of ordinary people whose world-making practices have been pathologized by state bureaucracy and minimized within social movement histories that privilege leaders and editors, and whose interiority can only be partially understood through available documentation.[33]

   While literary texts have long been recognized as a mode of diasporic community formation and social commentary, this article argues that novels offer a window into the daily lives, social spaces, and collective practices of Black diasporic readers in the interwar period that are less readily audible within archival repositories.[34] As the historian Lara Putnam has argued in her study of interwar Black internationalism in the Caribbean basin, "Novels offer glimpses of island streets where a shopkeeper might pass the time 'reading a two-days-old newspaper and talking politics with anyone who might drop in for a chat.'"[35] Building on this recognition, I suggest that literature is a cultural repository that—when studied judiciously and contextualized within and against available archival sources, memoirs, and periodicals—can offer invaluable insights into the imagined social questions and experiences that animate a specific historical conjuncture and generate new questions about the excesses and excisions of the archive itself.[36] If the study of transnational print culture "requires renewed attention to the radically transforming print ecology and new theoretical models and methodologies are required to make sense of it," then the discussion of literature and literary representations of the global Black press must feature centrally within historical analysis.[37] Reading literature along and against the archival grain is a generative research tool that not only redresses potential gaps within conventional historical archives but further indexes grounded and dynamic processes of political education and transformation and expands extant understandings of the relationship between revolutionary periodicals and other genres of print cultures.

The Question of "Authenticity" and the Duality of Readership in the Works of Claude McKay

Scholars have pointed to Claude McKay's portrayal of the "fleeting configurations" and "fragile translocal connections" that constitute diasporic politics as a source of conceptual strength that challenges tendencies to essentialize, dehistoricize, or obscure the historical specificities and uneven geographies of Black subject formation (fig. 2).[38] Although a work of fiction, *Banjo* was directly informed by the years McKay spent living in Marseilles from 1926 to 1928 and a promise he made to Lamine Senghor, the Senegalese Communist writer and seamen's organizer, to write "the truth about Negroes in Marseilles."[39] With both *Home to Harlem* and *Banjo*, McKay remained staunchly committed to writing multidimensional characters based on the people that he had met while doing manual labor, organizing workers, and covering working class struggles in New York, London, Paris, and Marseilles. Responding to negative reviews of *Home to Harlem*, McKay reflected in *A Long Way from Home*:

Figure 2. Photograph of Claude McKay taken for *Home to Harlem* promotion, ca. 1928. Harry Ransom Center Digital Archive, University of Texas, Austin.

I did not come to the knowing of Negro workers in an academic way, by talking to black crowds at meetings, nor in a bohemian way, by talking about them in cafes. I knew the unskilled Negro worker of the city by working with him as a porter and longshoreman and as a waiter on the railroad. . . . So when I came to write about the low-down Negro, I did not have to compose him from an outside view. Nor did I have to write a pseudo-romantic account, as do bourgeois persons who become working-class for a while and work in shops and factories to get material.[40]

McKay remained committed to a politics of authenticity that embraced the complexities and contradictions of modern Black subject formation against what he understood to be superficial, unidimensional, and utilitarian portrayals that failed to resonate with the daily lives of the transient peoples from across the world that he had met in the harbors of the imperial metropole.

McKay's characters emphasized the heterogeneity and contradictions of diasporic community formations, and his expressions of literary "authenticity" cannot be separated from his political activism and journalism. Born in rural Jamaica in 1889, Claude McKay migrated to the United States in 1912 to study agriculture. The historian Winston James describes McKay as

a free thinker, feminist, militant rationalist and Fabian socialist from his early childhood . . . , had earned a reputation as a poet before leaving Jamaica, [and] was further radicalized by the brutal racism (especially lynching) of the US he entered, the mindless slaughter of the First World War, the revolutionary ferment during and after the war, especially the outbreak of revolution in Russia, and the anti-colonial struggles sweeping the globe, especially in India and Ireland.[41]

For McKay, the Communist International was the primary vehicle for achieving world revolution that was simultaneously anticapitalist, anti-imperialist, and antiracist. He served as a member of the executive committee of the African Blood Brotherhood, a Harlem-based communist organization largely comprising West Indian radicals, and attended the Fourth Congress of the Communist International held in Moscow in 1922, where he and the Surinamese radical Otto Huiswoud argued the importance of the "Negro Question" for the Bolshevik movement.[42]

From 1919 to 1922 McKay worked to bridge the Black nationalism of the UNIA and revolutionary communism. Many of his most prescient articles were written from London, where he arrived in late 1919 against a backdrop of racial violence against Black, Arab, and South Asian workers in British port cities.[43] In a *Negro World* editorial, for example, McKay wrote fondly of the sense of community he derived from the library at the Drury Lane club for "all colored soldiers, sailors and nonmilitary men" in London, while also lamenting the shortage of high-quality reading material. He explained, "There isn't much to read in the little library" save for "a few copies of *The Crisis* and some old newspapers from America and the West Indies that had no guts," but in response to this shortage, he placed there "copies of the English and American *Nation*, *Workers Dreadnought*, *One Big Union* monthly, *Negro World*, and also some I.W.W. and other revolutionary literature."[44] His brief discussion of the library at the Drury Lane club demonstrates McKay's efforts to encourage club patrons and *Negro World* subscribers to read widely across geographical and political orientations.

Throughout this period, he published articles in labor periodicals such as the London-based *Workers Dreadnaught*, the unofficial organ of the British section of the Third International, which implored the white labor movement to build common cause with anticolonial nationalist movements and published articles in Marcus Garvey's *Negro World* on the importance of Bolshevism for the global Black freedom struggle. To the readers of *Negro World*, he emphatically encouraged "every Negro who lays claim to leadership to make a study of Bolshevism and explain its meaning to the colored masses, [as] it is the greatest and most scientific idea afloat in the world today."[45] Prior to his dispatch from London, McKay wrote a letter directly to Garvey in which he attached a clipping from the *Daily Herald*, a British socialist daily, as evidence that "the representative organ of British Labour denounced so strongly [the] imperial abomination and endorsed the self-determination of Britain's subject people" and, at the same time, proclaimed that "as I have said before in your paper, radical Negroes should be more interested in the white radical movement [in order to] meet on common ground against the common enemy."[46]

McKay's respect for the *Daily Herald* was short-lived, as less than one month after his letter was published in *Negro World*, the *Daily Herald* ran a series of sensational articles that perpetuated stereotypes of violent hypersexuality among colonial African soldiers and called for the "immediate withdrawal of the black troops and their return to Africa."[47] McKay subsequently cut ties with the paper and continued to write articles for the *Workers Dreadnought* on the struggles of "colored as well as white seamen" and synthesized labor stories from across the British empire.[48] He further used his journalistic platform to appeal to predominantly white segments of the international labor movement to support the struggles of African Americans in the US South, along with Irish and Indian independence. In 1920 he offered the clearest distillation of his position on the relationship between nationalism and communism: "Although an international Socialist, I am supporting the [UNIA] movement, for I believe that, for subject peoples, at least, Nationalism is the open door to Communism. Furthermore, I will try to bring this great army of awakened workers over to the finer system of Socialism."[49]

By the time McKay delivered his address to the Fourth Congress of the Communist International in the winter of 1922, he had become disillusioned with the incipient "white chauvinism" of the communist parties of the United States and Great Britain and called on the national parties to do more serious work with racialized communities.[50] Likewise, even as McKay thought the UNIA "repudiate[ed] all of the fundamentals of black workers' economic struggles" and "ignor[ed] all geographical and political divisions [to flatten] a vast continent of diverse tribes to a homogenous nation of natives," he held firm that the networks of the NAACP, African Blood Brotherhood, and UNIA could be mobilized by the Comintern to advance class conscious international movements.[51] His lived experience navigating the contradictions and polarities of interwar revolutionary struggles directly informed his literary compositions.

McKay first visited Paris in early 1924, and he lived in the south of France— Marseilles and Toulon— intermittently between 1924 and 1928.[52] In Paris, McKay met with the American literary editor Louise Bryant. The pair discussed the particular merits of "proletarian literature" and, as is detailed in McKay's memoir, his exchange with Bryant significantly influenced the composition of his early novels. McKay explains:

John Reed had written some early stories about ordinary people with no radical propaganda in them, she [Bryant] said, and suggested that I should do the same about my Negro stories—just write plain tales. And so now again in Paris, when she was sending me off to southern France for my health, Louise Bryant warned me: "Remember our conversation in New York, and don't try to force your stories with propaganda. If you write a good story, that will be the biggest propaganda."[53]

We can read McKay's fiction as an extension of his political journalism and broad efforts to appeal to the heterogeneous masses of the global working class rather than as a clear departure. His attempts to construct "authentic" characters were, at once, mediated by his experiences as a day laborer and writer living among Black workers in cities such as New York, London, and Paris and by his wider outlook on what he understood to be the two great international movements of his time: the Universal Negro Improvement Association and the Communist International. For McKay, true authenticity did not reside in the search for ideological purity, singular origins, or unidimensional explanations of political interests. Rather, his vision of authenticity lay in the material conditions and contradictions of daily life that mediate diasporic subjectivities. In embracing the lived struggles of the Black diaspora, McKay's *Banjo* illuminates a multiplicity of reader responses that shed light on print culture circulation and engagement, while also enriching extent understandings of interwar revolutionary movements. If, indeed, we read *Banjo* as a "good story" that is also a mode of propaganda, the messaging of the text is not a definitive call to join a particular organization so much as it is a clarion call to embrace the contradictory, ephemeral, and nonlinear qualities of political education that shape and constrain the possibilities for collective action and consciousness formation.

Negro World, *La race nègre*, and the Challenge of the Archive

The two periodicals referenced most extensively within *Banjo* are *Negro World*— the official organ of the UNIA— and *La race nègre* (*The Negro Race*)—the official organ of the Ligue de défense de la race nègre (LDRN), a French affiliate of the Communist International. Both papers emerged with in the "rising tide" of movements against racial and colonial oppression in the first half of the twentieth century. A rich body of research has examined the organizational histories of these respective movements, the political biographies of UNIA and LDRN leaders, and the editorial objectives and trajectories of *Negro World* and *La race nègre* with respect to gender, geographical differences, and debates on the meanings and mechanisms for achieving liberation. I will briefly discuss the key features of the periodicals and their organizational strategies before turning to an analysis of how these texts are discussed within the novel *Banjo* and the questions raised about diasporic readership.

 Negro World was established in August 1918 as "the indispensable weekly, the voice of the awakened Negro, reaching the masses everywhere."[54] With an estimated global membership of two million at its peak in the 1920s, the UNIA was largest Black internationalist movement of the twentieth century. With major outposts from New Orleans to Cape Town, Garvey's organization espoused a commitment to racial pride and self-determination that appealed widely to communities across the African diaspora, from "dockworkers in South Africa to sharecroppers in the United States, from cocoa farmers in Ghana to intellectuals in Nigeria, from ethnic mobilizers in Zimbabwe to activists in Cuba."[55] In 1923, members of the New Orleans chapter described the UNIA as "our church, our clubhouse, our theater, our fraternal order and our school."[56]

 With the primary aim of bringing "hope and light to our people in all corners of the world made dark by the deeds of the oppressors," issues of *Negro World* featured editorials written by Garvey, progress updates from UNIA chapters around the world, and appeals to the masses to join the movement for Black redemption and self-determination.[57] *Negro World* was unique among contemporaneous periodicals for its literary prose and columns about the revolutionary role of women (particularly those edited by Amy Jacques Garvey), even as the overall character of the paper reinforced masculinist narratives of Black nationalism.[58] *Negro World*'s spread and influence were magnified by regional newspapers such as the *Panama Workman, Belize Independent*, Kingston *Daily Gleaner*, and *Limón Searchlight*, which reprinted articles from Garvey's periodical and published forums and editorials in which local journalists debated the global dimensions of local injustices; the periodical was translated into languages including Spanish, French, and Zulu.

Deemed "more dangerous than rifles" by colonial officials from Trinidad to Dahomey (present-day Benin), *Negro World* was banned and criminalized across the African diaspora.[59] Yet the paper continued to circulate through clandestine channels and networks. In her incisive organizational history of the UNIA, Amy Jacques Garvey explains, "It [*Negro World*] was carried by trains, ships, smuggled in suitcase lining by seamen and students; concealed beneath garments being worn, or just the frontpage article hidden in a hat or cap lining." Teachers such as W. C. Parker—a Panamanian tutor who regularly traveled between New York City, Costa Rica, and Panama and was an influential mentor to the famed writer and editor Eric Walrond—spread word of the movement and distributed copies of *Negro World* in the Canal Zone. Sailors and dockworkers played a pivotal role in the newspapers' distributional networks.[60] Similarly, in the Gold Coast (present-day Ghana), *Negro World* was

an eye opener to the few educated elements, and others who rebelled against the imperialistic haphazard division of their continent into colonial territories for exploitation by Europeans. Discussion groups were formed. . . . The *Negro World* was banned; but some courageous Africans in various walks of life started to individually revolt against the slavish and tyrannical treatment of them by Europeans.[61]

Finally, in New York City, where Garvey gathered over 100,000 delegates from over twenty African countries for the landmark UNIA convention in 1920, police reports noted that "his followers stand in various groups in front of Liberty Hall until late at night discussing his various schemes."[62] Days later, officials lamented that despite attempts to infiltrate the UNIA meetings, agents could not discern the particulars of what transpired in the gatherings and could only infer from the members "chuckling audibly as they congratulated each other on a 'wonderful meeting.'"[63] Yet, despite the archival traces of the UNIA's material impacts in the form of official bans and established communities of readership, the specific features of conversations and deliberations surrounding specific texts and ideas—the process of consciousness formation—is difficult to recuperate within historical documents.

The same challenge can be seen in the historical records of the Ligue de défense de la race nègre (LDRN), another leading anti-imperial organization active in the interwar period. Founded in 1927 by the Senegalese activist Lamine Senghor and the French Sudanese agitator Tiémoko Garan Kouyaté , the LDRN was one of the most significant anti-imperial organizations with "global reverberations" founded by colonial subjects in interwar France.[64] It was established amid a split between the more reformist section of the Comité de défense de la race nègre and the more revolutionary faction—led by Senghor and Kouyaté—which advocated for national independence for African colonies and aligned itself with the Communist International, French Communist Party, and League Against Imperialism. The LRDN was established to "work for the revolutionary education, organisations and complete emancipation of the entire Negro race" and demanded freedoms of press, speech, association, and movement in French African colonies. In 1929, the LDRN mounted a strong campaign in solidarity with anticolonial uprisings in the French Congo. In public meetings, the organization advocated for "absolute and immediate independence" for the Congo and demanded that the French Communist Party offer meaningful support to national independence struggles in Africa and Asia; at the 1929 League Against Imperialism congress in Frankfurt it called for solidarity between the "national emancipation movement of the Negroes of Africa and the Negro movement for political and social emancipation in America."[65] The LDRN's membership was diasporic, and outside Paris the organization established chapters in Senegal, Togo, Gabon, Madagascar, Cameroon, Côte d'Ivoire, and Germany.[66]

It was through the LDRN's monthly periodical *La race nègre* that the organization's visions were most strategically circulated and consolidated. First published in June 1927, *La race nègre* was one of the most widely read Francophone anticolonial periodicals of the interwar period. As Silvester Trnovec has argued, "*La Race Nègre* offered a radically different picture of colonial reality than the official discourse of France's 'civilising mission' and was among the first press organs of African francophone intellectuals to demand the right to self-determination and independence for French colonial territories in sub-Saharan Africa."[67] From its inception, the periodical was plagued by internal tensions between "race first" approaches to Pan-Africanism and "class first" visions of the international proletarian struggle. From 1927 to 1929, issues of *La race nègre* regularly featured French translations of English language articles published in *Negro World*, which promoted the slogan "Africa for Africans," and in Lapido Solanke's *WASU*, the official organ of the London-based West African Student Union, a group that focused on "the awakening of a racial, not a territorial consciousness," along with eyewitness accounts of abuses committed by colonial officials and articles about the cultural achievements of Africans throughout history.[68] As Brent Hayes Edwards has argued, throughout its lifetime *La race nègre* expressed a "constant sense of searching" for a coherent ideological viewpoint; despite the protracted battles over editorial control, the paper's commitment to experimentation, debate, and fluctuation created an invaluable tool for dialogical learning.[69]

Despite persistent surveillance, raids, and infiltration by colonial officials, the LDRN still managed to circulate copies of *La race nègre* widely and developed innovative strategies to circumvent colonial surveillance systems. Students arriving from France hid revolutionary tracts in their schoolbooks, and, in some cases, members copied articles from *La race nègre* directly into handwritten letters handed to trusted friends.[70] The Cameroonian architect Joseph Bilé and other members of the German section smuggled copies of *La race nègre* into Cameroon, Togo, and Namibia by folding the periodicals into private letters addressed to friends and family, along with the socialist paper *Die rote Fahne* (*The Red Flag*).[71] African seamen in Marseilles, Le Havre, and Hamburg carried the periodical to various ports of call in West Africa. The Bamako postal worker Moudou Kouyaté, brother of Tiémoko Garan Kouyaté, received multiple copies of *La race nègre* that were distributed to LDRN sympathizers in the region. In 1928 the lieutenant governor of Ivory Coast wrote, "It is certain that the newspaper *La Race Nègre* is read by a large part of the literate native population along the lower coast and that an intense propaganda is underway to spread it throughout the colony."[72] Here again we learn of the existence of a committed readership whose consciousness has been transformed in part through engagements with *La race nègre*, but we know little about the specific questions and concerns raised by ordinary readers and audiences as the various papers printed in Europe changed hands along the railways of Senegal or the quays of Abidjan harbor.

Remarkably, *Banjo* presents a literary distillation of these respective political movements within the Vieux Port, Marseilles. Departing from the cursory references to distributive networks, traces of clandestine study groups, and well-formulated arguments published in periodicals, the novel indexes the sustained moments of struggle, debate, and dissensus among transient migrant and maritime workers from across the diaspora that converged in port cities (in this case Marseilles), which are otherwise only partially visible in the publications discussed above. From the literary account, we can extrapolate more generally about the patterns, processes, and contradictions that sailors navigated as they moved between ports and worked to forge diasporic solidarities, which McKay ultimately embraced as he articulated a politics of authenticity that pivoted on heterogeneity in and as struggle.

Banjo and the Exigencies of Diasporic Readership

Banjo is ostensibly a collection of episodic encounters between a group of sailors, soldiers, drifters, and deportees hailing from all corners of the African diaspora was they wander between waterfront cafes such as the Cairo Café, the Café African, and the Antilles Restaurant in search of cheap wine, good stories, lively debate, and late nights of music and debauchery. More than a recourse to naive idealism or apo-litical idleness, *Banjo* acts as a sort of cautionary tale against simplistic or utilitarian conceptualizations of political consciousness formation, a lesson that maintains political prescience today. Indeed, as the literary theorist Brent Hayes Edwards has argued in a rejoinder to W. E. B. Du Bois's initial review of the text, the episodes on the Marseilles docks are not incidental to philosophy, but rather "the episodes *are* the philosophy, and it is not an internationalism of coordinated social movement, but an internationalism of debate, miscommunication, and light-hearted and hot-headed accusation."[73] Through its depiction of the countercultural spaces and com-plex political subjectivities of ordinary people, *Banjo* offers a blueprint for the engaging informal spaces of debate and political education that emerged around and as a result of revolutionary periodicals as workers sought to link local concerns to global revolutionary praxis.[74]

While the characters share a general love of music and a loose desire to form a jazz band, their ideological positions, personalities, and conditions of (im)mobility differ tremendously. Lincoln Agrippa Daily, affectionately named "Banjo," is a vet-eran from the US South who is more interested in forming an "orchestra" than solv-ing the "race question." Ray is a Haitian writer with proletarian sensibilities. Taloufa, a Nigerian sailor who had been injured in the 1919 Cardiff race riots, is an avid Gar-vey supporter; so is Goosey, the "high yellow" flautist raised in a middle-class family in New Jersey. Bugsy is identified as a militant Black nationalist, as is the proprietor of the Café African, whose character is inspired by Pierre M'Baye, the celebrated Senegalese leader of the LDRN who helped forge solidarities between North Afri-can, West African, and South East Asian anticolonial movements and distributed *La race nègre* to seamen. *Banjo* offers insightful commentary on the cafes as spaces where the content of various periodicals was fiercely debated and where attempts by colonial officials to censor and repress liberatory movements were discussed, con-tested, and in some instances circumvented. Throughout the novel, it was in spaces such as Café African—much like the soldiers' and seamen's clubs in London whose libraries McKay curated and that, in part, shaped the formation of his political consciousness—that the characters' conceptions of Black radicalism were mediated by and shaped through articles the appeared in *Negro World* and *La race nègre.* Within these everyday spaces, contours of struggle, questions of solidarity, and the meaning of "civilization" were most acutely (re)defined.

Two scenes are particularly instructive for exploring the contours of debate and engagements with Black print culture in the Vieux Port. In the first instance, the proprietor of the Café African attempts to educate a Senegalese sailor after a fight breaks out between Italian and Senegalese dockworkers. Banjo, Ray, and Bugsy are also present in the café. The Senegalese sailor explains that "there was much jeal-ousy between the rival groups and the Senegalese aggressively reminded the Ital-ians that they were French and possessed the rights of citizens." The statement launches a wider debate into the geographies of racial injustice. The proprietor, a "fervid apostle of Americanism" argued that "there is no difference between Italians and Frenchmen. They are all the same white and prejudiced against Black skin," and on all accounts "America is better every time for a colored man." The sailor, "as if pinched behind to defense of his country," continues to defend the promise of French republicanism and the civilizing project of the French empire. After several rounds of shouting in French and Wolof, the proprietor brings down *La race nègre* from the shelf where it was "displayed conspicuously for sale" despite pushback from some clients and previous rebuke by a colonial official. Before discussing the contents of the issue of the paper, the proprietor proudly maintains his right to "remain master In his own café" by resisting efforts to censor his periodicals and explained that he "was not in West Africa where he had heard local authorities had forbidden the circulation of the *Negro World*."[75] The passage has been described as a "dramatization of the importance of sites like the Café African to the generation of anticolonial networks" and as a target of transimperial surveillance.[76] A closer reading of the scene further underscores the contradictions of colonial modernity and the "antinomy between universality and particularity that existed within both the metropolitan and colonial poles of the [French] imperial nation-state."[77]

As the scene progresses, the barkeeper "spread out the copy of *La Race Nègre* and began reading." Scanning through the pages, the proprietor reads aloud a list of violent offenses committed by French colonial officials in West Africa that included "forced conscription and young Negroes running away from their homes to escape into British African territory" and "native women insulted and their husbands humiliated before them." The café proprietor turns to the pages of the militant anticolonial periodical for evidence of the truth about how "Europeans treat Negroes in the colonies" before launching into a "discourse about Africa for the Africans and the rights of Negroes." The discussion devolves into a wider debate about the merits of Garveyism between the Senegalese proprietor, Ray, Banjo, and Bugsy, all of whom are present but remained silent through the discussion with the seaman. Most strikingly, there is no further response from the Senegalese sailor. We learn only that "he appeared crushed under the printed accounts."[78]

The scene indexes multiple contradictions within Black diasporic consciousness while emphasizing the importance of cafes as spaces of informal political education. Moving beyond the café as a site of circulation to a space of collective debate and dissensus brings the open-ended, ephemeral conditions of print encounters into sharp relief. It is unclear how and to what extent the Senegalese seafarer was transformed by the exchange, and there are numerous plausible interpretations for his appearance of being "crushed" by the printed accounts. He might simply have expressed defeat in a political debate with a well-read opponent. Perhaps the encounter with the proprietor and content of *La race nègre* precipitated a political awakening or transformed worldviews. It is also plausible that the sailor remained altogether unconvinced of this alternative political reality and opted to leave the bar rather than continue to engage in the conversation about the superiority of European versus American imperial powers. Would he go on to tell his shipmates who previously brawled with Italian seamen about the conversation and, if so, what might he say? Would the character seek out a secondhand copy of *La race nègre* the next time he was docked in Marseilles or try to connect with LDRN sympathizers in Dakar or Douala?[79]

The fictional encounter between the Senegalese proprietor and sailor in the Café African raises broader questions about the nature of political education in port cities and the processes of racial consciousness formation through dialogical encounters and exposure to radical print culture. Historically, both the UNIA and LDRN recruited heavily in port cities, and networks of politicized maritime workers were integral to the distribution of pamphlets and verbal transmission of news and ideas. While some seafarers passing through Marseilles would have made their way to the Comintern-affiliated International Seamen's Club at 10 rue Fauchier to "hear about the revolts and fights of the masses in China and in India" and "receive practical help against wage robbery," it was often only after informal debates and conversations that workers entered more formalized and structured spaces of revolutionary learning and mutual aid.[80] Many of the maritime workers who eventually attended these organized gatherings would have been initially or exclusively exposed to movement ideologies and strategies through informal encounters in cafes, on the docks, or on the streets in between, as had the Senegalese sailor in *Banjo*. The sailor's abrupt departure and the uncertainty around his response to the information presented by the proprietor are indicative of the ephemeral nature of encounters with Black radical print culture. Most often, discussions of ephemerality have focused on the material and aesthetic qualities of print production (e.g., cheap paper, lack of binding), the irregularity of whole issues or specific content such as advertisements or personal ads, or even how papers were put to use as kindling, insulation, or other practical purposes.[81] Unlike the boundedness, rigidity, and exclusion of book production, ephemeral weekly or monthly digests and newspapers such as *Negro World* and *La race nègre* enabled Black writers to be nimble, "to plunge into public conversation and get their views out nearly immediately" and to revise their worldviews in response to changing geopolitical circumstances.[82] While some newspapers deliberately crafted editorial structures designed to "encourage a style of reading that was patient, that paused rather than rushed ahead," the aspirational reading tempos were often out of sync with the material realities of the reading counterpublics.[83] Indeed, while studies have called for greater attentiveness to the most fleeting modes of expressive production, there is much more work to be done in order to understand how these texts were received and ascribed meaning by ordinary people whose exposure to radical beliefs was often through transient movements and ephemeral encounters like the one described here in fictional terms by McKay.

Such ephemerality was an organic aspect of diasporic life. Whether threatened by raids by colonial officials or interruptions by ship captains deputized as agents of empire, the rhythms of rail and shipping schedules, or the brevity and hypersurveillance of leisure time, the sociospatial capacities for collective debate had to be constantly renegotiated according to shifting conditions. Readers and audiences engaging with Black print culture had to make provisional spaces for radical study—both formal and informal—against the backdrop of racial violence. Neither oppression nor exposure to radical ideas inevitably result in internationalist consciousness. Rather, it is through distinct convergences and radical study that sturdy solidarities are formed. In arguing for a greater emphasis on the ephemeral qualities of print encounters, the point is not to flatten sociohistorical differences or advance an ontological argument about the liminality of Blackness. Rather, my goal is simply to argue that historians of Black radicalism in the interwar period currently lack a vocabulary for describing and accounting for the one-off, open-ended exposures to periodicals such as *La race nègre* or reckoning with the absence of readily identifiable resolution toward or congealment as liberatory consciousness. Such moments challenge linear, myopic understandings of political education and illuminate the messy, contradictory processes of grounded learning. To embrace the episodic qualities of brief encounters, as illustrated by McKay—the one-off acts of skimming through headlines in the Café African and the uncertain response to new information—is also to embark on the iterative and nonlinear processes of political education.

In another important scene in *Banjo*, the character Taloufa illustrates the multivalent processes whereby political consciousness was shaped through the combination of print culture, direct experiential knowledge of injustice, and informal dialogues and debate. Where the other characters have made a provisional home in Marseilles, Taloufa remains in the Vieux Port for only three days before disembarking on another shipboard voyage. While the previous example of the Senegalese seafarer foregrounds the importance of fleeting, ephemeral, and open-ended encounters within processes of political education, McKay's portrayal of the character Taloufa offers a prescient exploration of the ways in which transient workers developed decidedly internationalist and diasporic worldviews through the regimes of (im)mobility.

Nigerian-born Taloufa began his seafaring career at the age of thirteen after running away from the English Midlands, where he was employed as a boy servant in the multiethnic port city and center of Black internationalism, Cardiff. There he "found more contentment among the hundreds of colored seamen who lived in that port" until the infamous 1919 race riots wherein white soldiers and sailors indiscriminately attacked the city's Arab, African, and East Asian communities, burning

hostels and community centers.[84] The racial violence in British port cities referenced in *Banjo* coincided with McKay's time in London, and some scholars have
suggested that he "may well have based his fictional account of Taloufa's life and
the experience of the Cardiff rioting on incidents he had heard about while working
as a journalist in 1919."[85] After the riots, Taloufa shipped out to New York City,
where he jumped ship. In New York he joined the "Back-to-Africa crusade." Of
the "motley crew" depicted by McKay, Taloufa represents the most ardent supporter of the UNIA. Goosey explains that Taloufa "thinks colored people scattered
all over the world should come together and go back to Africa . . . and was even at
Liberty Hall for the big Manifestation [1919 UNIA convention]."[86] Here, again, we
can see the striking resonances between historical events and literary depictions in
McKay's work. At the November 1919 UNIA convention, for example, Garvey spoke
about the brutality of white vigilantes in Cardiff and other British port cities and
made direct reference to the critical coverage of the violence by newspapers such
as the *Trinidad Argos*.[87] It is notable that within McKay's narrative, the character
Taloufa is not politicized by a singular event (i.e., the riots), but rather through his
initial experience of state-sanctioned and extralegal violence and the subsequent
convention where Garvey and other UNIA officials drew connections in speeches
and editorials between mob violence in the United States and England and the
hypocrisies of the "white man's war for democracy."[88]

Taloufa's conviction about the UNIA movement was further shaped by his
seafaring travels through Africa. While Ray's and Banjo's critique of the UNIA
rested primarily on Garvey's individual scandals rather than the efficacy and reach
of the movement, the impact of Garveyism on the ground in West Africa dramati-
cally shaped Taloufa's outlook on the movement:

Taloufa maintained that the Back-to-Africa propaganda had worked wonders
among the African natives. He told Ray that all throughout West Africa the
natives were meeting to discuss their future, and in the ports they were no
longer docile, but restive, forming groups, and waiting for the Black Deliverer,
so that, becoming aroused, the colonial governments had acted to keep out all
propaganda, especially *Negro World*, the chief organ of the Back-to-Africa
movement.[89]

Here again, the scope and impact of colonial repression is palpable. More than a
reiteration of the anxieties expressed by the café proprietor about the ban of
Negro World in West Africa, Taloufa's statements upend the conventional geographies of anti-imperial knowledge production in the interwar period. While recent
studies have considered the routes along which knowledge was transmitted from
metropolitan centers such as Harlem, Berlin, Paris, and London through networks
of traveling students, sailors, and soldiers who spoke at meetings from Panama to
Bulawayo, there are fewer accounts of how the reports given by seamen such as

Taloufa were received among ordinary people upon their return to port cities in Europe and the United States.[90]

Taloufa's account of Garveyite mobilizations in West Africa is a critical source of grounded knowledge production in its own right that shifts discursive focus from Garvey's individual travails to the global architecture of repression and the expressions of agency and strategy by Africans on their own terms, even as they hold on to the promise of Garvey's imminent arrival.

Throughout his travels, Taloufa observed and ascribed political meaning to the shared struggles of colonial seafarers the world over. While many of these political connections were forged in the ports of call that he passed through on shipping contracts, he was also subject to numerous rounds of coerced mobility and regimes of deportation that brought him into contact with an even wider range of racialized communities. First, Taloufa "lived in the United States until after the passing of the new immigration quota laws," when he was subsequently arrested and deported due to the fact of his previously entering the country illegally. Later in the novel, Taloufa is deported from England. He discusses the latter instance with the other members of "the gang" at a seaman's bar in Marseilles, explaining that "colored subjects were not wanted in Britain. This was the chief topic of serious talk among colored seamen in all of the ports. Black and brown men being sent back to West Africa, East Africa, the Arabian coast, and India, showed one another their papers and held sharp and bitter discussions in the rough cafes of Joliette and the Vieux Port."[91] Through these bitter discussions, Taloufa, Goosey, Ray, and Banjo develop a wider critique of "the way of civilization with the colored man, especially the Black man," which links Taloufa's updates about deportation regimes with instances of criminalization that the others had recently faced on the docks of Marseilles. Where the conversation between the Senegalese proprietor and sailor indexes the antinomies of colonial modernity, Taloufa's multiple deportations present a "microcosm of the world of displaced colonial subjects and migrants" as well as a "world of color creating new performances of blackness on the global circuit."[92] In both instances, the cafés must be understood as a vital space of political education through which print materials were not only circulated but debated, ascribed meaning, and made legible in dialectic relation with experiential knowledges. If we understand periodicals as a forum for debate that moved geographically, then we must also insist that movement cannot be reduced to physical transfer across Cartesian coordinates. Rather, what is required is an awareness of the provisional—or, indeed, ephemeral—place-making practices through which ordinary people make space not only to discuss but to contest and create the material and imaginative contours of their daily lives amid regimes of coerced mobility and immobilization. Continued debate, commitment to continued questioning and inquiry, and carving out and creating space for political consciousness formation are all necessary preconditions for struggling toward diasporic solidarities and radical world making.

Conclusion

Returning to the initial challenge of the "audience" for studies of Black radicalism, the conversations at the Café African in *Banjo* offer a provisional guide for engaging archival collections. Rather than stitching together fragments and traces to reconstruct a fully formed political consciousness, scholars will do well to embrace the ephemeral qualities of print culture not as a source of incoherence but as an indication of the dynamic and multivalent dimensions of daily life and political education beyond what is readily accessible within traditional archival repositories. Thinking with and through *Banjo* provides a speculative, literary framework from which we can think more capaciously about the imperial antinomies, ruptures, ambivalences, and possibilities that structured daily lives in order to better understand how solidarities and subjectivities were forged within and beyond the pages of the *Negro World* and *La race nègre*. My objective in discussing *Banjo* is not to chart a monolithic account of interwar readership and Black print culture. Rather, attending to the characters' uneven mobilities, varied diasporic subject positions, and levels of engagement with print culture and social movements—all of which were crucial to McKay's early journalism and subsequent formulation of political "authenticity"— adds texture and nuance to discussions of circulation and consciousness formation. The novel's attentiveness to the episodic and shifting temporalities of encounter and transnational geographies of circulation illuminates the material challenges and urgencies of political education and contributes to wider conversations on "making freedom as a place."[93]

By political education, I do not mean a hierarchical or external process of learning but rather the empowerment of "oppressed people, ordinary people infusing new meanings into the concept of democracy and finding their own individual and collective power to determine their lives and shape the direction of history," and a practice that takes seriously the ways in which Black working-class people analyzed their world and capacities for leadership.[94] As militant intellectuals have taught us, revolutionary consciousness does not emerge spontaneously. It cannot be reduced to experience or explained as the formulaic outcome of crises or oppression. It is an iterative and ongoing process rather than an achievement or intellectual arrival before the fact of political practice.[95] While existing archival fragments provide a general guide for mapping the geographies of circulation and solidarities, the scope of dialogue, debate, and encounters that took place as periodicals changed hands, passed through neighborhoods, or were smuggled across oceans and deserts cannot be fully grasped from conventional archival records. As a historical artifact and archival methodology, then, *Banjo* challenges researchers to embrace the uncertainty of the archive and look beyond quantitative methods and cartographic nodes toward the iterative, collective practices through which spaces of political education are produced. Through his political journalism and literary works, McKay challenges readers to ask probing questions of the passing references and partial traces in intelligence files and editorials, and to search not only for coherence and consensus but for contestation among ordinary people and the dynamic multiplicity of collective engagements with diasporic print culture.

Mae A. Miller-Likhethe is assistant professor of global studies at the University of California, Santa Barbara. She is currently completing her first book manuscript, *Oceanic Groundings: Black Feminist Journeys through Insurgent Seas.*

Notes

1. Hill, "On Collectors," 51.
2. Putnam, *Radical Moves*; Davies, *Left of Karl Marx*; Haywood, *Let Us Make Men.*
3. Ewing, "Popular Pan-Africanism," 210.
4. Ardis and Collier, "Introduction"; Barber, "Hidden Innovators in Africa"; Gruber Garvey, *Writing with Scissors*; Hofmeyr, *Gandhi's Printing Press.*
5. Collier and Connolly, "Print Culture Histories"; Putnam, *Radical Moves*; Barber, "Hidden Innovators in Africa," 3–6; Miyonga, "We Kept Them to Remember," 102.
6. Hartman, *Wayward Lives*, 1.
7. Arondekar et al., "Queering Archives," 226.
8. Coleman, "Practices of Refusal in Images," 210; Carby, *Imperial Intimacies.*
9. Denning, *Noise Uprising*; Edwards, *Practice of Diaspora*; Stephens, *Black Empire.*
10. Davies, *Left of Karl Marx*, 72–73.
11. Putnam, *Radical Moves*, 126; see also Vogel, *Black Press.*
12. Fraser, "Emancipatory Cosmology," 274.
13. Gallon, *Pleasure in the News.*
14. Hill, "On Collectors," 51–54.
15. Vogel, *Black Press*, 2; Ardis and Collier, "Introduction."
16. Ardis and Collier, "Introduction"; Boyce Davies, *Left of Karl Marx*; Makalani, *In the Cause of Freedom.*
17. Putnam, *Radical Moves*; Stevens, *Red International and Black Caribbean.*
18. Ransby, *Ella Baker*, 70.
19. Dee, "Clements Kadalie."
20. Makalani, *In the Cause of Freedom*, 180.
21. Ransby, *Ella Baker*; Freire, *Pedagogy of the Oppressed*; Heatherton, *Arise!*
22. "The Firefly Responds," *Limón Searchlight*, September 12, 1931, 4.
23. *Negro World*, June 27, 1925.
24. "Bosses Afraid of the *Negro Worker*," *Negro Worker*, October–November 1931, No. 10/11, Volume 1, 40.
25. Nagar and Swarr, "Theorizing Transnational Feminist Praxis," 6.
26. Gruber Garvey, *Writing with Scissors*, chap. 3.
27. Barber, "Hidden Innovators in Africa," 7; Miyonga, "We Kept Them to Remember."
28. See Vinson, "Providential Design"; and Featherstone, *Solidarity.*
29. Keller, *Colonial Suspects*, 16, 51.
30. "Radicalism and Sedition among the Negroes as Reflected in Their Publications," J. Edgar Hoover to William L. Hurley, July 2, 1919, US National Archives, Records Group 59, file 000-612.
31. Haywood, *Let Us Make Men.*

32. Vogel, *Black Press*.

33. Hartman, *Wayward Lives*.

34. Higashida, *Black Internationalist Feminism*; Lee, "Repairing Police Action."

35. De Lisser, *Jane's Career*, 8, 17; cited in Putnam, *Radical Moves*, 137.

36. Nuttall, "Literature and the Archive"; Pasco, "Literature as Historical Archive."

37. Ardis and Collier, "Introduction," 2.

38. Edwards, *Practice of Diaspora*, 190; Featherstone, *Solidarity*, 41.

39. McKay, *Long Way from Home*, 214.

40. McKay, *Long Way from Home*, 175.

41. James, "Letters from London," 282–83.

42. Makalani, *In the Cause of Freedom*, 71–96.

43. Featherstone, *Solidarity*.

44. McKay, "Letter to the *Negro World*," *Negro World*, March 13, 1920; cited in James, "Letters from London," 288.

45. McKay, "Letter to the *Negro World*, September 20, 1919.

46. "McKay to Marcus Garvey, 17 December 1919," Columbia University Library, Rare Books and Manuscripts Library, Hubert H. Harrison Papers, Box 2, Folder 66.

47. E. D. Morel, "Black Scourge in Europe," *Daily Herald*, April 10, 1920; E. D. Morel, "Black Peril on the Rhine: Wave of Indignation," *Daily Herald*, April 12, 1920.

48. McKay, *Long Way from Home*, 63; see also Gopal, *Insurgent Empire*, 284–92.

49. Claude McKay, "Socialism and the Negro," *Workers Dreadnought*, January 31, 1920.

50. Claude McKay, "Report on the Negro Question," *International Press Correspondence*, January 5, 1923.

51. Claude McKay, "Garvey as a Negro Moses," *Liberator*, April 1922.

52. Edwards, *Practice of Diaspora*,187–89.

53. McKay, *Long Way from Home*, 196.

54. Garvey, *Garvey and Garveyism*, 23.

55. West and Wilkin, "Contours of the Black International," 11.

56. Harold, *Rise and Fall of the Garvey Movement*, 43–45.

57. Garvey, *Garvey and Garveyism*, 33.

58. Haywood, *Let Us Make Men*; Higashida, *Black Internationalist Feminism*; Stephens, *Black Empire*; Taylor, *Veiled Garvey*.

59. Ewing, "Popular Pan-Africanism"; James, "Letters from London."

60. Garvey, *Garvey and Garveyism*, 33.

61. Garvey, *Garvey and Garveyism*, 314.

62. "Report by Special Agent P-138," December 13, 1920, US National Archives, Record Group 65, BS 203677-33.

63. "Report by Special Agent P-138," December 13, 1920, US National Archives, Record Group 65, BS 203677-33.

64. Goebel, *Anti-imperial Metropolis*, 5.

65. Adi, *Pan-Africanism and Communism*, 223; Wilder, *French Imperial Nation-State*, 180; Makalani, *In the Cause of Freedom*, 157.

66. Trnovec, "The Black's Race Revolution," 288; Edwards, *Practice of Diaspora*, 245; Wilder, *French Imperial Nation-State*, 180.

67. Trnovec, "The Black's Race Revolution, 288.

68. Edwards, *Practice of Diaspora*, 293; Keller, *Colonial Suspects*, 157; Aitken, "From Cameroon."

69. Edwards, *Practice of Diaspora*, 252.
70. Keller, *Colonial Suspects*, 158, 164.
71. Aitken, "From Cameroon."
72. Keller, *Colonial Suspects*, 159, 60.
73. Edwards, *Practice of Diaspora*, 252.
74. Mahvish Ahmad, Koni Benson, and Hana Morgenstern, "Revolutionary Papers: Counterinstitutions, Counterpolitics, and Countercultures of Anticolonial Periodicals," in this issue.
75. McKay, *Banjo*, 73–74.
76. Featherstone, *Solidarity*, 41.
77. Wilder, *French Imperial Nation-State*, 3.
78. McKay, *Banjo*, 73.
79. McKay, *Banjo*, 72–76.
80. "The ISH and the International Seamen's Clubs," Box 1, Minority Movement, Working Class Movement Library, Salford, UK, p. 5.
81. Cocks and Rubery, "Margins of Print," 3–4.
82. Vogel, *Black Press*.
83. Hofmeyr, *Gandhi's Printing Press*, 4.
84. Featherstone, *Solidarity*.
85. Jenson, *Black 1919*, 10.
86. McKay, *Banjo*, 91.
87. Jenson, *Black 1919*, 192.
88. Marcus Garvey, Editorial Letter, *Negro World*, October 11, 1919; reprinted in the *Emancipator*, March 27, 1920.
89. McKay, *Banjo*, 102.
90. Makalani, *In the Cause of Freedom*; Matera, *Black London*.
91. McKay, *Banjo*, 311.
92. Stephens, *Black Empire*, 185.
93. Gilmore, "Abolition Geography," 227.
94. Ransby, *Ella Baker*, 5.
95. Ransby, *Ella Baker*, 5.

References

Adi, Hakim. *Pan-Africanism and Communism: The Communist International, Africa and the Diaspora, 1919-1939.* Trenton: Africa World Press, 2013.

Aitken, Robbie. "From Cameroon to Germany and Back via Moscow and Paris: The Political Career of Joseph Bilé (1892–1959), Performer, "Negerarbeiter" and Comintern Activist." *Journal of Contemporary History* 43, no. 4 (2008): 597–616.

Ardis, Ann, and Patrick Collier. "Introduction." In *Transatlantic Print Culture, 1880–1940: Emerging Media, Emerging Modernisms,* 1–13. New York: Palgrave Macmillan, 2008.

Arondekar, Anjali, Ann Cvetkovich, Christina B. Hanhardt, Tavia Nyong'o, Juana Maria Rodriguez, and Susan Stryker. "Queering Archives: A Roundtable Discussion." *Radical History Review,* no. 122 (2015): 211–31.

Barber, Karin. "Hidden Innovators in Africa." In *Africa's Hidden Histories: Everyday Literacy and Making the Self,* edited by Karin Barber, 1–23. Bloomington: Indiana University Press, 2006.

Boyce Davies, Carol. *Left of Karl Marx: The Political Life of Black Communist Claudia Jones.* Durham, NC: Duke University Press, 2008.

Carby, H. *Imperial Intimacies: A Tale of Two Islands.* London: Verso, 2019.

Cocks, H. G., and Matthew Rubery. "Margins of Print: Ephemera, Print Culture, and Lost Histories of the Newspaper." *Media History* 18, no. 1 (2011): 1–5.

Coleman, K. "Practices of Refusal in Images: An Interview with Tina Campt." *Radical History Review*, no. 132 (2018): 209–19.

Collier, Patrick., Connolly, James. "Print Culture Histories beyond the Metropolis: An Introduction." In *Print Culture Histories beyond the Metropolis*, edited by James J. Connolly, Patrick Collier, Frank Felsenstein, Kenneth R. Hall, and Robert G. Hall, 3–27. Toronto: University of Toronto Press, 2016.

Dee, Henry. "Clements Kadalie, the ICU, and the Transformation of Communism in Southern Africa, 1917–31." In *Revolutionary Lives of the Red and Black Atlantic since 1917*, edited by David Featherstone, Christian Høgsbjerg, and Alan Rice, 145–71. Manchester: Manchester University Press, 2022.

de Lisser, H. G. *Jane's Career: A Story from Jamaica*. New York: Mint Editions, 2021.

Denning, M. *Noise Uprising: The Audiopolitics of a World Musical Revolution*. New York: Verso, 2015.

Edwards, Brent Hayes. *The Practice of Diaspora: Literature, Translation, and the Rise of Black Internationalism*. Cambridge, MA: Harvard University Press, 2003.

Ewing, Adam. "Popular Pan-Africanism: Rumor, Identity, and Intellectual Production in the Age of Garvey." In *Global Garveyism*, edited by Ronald J. Stephens and Adam Ewing, 205–25. Gainesville: University Press of Florida, 2019.

Featherstone, David. *Solidarity: Hidden Histories and Geographies of Internationalism*. London: Zed Books, 2012.

Fraser, Gordon. "Emancipatory Cosmology: *Freedom's Journal, The Rights of All*, and the Revolutionary Movements of Black Print Culture." *American Quarterly* 68, no. 2 (2016): 263–86.

Freire, Paulo. *Pedagogy of the Oppressed*. New York: Penguin, 2017.

Gallon, K. *Pleasure in the News: African American Readership and Sexuality in the Black Press*. Urbana: University of Illinois Press, 2020.

Garvey, Amy Jacques. *Garvey and Garveyism*. Baltimore: Black Classic Press, 1963.

Gilmore, Ruth Wilson. "Abolition Geography and the Problem of Innocence." In *Futures of Black Radicalism*, edited by Gaye Theresa Johnson and Alex Lubin, 225–40. New York: Verso, 2017.

Goebel, Michael. *Anti-imperial Metropolis: Interwar Paris and the Seeds of Third World Nationalism*. New York: Cambridge University Press, 2015.

Gopal, Priyamvada. *Insurgent Empire: Anticolonial Resistance and British Dissent*. London: Verso, 2019.

Gruber Garvey, Ellen. *Writing with Scissors: American Scrapbooks from the Civil War to the Harlem Renaissance*. Oxford: Oxford University Press, 2013.

Hartman, Saidiya. *Wayward Lives, Beautiful Experiments: Intimate Histories of Social Upheaval*. New York: Norton, 2019.

Haywood, D. *Let Us Make Men: The Twentieth Century Black Press and a Manly Vision for Racial Advancement*. Chapel Hill: University of North Carolina Press, 2018.

Heatherton, Christina. *Arise! Global Radicalism in the Era of the Mexican Revolution*. Oakland: University of California Press, 2024.

Higashida, Cheryl. *Black Internationalist Feminism: Women Writers of the Black Left, 1945–1995*. Urbana: University of Illinois Press, 2013.

Hill, Robert. "On Collectors, Their Contributions to the Documentation of the Black Past." In *Black Bibliophiles and Collectors*, edited by Elinor Des Verney Sinette, W. Paul Coates, and Thomas C. Battle, 46–56. Washington, DC: Howard University Press, 1990.

Hofmeyr, Isabel. *Gandhi's Printing Press: Experiments in Slow Reading*. Cambridge, MA: Harvard University Press, 2013.

James, Winston. "Letters from London in Black and Red: Claude McKay, Marcus Garvey, and the *Negro World*." *History Workshop Journal* 85 (2018): 281–93.

Jenson, Jacqueline. *Black 1919: Riots, Racism, and Resistance in Imperial Britain*. Liverpool: Liverpool University Press, 2009.

Keller, Kathleen. *Colonial Suspects: Suspicion, Imperial Rule, and Colonial Society in Interwar French West Africa*. Lincoln: University of Nebraska Press, 2018.

Lee, A. J. Yumi. "Repairing Police Action after the Korean War in Toni Morrison's *Home*." *Radical History Review*, no. 137 (2020): 119–40.

Makalani, Minkah. *In the Cause of Freedom: Radical Black Internationalism from Harlem to London, 1917–1939*. Chapel Hill: University of North Carolina Press, 2011.

Matera, Marc. *Black London: The Imperial Metropolis and Decolonization in the Twentieth Century*. Berkeley: University of California Press, 2015.

McKay, Claude. *Banjo*. Orlando: Harper and Brothers, 1929.

McKay, Claude. *A Long Way from Home*. New Brunswick, NJ: Rutgers University Press, 2007.

Miyonga, Rose. "We Kept Them to Remember: Tin Trunk Archives and the Emotional History of the Mau Mau War." *History Workshop Journal* 96 (2023): 96–114.

Nagar, Richa, and Amanda Swarr. "Introduction: Theorizing Transnational Feminist Praxis." In *Critical Transnational Feminist Praxis*, edited by Amanda Lock Swarr and Richa Nagar, 1–21. Albany: State University of New York Press, 2010.

Nuttall, Sarah. "Literature and the Archive: The Biography of Texts." In *Refiguring the Archive*, edited by Carolyn Hamilton, Verne Harris, Michèle Pickover, Graeme Reid, Razia Saleh, and Jane Taylor, 283–99. Dordrecht: Kluwer Academic, 2002.

Pasco, Allan H. "Literature as Historical Archive." *New Literary History* 35, no. 3 (2004): 373–94.

Putnam, Lara. *Radical Moves: Caribbean Migrants and the Politics of Race in the Jazz Age*. Chapel Hill: University of North Carolina Press, 2013.

Ransby, Barbara. *Ella Baker and the Black Freedom Movement: A Radical Democratic Vision*. Chapel Hill: University of North Carolina Press, 2003.

Stephens, Michelle. *Black Empire: The Masculine Global Imaginary of Caribbean Intellectuals in the United States, 1914–1962*. Durham, NC: Duke University Press, 2005.

Stevens, Margaret. *Red International and Black Caribbean: Communists in New York City, Mexico, and the West Indies, 1919–1939*. London: Pluto Press, 2017.

Taylor, Ula Y. *The Veiled Garvey: The Life and Times of Amy Jacques Garvey*. Chapel Hill: University of North Carolina Press, 2002.

Trnovec, Silvester. "The Black's Race Revolution: The Journal 'La Race Nègre' and the Circulation of Radical Ideas in French West Africa in 1927–1930." *Asian and African Studies* 31, no. 2 (2022): 277–97.

Vinson, Robert Trent. "Providential Design: American Negroes and Garveyism in South Africa." In *From Toussaint to Tupac: The Black International Since the Age of Revolution*, edited by Michael O. West, William G. Martin, and Fanon Che Wilkins, 130–53. Chapel Hill: University of North Carolina Press, 2009.

Vogel, Todd, ed. *The Black Press: New Literary and Historical Essays*. New Brunswick, NJ: Rutgers University Press, 2001.

Wilder, G. *The French Imperial Nation-State: Negritude and Colonial Humanism between the Two World Wars*. Chicago: University of Chicago Press, 2005.

Fighting Fascism on Empire's Doorstep

Mediodía and Popular Front Politics in 1930s Cuba

Tony Wood

Between its launch in 1936 and its closure in 1939, the Cuban magazine *Mediodía* (*Midday*) became an important fixture in the intellectual life of the island's Left. More than a publishing venture, the magazine saw itself as a political project. "*Mediodía* is not a business, it is A CAUSE!," declared an announcement in the July 1937 issue; it went on to clarify: "The cause of Cuban democracy and of a new national independence."[1] Yet, although it was deeply concerned with Cuban politics, and in particular with struggles for democratic representation and for racial equality, for *Mediodía*'s editors these battles could not be separated from the broader turbulence afflicting the world in the 1930s.

In its editorial approach, *Mediodía* embodied a Cuban version of the Communist International's "Popular Front" strategy. Adopted in 1935, this urged Communist parties and Communist-aligned organizations to make alliances beyond their own ranks in a common battle against fascism and imperialism. In line with this approach, *Mediodía* was edited by people close to the Cuban Communist Party (Partido Comunista de Cuba, PCC) but drew contributors and readers from among other leftists and progressives. Across more than a hundred issues, it published a dazzling constellation of authors—including Latin American, US, and European radical writers such as Langston Hughes, César Vallejo, André Malraux, and Isaak Babel, as well as Cuban luminaries such as the anthropologist Fernando Ortiz, the feminist activist Ofelia Domínguez Navarro, the novelist Alejo Carpentier, and the

Radical History Review

Issue 150 (October 2024)   DOI 10.1215/01636545-11257408

© 2024 by MARHO: The Radical Historians' Organization, Inc.

Afro-Chinese Cuban poet Regino Pedroso. Although it began as a Cuba-focused literary monthly, it quickly became a weekly current affairs magazine with an internationalist outlook. Reportage on the Spanish Civil War nestled alongside essays on racism in Cuba; accounts of Chinese resistance to Japanese occupation appeared next to warnings of Nazi Germany's threats to Czechoslovakia.

Mediodía has received little scholarly attention to date, especially in the English-speaking world.[2] As a case study in imaginative radical publishing, it would be worthy enough of further discussion. But *Mediodía* sheds light on two issues with wider relevance to the study of radical movements. First, it helps us think about the cultural politics of left movements in the 1930s. The Popular Front strategy implied the creation of a broad public consensus against fascism. In some places, Communist parties were able to express their ideas openly, and in France and Chile, for example, they put together successful Popular Front electoral coalitions. Yet elsewhere, Communist parties were tightly constrained: most were illegal and had to operate clandestinely. Under such conditions, the Popular Front could not take organized political form. It therefore remained confined to the cultural realm, expressing the ideas of a counterhegemonic force that had yet to cohere. What did an antifascist consensus look like when many of its key premises—in particular any sympathy with Communism—had to remain unspoken?

In the United States in the 1930s, the Popular Front involved a powerful upsurge in the power of organized labor as well as what Michael Denning has called the "laboring of American culture"—the take-up of prolabor themes across the field of cultural production.[3] The case of *Mediodía*, however, shows a different path: in Cuba, Popular Front culture developed predominantly through the articulation of a leftist internationalism. In mid-1930s Cuba, urgent questions about imperialism, sovereignty, racial inequality, and social injustice were in the air.[4] Yet, with press freedom limited, domestic issues could not be debated openly. Coverage of international affairs provided avenues for much freer expression of radical impulses and solidarities, allowing the magazine to give voice to a leftist counterpolitics that extended the boundaries of what was sayable in 1930s Cuba and helped to inform and expand a radical counterculture.[5] By the end of the decade, when the government relaxed restrictions on the press, *Mediodía* had already established itself as a venue from which the Cuban Left could address the island's internal politics.

The central role played by foreign affairs coverage in *Mediodía* highlights a second set of insights to be gained from studying the magazine, concerning left internationalism. *Mediodía*'s outward orientation was not itself a novelty, either on the Left or in Cuba: internationalism had been synonymous with socialist and labor movements since the nineteenth century, and the entanglement of the local and the global was a recurrent feature of Cuba's history, from its time as a slaveholding Spanish colony to its early twentieth-century absorption into the informal US empire. What was distinctive about *Mediodía*, rather, was the particular manner in which the local and the global were interwoven. For the magazine's editors, the boundary between internal questions and global issues was permeable; the anti-imperialist, antifascist, and antiracist struggles were bound together into a single battle with many interlinked fronts. More than a matter of solidarity or connection, this form of internationalism insisted on the systemic nature of the struggles being waged. Events in Nanjing or Barcelona mattered to readers in Havana not only because of an abstract belief in a common humanity but because of the concrete oppressions they shared. This solidaristic orientation was a core part of the anti-imperialist and antifascist counterpolitics *Mediodía* articulated.

Finally, *Mediodía* opens a window onto an often-overlooked period in the life of the Cuban Left. The systemic solidarity the magazine expressed in the 1930s marked a step change in the Cuban Left's contacts with global left political culture. This in turn laid crucial groundwork for the better-known surge of internationalism of the 1960s. *Mediodía*'s pages allow us to recover a key piece of the Cuban Revolution's political and intellectual genealogy and to better appreciate the long gestation of the struggles that burst into the open in the late 1950s.

Drawing on a close reading of *Mediodía*'s hundred-plus issues, as well as on memoirs, biographies, published interviews, and a range of secondary materials, I offer the first full account of the magazine's origins and its place within Cuba's political and intellectual landscape. While *Mediodía*'s contents are the guiding thread in my analysis, a broader array of sources was needed to capture the specificity and range of its interventions. I begin by outlining the context in which the magazine emerged and describe its beginnings before situating it within Cuban publishing. I then explore the magazine's specific brand of Popular Front politics, expressed initially in its internationalism. I track *Mediodía*'s coverage of global developments—especially the Spanish Civil War—noting the interconnections it made between distant struggles but also its political blind spots. I then turn to domestic themes, which *Mediodía* took up with increasing vigor amid a political opening in the later 1930s. I focus in particular on its approach to race and national identity, examining its contributions to debates around Blackness in Cuba and the island's new constitution. I conclude by highlighting how the ideological alignments and relationships that developed in the 1930s carried over into subsequent decades, making *Mediodía* and the Popular Front experience crucial precursors for Cuba's post-1959 revolutionary culture.

The Cuban Context

Cuba in the 1930s was rich in political possibilities and at the same time ripe with frustration. Pro-independence forces had waged a long struggle against Spain in the nineteenth century, including three wars between 1868 and 1898 that brought an end to slavery. In the process, they forged a new nationalism that sought to overcome the island's deep racial divisions.[6] But when Cuba was on the brink of gaining sovereignty in 1898, the United States intervened and made it a virtual protectorate. Thereafter, although Cuba became formally independent in 1901, its northern neighbor exerted a decisive influence on its affairs. This made imperialism and national sovereignty central to Cuban political and intellectual discussions throughout the first half of the twentieth century.

The most egregious example of the US hold on Cuba was the Platt Amendment, which the United States forced Cuban lawmakers to include verbatim in the island's constitution, and which authorized the United States to send troops to Cuba to secure "the maintenance of a government adequate for the protection of life, property, and individual liberty."[7] Though US forces left the island in 1902, they returned to occupy Cuba again in 1906–9, 1912, and 1917–22.[8] Washington's political sway over Cuba was accompanied by an intensifying economic dominance, as US banks and investors expanded their presence on the island. By 1916 Cuba was providing half of the United States' sugar, while by 1923 foreign banks held over three-quarters of Cuban deposits.[9]

Sudden fortunes were made from a dizzying rise in prices during and after the First World War, with a select few Cubans invited to join the "Dance of the Millions" alongside US capitalists. Yet this prosperity proved short-lived. The Wall Street crash of 1929 and the Great Depression hit the island hard; the value of its annual sugar crop plummeted, wages slumped to their "lowest since the days of slavery," and unemployment and poverty became widespread.[10]

Amid growing economic discontent, political turbulence mounted. Since 1925, Cuba had been ruled by Gerardo Machado, who made extensive use of police spies and hired thugs to tamp down dissent, forcing many Cuban leftists into exile. Yet the president's strong-arm tactics failed to quell the discontent, and from 1930 onward there were waves of labor strikes and political violence. In August 1933 these pressures culminated in a general strike that within days led to Machado's ouster. (He and his retinue fled to the Bahamas on a plane, some of them reportedly carrying bags of gold while still in their pajamas.)[11]

The revolution of 1933 was a formative experience for an entire generation in Cuba. It unleashed a flood of popular energies, yet its democratizing impulses were blocked by the restoration of a heavy-handed pro-US regime. Soon after Machado's ouster, a progressive government led by Ramón Grau San Martín took office. His tenure was brief, in large part due to pressure from Washington. Yet the Grau administration—known as the "Government of a Hundred Days," since it lasted from September 1933 to January 1934—laid down some crucial markers. It abrogated the Platt Amendment and introduced legislation for an eight-hour working day and for women's suffrage, as well as a law requiring that half of all employees in most businesses be Cuban nationals. Known as the "50% Law," this was hugely popular in the context of rampant unemployment. But it was also laden with national and racial tensions; though directed against Spanish immigrants who held skilled posts in the cities, it would mainly be implemented against Haitian and Jamaican migrant workers who cut cane in the countryside.[12]

By 1935 Cuban elites had managed to contain the ferment provoked by the 1933 revolution, suppressing a general strike that March. Though Cuba's leaders were still nominally elected, the real power behind the throne was now Fulgencio Batista, head of the Cuban army, who had helped the United States to broker Grau's ouster. The outward forms of democracy were still observed, but the political climate became more restrictive. Tight limits were placed on radical student organizations and leftist groups such as the Communist Party, which had mostly operated clandestinely since its foundation in 1925. Yet the promise of 1933 had not yet vanished, and a range of political tendencies continued to agitate for that stalled agenda to be implemented. This included a wide array of Black social organizations—known as *sociedades de color*—which continued to push for racial equality.[13] When *Mediodía*'s first issue appeared in 1936 the island was still abuzz with political debate and tension, but many of the avenues for public expression and action had been blocked, generating a heady mix of creativity and frustration.

Beginnings

Mediodía was a product of this tense moment and of the Cuban Left's attempt to make its voice heard despite the constraints. It was a daunting climate for publishing, because of the weakness of the island's publishing infrastructure and due to the vagaries of censorship. Cuba at this time had few publishers—the vast majority of books were imported—and most of its cultural life unfolded through magazines and *tertulias*, informal literary salons.[14] Yet these magazines tended to be short-lived, since they often fell afoul of capricious censors. It was not illegal to *sell* "subversive" literature in Cuba, but it was illegal to *read* it.[15] And while bookstores were immune, magazines printing such material were frequently raided and shut down by police.

From the 1920s through the 1930s, the Cuban government scotched a string of radical magazines. The vanguard magazine *Revista de avance* published a remarkable range of Cuban and international authors between 1927 and 1930, before being closed down for supposedly instigating student protests. In 1927 the Cuban Anti-imperialist League only published a few issues of its organ *América libre* before its editors were all arrested.[16] In May 1934 the League launched a new monthly, *Masas* (*Masses*), but in early 1935 the government ordered its closure. Its editor, the Marxist intellectual Juan Marinello, had been among the editors of the defunct *Revista de avance*. In 1935 he was also the editor of the daily newspaper *La palabra* (*The Word*), which was radical in sympathies without overt ties to the Communist Party. This too was shut down after the March 1935 general strike, and Marinello was jailed for six months.[17]

Against this backdrop, *Mediodía* stands out as the most sustained and successful left periodical in 1930s Cuba. Other radical magazines managed only a few issues before vanishing: *Masas* in 1934–35, *Resumen* (*Summary*) in 1935, *Islas* (*Islands*) in 1936, and *Baraguá* in 1937–38.[18] *Mediodía*, by contrast, established itself and even increased its frequency from monthly to weekly. It began with a print run of five hundred but by mid-1937 it claimed a circulation of ten thousand.[19] This was much smaller than the readership of *Bohemia*, Cuba's most popular magazine, which in October 1933 had an audited circulation of fifty thousand.[20] But it dwarfs the print runs of peer publications for which data are available; in the 1940s, for example, the influential left literary magazine *Gaceta del Caribe* had a circulation of one thousand copies.[21]

Mediodía's early days were far from smooth. It emerged from the ruins of another magazine, the weekly *Resumen*, which lasted two months before it was shut down by the censors in the summer of 1935. But *Resumen* laid some important groundwork: it brought together the core of the team that was behind *Mediodía* a year later. Among those closely involved in *Resumen* were the young Marxist intellectual Carlos Rafael Rodríguez; Ángel Augier, a journalist and poet from eastern Cuba; and Nicolás Guillén, one of Cuba's leading poets. Though not a member of the Communist Party, Guillén moved in the same circles as radical Marxist intellectuals. His verses combining modernist forms with motifs from Afro-Cuban traditions were widely popular, and his prestige made him the ideal figurehead for the next attempt to produce a leftist magazine.

By mid-1936 the *Resumen* team felt the moment was ripe to try again. In late 1935 the PCC had made a major policy shift in line with the Comintern's "Popular Front" strategy. Announced at the Comintern Congress in Moscow in July 1935, this new strategy prioritized the struggle against fascism over the Comintern's previous insistence on class antagonism, encouraging Communist parties across the world to seek out alliances with social democrats, progressive nationalists, and anti-imperialists.[22]

In this new context, *Mediodía* aimed to be the rallying point for a broader array of leftist writers. As Augier put it, the magazine would be the "tribune of writers militantly attached to Marxism or with sympathies towards that powerful current in political thought."[23] Given the climate of censorship, however, it could not announce itself as such. Rodríguez later recalled the balancing act of producing a magazine that would be "legal, that is, not too audacious" but at the same time "sufficiently clear for the masses to understand our message."[24] The need for caution explains the oblique phrasing of the editorial statement in its first issue, tucked away at the bottom of the fifth page, which announced no explicit goals, instead asserting that the editors preferred to "demonstrate the intention behind [the magazine] without declaring it in advance."[25] Still, the masthead would have made the magazine's sympathies obvious: besides Guillén, the editorial team included well-known leftists such as Augier, Marinello, Rodríguez, and the artist Jorge Rigol, as well as the literary critic José Antonio Portuondo, the novelist Carlos Montenegro, the journalist Aurora Villar Buceta, and Communist militant Edith García Buchaca.[26]

The magazine's first incarnation was very different in style and tone from those it would adopt for most of its existence—both more literary and more indirect in its politics. The first issue appeared in June 1936, its cover featuring a line drawing of a factory worker by Rigol. Its contents firmly placed the magazine on the left of Cuba's literary and artistic vanguard, but without addressing Cuban politics. Alongside Guillén's poem "Elegy for a Living Soldier," for example, it included a translation of an essay by the Hungarian Marxist Georg Lukács on Friedrich Engels's literary criticism. It also included an essay by Juan Marinello on Alejo Carpentier's novel *Écue-yamba-ó* (1933) and a text by Carlos Rafael Rodríguez surveying Black Cuban poetry. In its engagement with Cuba's African heritage, the magazine echoed broader attempts being made at the time to emphasize and validate African contributions to Cuban identity.[27] One of the foremost exponents of this impulse was the anthropologist Fernando Ortiz, who also contributed to *Mediodía*'s first issue. His text, titled "Economic Contrast between Sugar and Tobacco," was an early draft of what would, four years later, become the seminal book *Cuban Counterpoint*.[28]

Yet even with this literary approach, after only three issues *Mediodía* almost met the same fate as its short-lived predecessors. Its August 1936 issue included an extract from a novel by Carlos Montenegro called *Hombres sin mujer* (*Men without Women*), an unsparing depiction of life in prison. The Cuban authorities accused the magazine of "pornography and subversive propaganda" and ordered the arrest of the entire editorial committee. In the end, only Guillén was jailed, and he was cleared at his trial in September. But he lost his job at the Havana municipality and was evicted from his apartment.[29]

This was a turning point for the magazine. The successful trial defense allowed it to resume publication, but the personal pressures on Guillén led him to seek a change of scene, and in January 1937 he left for Mexico. For some time thereafter he would only be in Cuba for short spells. This meant that, although Guillén remained *Mediodía*'s nominal editor, in practice the job fell to Carlos Rafael Rodríguez, who quickly modified the magazine's approach.

Situating *Mediodía*

In January 1937 *Mediodía* adopted the format and focus that would define it for the rest of its existence. As Rodríguez later put it, the idea was "to transform an intellectual publication into a popular one," aimed at a broader public.[30] While it still addressed literary themes, *Mediodía* now gave much more emphasis to politics and current affairs, both in Cuba and internationally. In its new incarnation, *Mediodía* was published with greater frequency: every ten days at first, then weekly from July 1937 onward. The cover price halved, from ten centavos to five, making it more affordable, though this also meant it had to be printed on cheaper paper. Its visual

Figure 1. *Mediodía*'s changing graphic style. Covers of *Mediodía* (*left to right*): no. 3 (August 1936); no. 23 (July 6, 1937); and no. 99 (December 12, 1938). Instituto de Historia de Cuba, Havana. Photographs by author.

style also mutated, going from a spare aesthetic to a more assertive and colorful idiom. Its covers tended to include topical art or political cartoons, often in black and white, inset alongside text signaling the issue's contents, all against a background of vibrant color. As the magazine reached the end of its cycle, graphic elements came to dominate, eventually displacing text altogether (fig. 1).

Mediodía's main readership would have been concentrated in Havana and Santiago de Cuba, the country's two largest cities, but it was clearly read across the island. The January 17, 1938, issue listed its "best agents" in twenty locations, including many in the sugar-cultivating zones of Santa Clara and Oriente Provinces.[31] As a publication closely linked to the Communist Party and the labor movement, it had many working-class readers. In January 1938 it ran anniversary greetings to the magazine from transport unions in Havana, a shoe factory in Manzanillo, hairdressers in Santa Clara, and sugar workers in Mabay, Oriente.[32]

The magazine's geographical and social reach reflected its quick rise to prominence within Cuba's media landscape. *Mediodía*'s connection to the radical Left contributed centrally to this success. Throughout, the magazine drew much of its political orientation from the PCC—albeit tacitly, since the party was illegal for most of *Mediodía*'s existence.[33] The PCC's leader, Blas Roca, wrote frequently for the magazine under pseudonyms and drafted many of its editorials.[34] But as the "tribune," as Augier put it, for a broader Left, *Mediodía* had a more capacious agenda than the PCC itself and could publish a range of opinions, including those of progressives and liberals such as Fernando Ortiz and Emilio Roig de Leuchsenring. Its political agenda likewise looked for common ground with political formations outside the Left such as Grau's Cuban Revolutionary Party (Partido Revolucionario Cubano, PRC). The magazine also prominently featured the activities of labor unions and social movements, from *sociedades de color* to the organizers of the 1937 National Women's Congress.

Yet while *Mediodía* engaged closely with Cuban affairs, it was resolutely internationalist in outlook, devoting a significant proportion of its pages to world events. As a result, it constantly moved back and forth between national and global frames; reports on land struggles in eastern Cuba were followed by commentary on the Moscow show trials, while coverage of water supply issues in Havana sat alongside an item on the Nazi takeover of Austria.[35] This interweaving of local and global perspectives was central to the magazine's identity, expressing the profound conviction that events in Cuba were inextricably bound up with developments everywhere else.

Storm Clouds

Mediodía's two-and-a-half-year run coincided with a period of global turbulence that culminated in the Second World War. In Europe, fascism was in the ascendant, and in the Far East, Japan launched a full-scale invasion of China in 1937. For *Mediodía*, these developments were not aberrations but symptomatic outgrowths of capitalism and imperialism in the crisis conditions of the Great Depression. While the specific effects of this worldwide crisis varied, *Mediodía*'s internationalism was premised on the idea that they had common roots and that international solidarity therefore was not just desirable on moral-ethical grounds: it was a strategic imperative.

This is why, in *Mediodía*'s pages, the distance between Havana and Manchuria was no greater or smaller than that between Mexico and the Sudetenland. The imperialism from which Cuba suffered was tied to the global sway of the major capitalist powers, which strove to uphold exclusionary and racist forms of domination. The magazine's programmatic entwinement of the global and the national makes any attempt to survey *Mediodía*'s output especially challenging; separating out its coverage into distinct topics would in many ways misrepresent what it was like to read it. Nonetheless, several key themes and concerns stand out.

One was its sustained attention to the Far Right in Europe and beyond. The fascist regimes in Italy and Germany forged the Rome-Berlin Axis in October 1936; Hitler annexed Austria in March 1938 and by September had forced Czechoslovakia to capitulate to his demands; a month later, German troops marched into Sudetenland. The Nazi persecution of Jews also accelerated in the later 1930s, as did anti-Jewish violence. The magazine covered these events extensively, condemning the Nazis' racism and expansionism.[36] At the same time, it also framed many key developments in Latin America in terms of the struggle against fascism, explicitly identifying the stakes as being equivalent to those in Europe. It understood Getúlio Vargas's November 1937 coup in Brazil as making the country into a "Trojan horse for fascism" in the Americas and characterized the right-wing regime in Guatemala as a "Nazi instrument."[37]

Against these examples of the Right's advance, *Mediodía* also found positive models within Latin America, for example in the victory of the Popular Front coalition in the October 1938 Chilean elections.[38] The magazine was also fascinated by Mexico, which had provided a home for radical exiles from across the region in the 1920s and 1930s—including Guillén and many of *Mediodía's* contributors. After taking office in 1934, the Mexican president Lázaro Cárdenas had accelerated agrarian reform and endorsed "socialist education." In 1938 he even faced down the United States, nationalizing Mexico's oil and expropriating the assets of US oil companies. All these measures received approving coverage in *Mediodía*, which saw Cárdenas's brand of left populism as a model for Cuba to emulate.

Yet the magazine's coverage underplayed Mexico's differences from Cuba. Independent for eighty years longer, Mexico had undergone a decade of revolutionary upheaval from 1910 to 1920. By the 1930s it was in the process of becoming a one-party state, in which the radical Left was at best a subordinate partner and at worst the target of state repression. Far from showing Popular Front politics in action, Mexico was an example of the Left's neutering and co-optation. The blurring of these differences points to one of the perils of *Mediodía's* eagerness to make connections: it could portray temporary gains or expedient accommodations as major strategic advances, giving an exaggerated impression of the Left's strength.

A different kind of occlusion took place in *Mediodía's* coverage of China, where from 1937 to 1945 an alliance of Kuomintang (KMT) Nationalists and Communists waged a war of resistance against Japan. China had been central to global Communism's vision of world revolution since the early 1920s. In 1923, the Comintern instructed the fledgling Chinese Communist Party (CCP) to align itself with the KMT—a strategy that backfired disastrously four years later, when the KMT massacred its former allies and launched a "White Terror" that lasted several years.[39] The Japanese invasion of 1937 prompted a new KMT-Communist alignment, which formed the basis for a joint campaign of resistance. But the unity was always tenuous, and it would quickly disintegrate in the 1940s.

Mediodía published more than thirty separate items about China, making it among the topics it most frequently addressed. Yet little of the tension between the CCP and KMT surfaced in these articles, which skirted around the differences between the Communists' and Nationalists' agendas.[40] Where the CCP called for sweeping agrarian revolution, for example, the KMT sought to preserve landlord power as the basis for a national industrialization drive.[41] For *Mediodía*, the immediate demands of anti-imperial struggle meant that these divergences should be played down. But at moments like this the magazine's loyalty to the Popular Front line overrode its commitment to critical analysis, undercutting its claim to speak to and for a more broadly defined left audience.

Mediodía's coverage of China was also distinctive in its emphasis on the connections between China and Cuba, both literal and metaphorical. Since the late

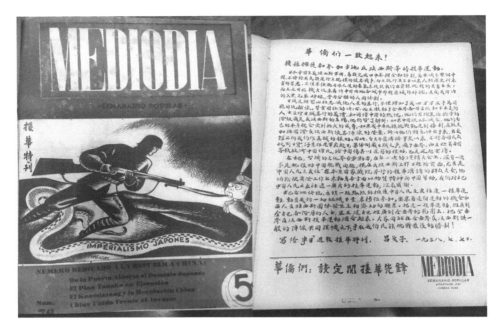

Figure 2. Cover and page from *Mediodía* no. 76 (July 11, 1938). Instituto de Historia de Cuba, Havana. Photographs by author.

nineteenth century, the island had been home to a substantial population of Chinese migrants. Many had joined the fight for independence from Spain; Emilio Roig de Leuchsenring emphasized "Cuba's debt to the Chinese people" in a 1938 article for *Mediodía*.[42] Their presence made Popular Front politics in China directly relevant to the Cuban Left; Chinese-speaking communities in Cuba retained strong ties to the Chinese mainland, including to organizations such as the KMT.[43] For Chinese Cubans, the question of how to help the struggle from afar was a pressing and often personal one. As well as closely following events in China, *Mediodía* addressed Chinese Cubans directly: the July 11, 1938, issue carried a full-page announcement in Chinese exhorting all overseas Chinese to join a broad antifascist movement (fig. 2).[44]

Cuban solidarity with China was also underpinned by a strong sense of parallels between the two countries' fortunes. An editorial in the July 11, 1938, issue asserted that "the Cuban people feel connected to China not only because many Chinese gave their blood generously for our freedom, but also because the Chinese, tilling our soil and working in the industry of our cities, have suffered the same oppression as the Cubans."[45] The two peoples shared a vulnerability in the face of outside powers. For *Mediodía*, Cuba's continued subordination to the United States could be set alongside China's shattered sovereignty in the 1930s. Here again, the conception of imperialism as a global phenomenon tightened the link between

Cuba and China. Their fates were not simply parallel but interconnected thanks to the systemic nature of the forces in play.

Conversely, this merging of local and global frames also meant that resistance to imperialism needed to be conceived as a single struggle distributed across many fronts. This is why, for example, *Mediodía* could so closely identify the cause of Chinese national resistance with the defense of popular sovereignty and democracy across the globe and with the magazine's own commitment to Cuba's democratization. An advertisement on the back cover of *Mediodía*'s one hundredth issue showcases that identification: alongside a description of the magazine as "democracy's militiaman [*miliciano de la democracia*]" stands an image of a Chinese soldier.[46]

"Look at Her, Spain, Broken!"

The most potent demonstration of the interweaving of the local and the global came with *Mediodía*'s coverage of the Spanish Civil War. The war mapped closely onto the magazine's life span: the Nationalist uprising began in July 1936, a month before its first issue appeared, and the war ended with the Republican side's defeat in April 1939, three months after it ceased publication. *Mediodía* tracked events in Spain closely: in total, the magazine ran 129 items on the war, making it by far the most dominant single theme. The centrality of Spain to a left publication, especially in Latin America, is not surprising. What was distinctive about *Mediodía*'s coverage was the close connections it drew between the struggle against fascism in Europe and the battle for democracy and against racism in Cuba.

Spain figured prominently in Cuban readers' minds even before the Civil War. Thousands of Spanish migrants had continued to move to Cuba after independence, and in the late 1930s a sizeable share of its population was either born in Spain or had at least one Spanish parent. For the Cuban Left, there were further affinities. The inauguration of the Second Spanish Republic in 1931 drew radical sympathies across the Spanish-speaking world, and in February 1936, a coalition of progressive republicans, socialists, Communists, and Catalan and Galician nationalists won power in elections—seemingly a resounding validation of the Popular Front strategy. Yet within months, the new government was threatened by a right-wing rebellion led by General Francisco Franco.

Cuban radicals identified especially closely with Republican Spain. When the Civil War broke out, defending the Republican cause became an outlet for pent-up political energies on the island. As Ariel Mae Lambe has argued, with the defeat of the March 1935 general strike a broad sense of frustration took hold.[47] Faced with what seemed immovable domestic obstacles, many Cuban leftists and progressives began to channel their energies outward. One avenue was solidarity efforts with Ethiopia, which in 1935–36 preoccupied Black social organizations and PCC cells as well as the future *Mediodía* editorial team member Ángel Augier.[48] By May 1936, however, Italian forces had taken the Ethiopian capital and deposed

Figure 3. Cover of
Mediodía no. 77
(July 18, 1938). Instituto
de Historia de Cuba,
Havana. Photograph
by author.

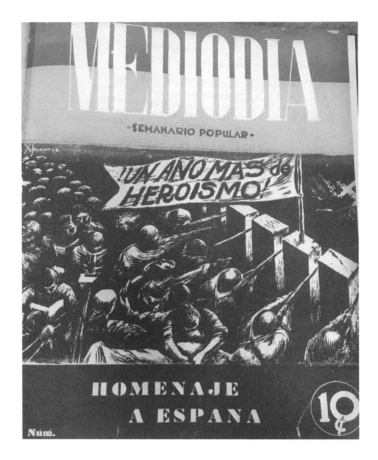

the emperor. The outbreak of hostilities in Spain two months later was another
chance to contribute to what was framed as a global antifascist cause. Many Cubans
would have echoed the words of African American volunteers who fought in Spain:
"This ain't Ethiopia but it'll do."[49]

     Mediodía's coverage of Spain took a number of forms, from frontline report-
age to literary works to profiles of Spanish Republican army officers, politicians and
intellectuals. But across these genres, bolstering the Republican effort was the
overall goal. Its July 18, 1938, issue, billed as a "homage to Spain," bore the colors
of the Republican flag on either side of an illustration by the Mexican artist Xavier
Guerrero featuring the words "One more year of heroism!" (fig. 3).

     For many Cuban leftists, events in Spain were not a distant object of concern
but a spur for action in the here and now. *Mediodía* paid frequent attention to Cuban
solidarity efforts, proudly noting the huge turnouts at pro-Republican rallies: some
sixty thousand people attended one such event at La Polar stadium in Havana in
September 1937.[50] The magazine also often wrote about Cubans who traveled to
Spain to fight. Many of them joined the Republican Army directly, while others

served in the International Brigades.[51] In all, over one thousand Cubans fought in Spain, more than from any other Latin American country.[52] *Mediodía* published photographs of Cuban fighters and news of casualties.[53] It also ran profiles, including Guillén's portrait of Basilio Cueria, a Cuban baseball player who served as a captain in the Spanish Republican Army.[54]

It was Guillén who most powerfully captured the multiple meanings of the Spanish Civil War for Cubans. He was one of many writers to spend time in Spain reporting on the war. He and Juan Marinello attended the Second International Congress of Writers for the Defense of Culture, held in Valencia, Barcelona, and Madrid in July 1937, which drew more than two hundred writers aligned with the Republican cause. Many of them stayed on to chronicle the war, including Guillén, who remained until February 1938.[55] During those months he produced striking pieces of reportage for *Mediodía*, including interviews with frontline soldiers and an account of the bombing of Madrid. The magazine also published evocative fragments of poems Guillén wrote there:

Look at her, Spain, broken!
And birds flying over ruins,
and fascism and its boot
and streetlights with no electricity on the corners,
and fists raised in the air . . . [56]

For Guillén, Spain's ordeal was not only worthy of solidarity and support in its own right. It was part of a worldwide struggle against racism in all its forms. In his speech at the July 1937 Writers' Congress, reprinted in *Mediodía* a few weeks later, he emphasized the racism inherent to fascism, describing the very idea of racial superiority as being designed to maintain a "brutal, vicious circle" of exploitation.[57] He was speaking, he said, as the representative of a group that was enclosed in that circle: "I come as a Black man," Guillén said, "as a man who cares for his freedom, and who knows, like his brothers of the same race, that only by toppling the walls between the present and the future can he obtain [that freedom] in full."[58]

Guillén then asserted that there was a more specific affinity between Black Cubans and Spain. This was partly cultural, rooted in centuries of Spanish colonial rule over the island, thanks to which, as Guillén put it, Black Cubans received and assimilated elements of Spanish culture—along with slavery and "strokes of the master's lash."[59] Tainted with violence, this legacy would seem to be a shaky basis for solidarity. But for Guillén, the colonial past was not the only or even the main source of connection. There were also strong political and class grounds for Cubans to sympathize with Spain. According to Guillén, Black Cubans "live the tragedy of Republican Spain because they know that this moment we are passing through is only an episode in the battle between democratic forces, of which the Black . . . is

part, and the conservative classes that have already enslaved him once and are looking to enslave him always."[60] In Guillén's framing, a struggle for democracy was
unfolding both in Spain and in Cuba, and defeat for progressives would allow the
victorious Right to turn back the clock of history.

Many Black Cubans seemed to share this sense that Spain's resistance to fascism was closely linked to the broader movement against racism. There was plenty of
evidence to support the idea that Cuba's working classes and Spanish Republicans
were up against the same enemy: conservative Spanish emigres in Cuba formed local
branches of the fascist Falange organization in several provinces. According to US
diplomatic correspondence, by 1938 some had several hundred members, including
local elites—"professional men, merchants, and more or less substantial people."[61]
Many of these men would have been the visible face of Cuba's systems of racialized
economic domination. *Mediodía* readily made the connection between Spain's
and Cuba's own internal struggles, noting the Francoist sympathies of some Spanish-
born Cuban landlords, and assailing the "fascist" methods they used to expel Cuban
tenants.[62]

Mediodía framed the civil war in Spain as one front in a broader battle for
democracy. The magazine's international coverage enabled it to link Cuban struggles against imperialism and racism with conflicts in Europe and East Asia, and thus
to emphasize the systemic character of the obstacles to be overcome. According to
Mediodía's de facto editor, moreover, the resonance of international issues such as
the Spanish Civil War and Mexican oil nationalization opened up space for the
Cuban Left domestically. Rodríguez later recalled that the war in Spain created
"such a strong connection of our people, our working class, with the struggle against
fascism and such a broad political unity that this enabled us to act with a certain freedom, which only increased."[63] *Mediodía* itself reflected that growing latitude, the magazine becoming bolder in its coverage of domestic questions, especially from 1938
onward, as momentum gathered behind demands for a new constitution.

Race and the Remaking of Cuba

Cuba's first independent constitution, drafted in 1901, had enshrined the legal equality of its citizens. But in practice, vast inequalities of power and wealth remained,
including those created between Black and white Cubans by centuries of slavery.
The constitution had also codified Cuba's subordination to the United States
through the Platt Amendment, which accorded the United States the unilateral
right to intervene in Cuban affairs. The amendment had been abrogated after the
1933 revolution, but dissatisfaction with the country's institutions lingered. In the
late 1930s, Cuban leftists and progressives united behind calls for a Constituent
Assembly to draft a new charter. Even Batista recognized, in January 1937, that a
new constitution was needed to solidify the "definitive structure of the state."[64] But
what kind of state would it be, and who would decide?

Race featured prominently in these debates. In postindependence Cuba, an "ideology of raceless nationality" had predominated in which racial distinctions had supposedly been transcended.[65] In practice, this meant that the political space for discussion of racial inequality and discrimination narrowed even as these phenomena stubbornly persisted, and those who raised such issues were accused of undermining national unity. For Cuban radicals and progressives, the drafting of a new charter was an opportunity to make concrete moves toward undoing racial injustices as well as to think about the meaning and substantive content of "democracy."

Mediodía's coverage formed part of a wider conversation, led above all by Black social organizations—*sociedades de color*.[66] For *Mediodía* as for the broader Cuban Left, antiracism was part of a broader agenda for social transformation that involved a more inclusive redefinition of Cuban national identity and a greater emphasis on economic equality. "Democratization" in this context meant not only meaningful participation in elections but expanded access to social and welfare rights.[67]

Mediodía published a total of thirty-eight items relating to the new constitution, ranging from editorials to brief surveys to in-depth analyses. The very first item set the tone. The August 1936 issue included a substantial article by the prominent PCC leader Martín Castellanos arguing that Cuba's new founding charter needed to combine effective sovereignty with social guarantees for workers and peasants, drawing on the example of Mexico's 1917 constitution.[68] Castellanos, who was of African descent, was the PCC's main spokesman on race and was centrally involved in the party's adoption of antiracism as a key element in its platform in the 1930s.[69] The PCC's emphasis on racial equality enabled it to forge alliances with left-wing *sociedades de color* and to considerably expand its support base among the island's population of African descent.[70] In his 1936 *Mediodía* text, as in his contributions to internal party debates, Castellanos emphasized the existing Cuban constitution's failure to guarantee equal rights in practice for the island's Black population. Rather than merely asserting racial equality on paper, Castellanos argued, the new constitution should actively punish discrimination.[71]

But for Castellanos, the question of the constitution was also bound up with systemic issues, ranging from Cuba's curtailed sovereignty to racism and from workers' rights to agrarian reform. Anti-imperialism and antiracism could not be separated from each other or from a radical socioeconomic agenda. Other contributions to *Mediodía* displayed a similar sense of interconnection, with several of the respondents to a 1938 survey calling for expanded social rights to be included in the new constitution, while Pedro Portuondo Calá echoed Castellanos's earlier call for an antidiscrimination provision.[72] For Enrique Llarch, the drafting of a new constitution was a moment for Cuban Blacks to "fulfill their duty in defense of democracy" and to realize the promises of the struggle for independence in the nineteenth century, achieving Cuba's "full liberty and sovereignty."[73] For Llarch, the Constituent Assembly was not only a means of redressing Cuba's racial inequalities; it was also an opportunity to fulfill the thwarted aspirations of the Cuban independence movement. Here, the idea of "democracy" that was at stake involved racial equality and national sovereignty, the realization of which implied substantial changes in Cuba's internal social order as well as its external orientation.

The debates around the Constituent Assembly were accompanied by profound efforts to rethink Cuban national identity—and here, too, race featured prominently. What defined *cubanidad* (Cubanness) and how should the African contributions to Cuban culture and society be weighed? Some participants in these debates insisted on singling out and honoring African components of Cuban culture (a tendency known as "Afrocubanismo"), while others argued that African elements were so fundamental to Cuba's sense of itself that it made no sense to distinguish them within the mix.[74] These discussions unfolded in a range of venues, from Black social clubs to the magazines several of them published, such as *Adelante*. *Mediodía* was another key forum, carrying a string of articles that grappled with the relation between race and *cubanidad*. Guillén, for example, frontally attacked racist arguments that continued to affirm the notion of Blacks' supposed inferiority, arguing for Blacks' central contribution to Cuban history and culture.[75] The public intellectual and PCC militant Salvador García Agüero likewise affirmed the historic depth of Blacks' prominence in Cuban culture.[76] Ángel Pinto, meanwhile, rebutted claims made by fellow Black writer Gustavo Urrutia in the conservative daily *Diario de la marina* that Blacks should not be drawn to socialism.[77] For Pinto, it was in any case not socialist ideology that appealed to him but the Left's commitment to finally realizing the promise of racial equality. Subsequent events partially ratified this view; when elections to the Constituent Assembly were eventually held in late 1939, three of the five nonwhite delegates were Communists, and they played a prominent role in getting antidiscrimination provisions written into Article 23 of the island's 1940 constitution.[78]

A Vital Precursor

Mediodía's September 19, 1938, issue carried news that may have electrified its readers but that at the same time prefigured the magazine's demise. The PCC, having worked underground since the fall of Grau, had finally been legalized.[79] Subsequent issues carried photographs of celebratory PCC meetings in Havana, Santa Clara, Manzanillo, Yaguajay, and other towns.[80] While the Popular Front strategy that had impelled the creation of *Mediodía* still obtained, the party could now afford to be more overt in its approach to publishing. As Carlos Rafael Rodríguez would later recall, in these new circumstances the party decided to shift energy and resources to another project: a daily newspaper, *Noticias de hoy*, which it had launched in April 1938.[81] The two publications existed alongside each other for several months, but the PCC's resources could not cover both, and *Mediodía* was the casualty. It ceased publication at the end of January 1939.

As the most successful of Cuba's radical magazines of the 1930s, *Mediodía* played a vital role in establishing the public legitimacy of leftist ideas at a time when censorship had otherwise blocked their expression. As Rodríguez put it, "at a moment when hardly anyone could say what the people thought . . . [w]e managed to say it."[82] In providing a platform for writers and employment for editors, it also enabled Cuba's intellectual Left to maintain a sense of continuity, creating the infrastructure and cultivating the readership for left publishing ventures such as the newspaper *Hoy* and its literary magazine as well as the *Gaceta del Caribe*.[83]

Over the course of its 104 issues, *Mediodía* embodied the Cuban version of Popular Front politics, as a Communist-led publication that played host to a range of opinions and sought to build a broad left counterpolitics. Anti-imperialism, antifascism, and antiracism were central to that agenda, not as discrete concerns but as interlocking components of a single, all-encompassing struggle. The magazine's coverage and layout reflected a constant impulse to connect seemingly disparate developments. Racial oppression in Cuba was of a piece with the advance of the Spanish Right; Chinese resistance to Japanese imperialism needed to be seen alongside Latin American attempts to fend off US dominance. This form of internationalism, rooted in a systemic understanding of the connections between far-flung places, enabled *Mediodía*'s editors to articulate a radical counterpolitics while avoiding attacks from the Cuban censors. In the process, they created a space from which the Left could more frontally address Cuba's internal issues when domestic conditions softened.

Mediodía's two-and-a-half-year run was also a crucial episode in the development of the Cuban Left. The Popular Front years, with their urgent sense of global struggle, were formative for a generation of leftists, including many of the contributors to *Mediodía*. That generation would go on to play prominent roles in Cuban public life after the 1959 revolution. *Mediodía*'s editors Nicolás Guillén and Carlos Rafael Rodríguez were among the most visible public intellectuals of the post-1959 era, and several of the magazine's contributors were closely involved in the new state. Rodríguez himself served in a range of key government positions, and would later become vice president of the Council of Ministers; Raúl Roa became the Cuban foreign minister; Blas Roca was secretary general of the PCC until 1962 and remained a member of its politburo under Fidel Castro in the 1960s and 1970s, as well as heading Cuba's National Assembly from 1976 to 1981.[84]

For figures such as these, the revolution of 1959 represented at least in part the fulfilment of the agenda they had promoted through *Mediodía*. As Rodríguez recalled, the magazine's role in the 1930s had been to show how the struggle for democracy was "an inevitable step in the struggle for socialism," which in his view had then been taken up and driven forward by Fidel Castro's rebel movement.[85] Indeed, the convergence that took place in *Mediodía*'s pages anticipated some of the ideological alliances behind the early consolidation of the Cuban Revolution. Understanding those alliances in the light of the 1930s' Popular Front gives deeper context for the enduring commitment of many of these figures to the post-1959 dispensation. *Mediodía*'s internationalism also provides a strong precedent for Cuba's distinctive anti-imperialist alignments in the 1960s and beyond. While the magazine was only one component within Cuba's broad and active Left, its contribution to sustaining and expanding the horizons of that counterculture was vital. As well as shedding light on the role of internationalism in articulating Popular Front politics in the 1930s, the history of *Mediodía* is integral to the genealogy of Cuba's revolutions.

Tony Wood is assistant professor of history at the University of Colorado Boulder. His research focuses on the Latin American radical Left in the interwar period, tracing connections between Mexico, Cuba, and the Soviet Union. Initially trained as a specialist on Russia and the former Soviet Union, he is the author of *Chechnya: The Case for Independence* (2007) and *Russia without Putin: Money, Power and the Myths of the New Cold War* (2018).

Notes

I would like to thank the editors of this special issue and the two anonymous readers for their invaluable feedback, which helped me clarify and improve the text. Any errors or oversights are my own.

1. *Mediodía*, "'Mediodía no es una empresa.'"
2. It is discussed briefly as part of a broader radical left publishing scene in Smorkaloff, *Readers and Writers*, 43–45; and Lambe, *No Barrier Can Contain It*, chap. 3; and as a forerunner to the 1940s literary magazine *Gaceta del Caribe* in Seligmann, *Writing the Caribbean*, 59.
3. Denning, *Cultural Front*.
4. On Cuban politics in the 1930s, see Whitney, *State and Revolution*; for Cuban antifascism, see especially Lambe, *No Barrier Can Contain It*.
5. On the concept of the counterpolitical, see Ahmad, Benson, and Morgenstern, "Editors' Introduction."
6. Ferrer, *Insurgent Cuba*, 9.
7. Pérez, *Cuba under the Platt Amendment*, 52.
8. Ferrer, *Cuba*, 204–5, 210, 217–19.
9. Ayala, *American Sugar Kingdom*, 68–69, table 3.4; Aguilar, *Cuba 1933*, 46.
10. Ferrer, *Cuba: An American History*, 229.
11. Ferrer, *Cuba: An American History*, 231.
12. Giovannetti-Torres, *Black British Migrants*, 196–213.
13. Pappademos, *Black Political Activism*, 178–86.
14. Smorkaloff, *Readers and Writers*, 46, 49; Seligmann, *Writing the Caribbean*, 58.
15. Smorkaloff, *Readers and Writers*, 45–46.
16. Kersffeld, *Contra el imperio*, 164–65.
17. Simón and Pérez, *Recopilación*, 363.
18. Smorkaloff, *Readers and Writers*, 43.
19. Roche, "La revista *Mediodía*," 42; *Mediodía*, "'Mediodía no es una empresa.'"
20. *Bohemia*, "*Bohemia* ya es miembro del Audit Bureau of Circulations."
21. Seligmann, *Writing the Caribbean*, 61.

22. Broué, *Histoire de l'Internationale*, 492–521.

23. Augier, *Nicolás Guillén*, 17.

24. Roche, "La revista *Mediodía*," 42.

25. *Mediodía*, [untitled].

26. Augier, *Nicolás Guillén*, 17.

27. Moore, *Nationalizing Blackness*, 1–3, 122–27.

28. Ortiz, "Contraste económico"; Ortiz, *Cuban Counterpoint*.

29. Augier, *Nicolás Guillén*, 19.

30. Roche, "La revista *Mediodía*," 42.

31. *Mediodía*, "Los mejores agentes."

32. *Mediodía*, "Saludos a Mediodía."

33. Roche, "La revista *Mediodía*," 40, 42; Rodríguez, *Letra con filo*, 558. It seems more than likely the party also funded the magazine, though I have been unable to find direct confirmation of this.

34. Roche, "La revista *Mediodía*," 45.

35. These examples are drawn from *Mediodía* no. 11 (March 5, 1937); and no. 85 (September 12, 1938).

36. See, for example, *Mediodía* no. 9 (February 15, 1937); no. 37 (October 11, 1937); no. 54 (February 7, 1938); no. 57 (February 28, 1938); no. 64 (April 18, 1938); no. 80 (August 8, 1938); no. 88 (October 3, 1938); and no. 104 (January 23, 1939).

37. Martínez, "Brasil"; González, "Guatemala."

38. Brown, "Chile."

39. Karl, *China's Revolutions*, 74.

40. See, for example, Field, "El Frente Unico."

41. Contention over this issue would recur in many contexts; on different socialist strategies adopted in the developing world during the Cold War, see Friedman, *Ripe for Revolution*.

42. Roig de Leuchsenring, "Los chinos en Cuba."

43. The KMT had been aligned with the Cuban Communists in the 1920s and collaborated with the Cuban Anti-Imperialist League. See López, *Chinese Cubans*, 198–99.

44. *Mediodía*, [Overseas Chinese unite!].

45. *Mediodía*, "El heroísmo de un pueblo."

46. *Mediodía* no. 100 (December 26, 1938).

47. Lambe, *No Barrier Can Contain It*, 1–3, 49–53.

48. Augier, *Nicolás Guillén*, 15.

49. Kelley, *Race Rebels*, 123–60.

50. Augier, "Marcelino Domingo."

51. For an overall English-language history of the "Internationals," see Tremlett, *International Brigades*.

52. Citing the work of Denise Urcelay-Maragnès, Lambe gives a total figure of 1,067 (*No Barrier Can Contain It*, 88).

53. For photographs, see, for example, *Mediodía* no. 15 (April 15, 1937); no. 18 (May 15, 1937); and no. 39 (October 25, 1937). For casualty lists, see no. 14 (April 5, 1937); and no. 77 (July 18, 1938).

54. Guillén, "Un pelotero."

55. *Mediodía* published one of the first translations of Hughes's "Song of Spain": Hughes, "El canto de España."

56. Guillén, "España."
57. Guillén, "Discurso del delegado por Cuba," 9.
58. Guillén, "Discurso del delegado por Cuba," 9.
59. Guillén, "Discurso del delegado por Cuba," 18.
60. Guillén, "Discurso del delegado por Cuba," 18. Guillén's reasoning here ran parallel to the thinking of Langston Hughes, who in his speech to the same gathering described fascism as a continuation of white supremacy: Hughes, "Too Much of Race," 3.
61. Arthur Jukes to J. Butler Wright, Nuevitas, August 23, 1938, National Archives and Record Administration, RG 59, 837.00 F3.
62. *Mediodía*, "Fascista."
63. Roche, "La revista *Mediodía*," 43.
64. Quoted in Whitney, *State and Revolution*, 129.
65. Ferrer, *Insurgent Cuba*, 9.
66. The Adelante Association was one of these social organizations; for a discussion of its magazine, also called *Adelante*, and its role in debates around Blackness and antiracism, see Vásquez, "*Adelante*."
67. On Latin American conceptions of social rights, as distinct from the Anglo-American emphasis on individual property rights, see Grandin, "Liberal Traditions."
68. Castellanos, "Notas sobre la Constituyente," 4.
69. On Castellanos and his role in PCC debates, see Wood, "Another Country," 657–61, 665–66.
70. De la Fuente, *Nation for All*, 215–16.
71. Castellanos, "Notas sobre la Constituyente," 4.
72. *Mediodía*, "Cuba y la Constituyente"; and Portuondo Calá, "Sobre la Constituyente."
73. Llarch, "El negro y la próxima Constituyente," 12.
74. For excerpts from contributions to these discussions, see Vásquez, "Adelante."
75. Guillén, "Racismo y cubanidad."
76. García Agüero, "El negro en nuestra cultura."
77. Pinto, "Lo que debe guiar al negro."
78. De la Fuente, *Nation for All*, 216–22.
79. *Mediodía*, "La legalidad del Partido Comunista." A PCC front organization, the Unión Revolucionaria, had been able to operate legally since March 1937, but not the PCC as such.
80. See *Mediodía* no. 87 (September 26, 1938); no. 89 (October 10, 1938); no. 92 (October 31, 1938); and no. 94 (November 14, 1938).
81. Rodríguez, *Letra con filo*, 559.
82. Roche, "La revista *Mediodía*," 43.
83. Smorkaloff, *Writers and Readers*, 45; Seligmann, *Writing the Caribbean*, 58–59.
84. On Blas Roca, see Jeifets and Jeifets, *América Latina en la Internacional Comunista*, 211, 537.
85. Roche, "La revista *Mediodía*," 44.

References

Aguilar, Luis. *Cuba, 1933: Prologue to Revolution*. Ithaca, NY: Cornell University Press, 1972.
Ahmad, Mahvish, Koni Benson, and Hana Morgenstern. "Revolutionary Papers: Counterinstitutions, Counterpolitics, and Countercultures of Anticolonial Periodicals from the Global South." *Radical History Review*, no. 150 (2024): 1–32.

Augier, Ángel. "Marcelino Domingo en la Polar." *Mediodía* no. 34 (September 21, 1937): 13, 16.

Augier, Ángel. *Nicolás Guillén: Notas para un estudio biográfico-crítico*. Vol. 2. Santa Clara: Dirección de Publicaciones, Universidad Central de las Villas, 1962.

Ayala, César J. *American Sugar Kingdom: The Plantation Economy of the Spanish Caribbean, 1898–1934*. Chapel Hill: University of North Carolina Press, 1999.

Bohemia. "*Bohemia* ya es miembro del Audit Bureau of Circulations." Vol. 25, no. 34 (October 1, 1933): back cover.

Broué, Pierre. *Histoire de l'Internationale communiste, 1919–1943*. Paris: Fayard, 1997.

Brown, Helen. "Chile entre la democracia y el fascismo." *Mediodía* no. 91 (October 24, 1938): 9, 18.

Castellanos, Martín. "Notas sobre la Constituyente." *Mediodía* no. 3 (August 1936): 3–4.

de la Fuente, Alejandro. *A Nation for All: Race, Inequality, and Politics in Twentieth-Century Cuba*. Chapel Hill: University of North Carolina Press, 2001.

Denning, Michael. *The Cultural Front: The Laboring of American Culture in the Twentieth Century*. London: Verso, 1996.

Ferrer, Ada. *Cuba: An American History*. New York: Scribner, 2021.

Ferrer, Ada. *Insurgent Cuba: Race, Nation, and Revolution, 1868–1898*. Chapel Hill: University of North Carolina Press, 1999.

Field, Frederick V. "El Frente Unico en China." *Mediodía* no. 24 (July 13, 1937): 8, 19.

Friedman, Jeremy. *Ripe for Revolution: Building Socialism in the Third World*. Cambridge, MA: Harvard University Press, 2021.

García Agüero, Salvador. "El negro en nuestra cultura." *Mediodía* no. 6 (January 15, 1937): 10, 16.

Giovannetti-Torres, Jorge L. *Black British Migrants in Cuba: Race, Labor, and Empire in the Twentieth-Century Caribbean, 1898–1948*. Cambridge: Cambridge University Press, 2018.

González, Arturo. "Guatemala, el Portugal de América." *Mediodía* no. 67 (May 9, 1938): 8, 16.

Grandin, Greg. "The Liberal Traditions in the Americas: Rights, Sovereignty, and the Origins of Liberal Multilateralism." *American Historical Review* 117, no. 1 (2012): 68–91.

Guillén, Nicolás. "Discurso del delegado por Cuba." *Mediodía* no. 29 (August 17, 1937): 11, 18.

Guillén, Nicolás. "España: Fragmento." *Mediodía* no. 36 (October 4, 1937): 10.

Guillén, Nicolás. "Racismo y cubanidad." *Mediodía* no. 6 (January 15, 1937): 4, 19.

Guillén, Nicolás. "Un pelotero, capitán de ametralladoras." *Mediodía* no. 45 (December 6, 1937): 10.

Hughes, Langston. "El canto de España." *Mediodía* no. 40 (November 1, 1937): 9.

Hughes, Langston, "Too Much of Race." *The Volunteer for Liberty* no. 1 (August 23, 1937): 3–4.

Jeifets, Lazar, and Víctor Jeifets. *América Latina en la Internacional Comunista, 1919–1943: Diccionario biográfico*. Santiago de Chile: Ariadna Ediciones, 2015.

Karl, Rebecca. *China's Revolutions in the Modern World: A Brief Interpretive History*. London: Verso, 2020.

Kelley, Robin D. G. *Race Rebels: Culture, Politics, and the Black Working Class*. New York: Free Press, 1994.

Kersffeld, Daniel. *Contra el imperio: Historia de la Liga Antimperialista de las Américas*. Mexico City: Siglo Veintiuno, 2012.

Lambe, Ariel Mae. *No Barrier Can Contain It: Cuban Antifascism and the Spanish Civil War*. Chapel Hill: University of North Carolina Press, 2019.

Llarch, Enrique. "El negro y la próxima Constituyente." *Mediodía* no. 32 (September 7, 1937): 8, 12.

López, Kathleen. *Chinese Cubans: A Transnational History.* Chapel Hill: University of North Carolina Press, 2013.

Martínez, R. A. "Brasil: El Caballo de Troya del fascismo." *Mediodía* no. 46 (December 13, 1937): 11.

Mediodía. "Cuba y la Constituyente." No. 69 (May 23, 1938): 8–11, 18.

Mediodía. "El heroísmo de un pueblo." No. 76 (July 11, 1938): 3.

Mediodía. "Fascista que despoja a un campesino." No. 45 (December 6, 1937): 15.

Mediodía. "La legalidad del Partido Comunista." No. 86 (September 19, 1938): 13.

Mediodía. "Los mejores agentes de Mediodía." No. 51 (January 17, 1938): 16.

Mediodía. "'Mediodía' no es una empresa, ¡es una causa!" No. 23 (July 6, 1937): 15.

Mediodía. [Overseas Chinese unite!] No. 76 (July 11, 1938): 15.

Mediodía. "Saludos a Mediodía." No. 51 (January 17, 1938): 13; and no. 53 (January 31, 1938): 15.

Mediodía. "Sintonice." No. 5 (January 18, 1938), 20; and no. 66 (May 2, 1938): inside back cover.

Mediodía. [Untitled]. No. 1 (July 1936): 5.

Moore, Robin. *Nationalizing Blackness: Afrocubanismo and Artistic Revolution in Havana, 1920–1940.* Pittsburgh, PA: University of Pittsburgh Press 1997.

Ortiz, Fernando. *Cuban Counterpoint: Tobacco and Sugar.* Translated by Harriet de Onis. Durham, NC: Duke University Press, 1995.

Ortiz, Fernando. "Contraste económico del azúcar y el tabaco." *Mediodía* no. 1 (July 1936): 7–8.

Pappademos, Melina. *Black Political Activism and the Cuban Republic.* Chapel Hill: University of North Carolina Press, 2014.

Pérez, Louis A., Jr. *Cuba under the Platt Amendment, 1902–1934.* Pittsburgh, PA: University of Pittsburgh Press, 1986.

Pinto, Ángel. "Lo que debe guiar al negro." *Mediodía* no. 26 (July 27, 1937): 10.

Portuondo Calá, Pedro. "Sobre la Constituyente." *Mediodía* no. 71 (June 6, 1938): 13.

Roche, José Antonio. "La revista *Mediodía*: Un testimonio de Carlos Rafael Rodríguez." *Bohemia*, no. 24 (June 13, 1986): 40–45.

Rodríguez, Carlos Rafael. *Letra con filo.* Vol. 2. Havana: Editorial de Ciencias Sociales, 1983.

Roig de Leuchsenring, Emilio. "Los chinos en Cuba." *Mediodía* no. 76 (July 11, 1938): 9, 16.

Seligmann, Katerina Gonzalez. *Writing the Caribbean in Magazine Time.* New Brunswick, NJ: Rutgers University Press, 2021.

Simón, Pedro, and Trinidad Pérez. *Recopilación de textos sobre Juan Marinello.* Havana: Casa de las Americas, 1979.

Smorkaloff, Pamela Maria. *Readers and Writers in Cuba. A Social History of Print Culture, 1830s–1990s.* New York: Garland, 1997.

Tremlett, Giles. *The International Brigades: Fascism, Freedom, and the Spanish Civil War.* London: Bloomsbury, 2020.

Vásquez, Jorge Daniel. "*Adelante*: Blackness and Anti-Racism in Cuba." Revolutionary Papers, updated October 12, 2022. https://revolutionarypapers.org/teaching-tool/adelante-blackness-and-anti-racism-in-cuba/.

Whitney, Robert. *State and Revolution in Cuba: Mass Mobilization and Political Change, 1920–1940.* Chapel Hill: University of North Carolina Press, 2001.

Wood, Tony. "Another Country: Cuban Communism and Black Self-Determination, 1932–36." *Hispanic American Historical Review* 102, no. 4 (2022): 643–72.

Congress Militant

Revolutionary Papers as Political Organizers

Noor Nieftagodien

Inqaba ya basebenzi and *Congress Militant*, the journal and newspaper of the Marxist Workers' Tendency of the African National Congress (hereinafter the Tendency), were products of revolutionary times. They were launched, respectively, at the beginning and end of the 1980s, a decade characterized by mounting mass struggles against apartheid led by numerous local and national movements. These counterhegemonic movements were spaces of burgeoning radical ideas and practices, where critiques of apartheid and capitalism and experiments with building democratic organizations and mobilizing various repertoires of struggles were formulated and elaborated. The resistance press, including revolutionary publications such as *Inqaba ya basebenzi* and *Congress Militant*, reflected and contributed to this fertile milieu of dissent and radicalism. The former was published in exile and the latter, from 1990, inside the country. This article is principally concerned with examining the role of *Congress Militant* as a tool of political organizing of the Tendency in a period of intensified mass struggles, negotiations, and violence. The character and tempo of the anti-apartheid struggle, as well as the Tendency's growth inside the country, determined the organization's conception of the specific roles of its publications. In other words, political context was crucial in shaping the form and content of the Tendency's publications.

The period from the late 1970s to the early 1980s witnessed the revival of the internal anti-apartheid movement, following a brief hiatus caused by state

Radical History Review
Issue 150 (October 2024)   DOI 10.1215/01636545-11257421
© 2024 by MARHO: The Radical Historians' Organization, Inc.

repression in response to the 1976 student uprising. New national movements were established, such as the Azanian People's Organization, the Federation of South African Trade Unions (FOSATU), the Azanian Students' Organization, and the Congress of South African Students. Simultaneously, local movements proliferated, especially civic associations, which campaigned on socioeconomic problems facing poor Black communities. This process of reconstituting movements also involved widespread and intense deliberations on liberation politics, from debates on the character of state and society, the nature of trade unions, and the role of the Black working class, to contestations over appropriate strategies and tactics. *Inqaba ya basebenzi* was the main forum in which the Tendency engaged in these discussions, focusing initially on clarifying its theoretical standpoint and analysis of the emerging crisis of apartheid. Written in exile, these interventions established a broad framework for its political program throughout the 1980s. A salient thread running through this body of political material was the Tendency's assertion that the mass resistance by the Black population nationally was creating favorable conditions for the overthrow of apartheid and capitalism.

However, in the 1990s the politics of negotiations predominated, culminating relatively soon in the country's first democratic elections in 1994. At the same time mass mobilization, especially by unions, also reached new heights, while the civil war in Natal (now KwaZulu Natal) and the townships of Pretoria-Witwatersrand-Vereeniging (now Gauteng Province) posed a serious threat to the efforts to produce a negotiated settlement. These issues inevitably determined the content and tenor of *Congress Militant*, which from 1990 effectively replaced *Inqaba ya basebenzi* as the principal publication of the Tendency. In this new, post-exile era, with editors back in South Africa, the paper could be produced inside the country and circulated openly.

Following the examples of revolutionary organizations throughout the twentieth century, the Tendency's ideas about the role of its paper derived from Lenin's exposition of the purposes of *Iskra*. Writing in the early twentieth century, the leader of the Bolsheviks advocated the view that "[a] newspaper is not only a collective propagandist and a collective agitator, it is also a collective organizer." Elaborating on this core idea, he explained that a paper "may be compared to the scaffolding erected around a building under construction; it marks the contours of the structure and facilitates communication between the builders, permitting them to distribute the work and to view the common results achieved by their organized labor."[1] In this approach, papers are political organizers and integral to the life of a party, acting as forums for theorization, political analysis, agitation, propaganda, and internal communication. Revolutionary papers are material and public manifestations of the ideas and practices of revolutionary organizations. Produced in various formats such as journals, broadsheets, and pamphlets, their role as organizing tools are determined by mutually constitutive internal and external functions. Arguably, their key internal role is to nurture revolutionary cadres through political education comprising the elaboration of theories, political-economic analyses, and perspectives. Their external objectives are usually to delineate an organization from others and to disseminate its ideas, program, and strategies in order to recruit new members. Importantly, they are tools of mobilization against class adversaries by offering critiques of capitalism and contributing to struggles against all manifestations of oppression and exploitation. Both of the Tendency's publications effectively carried out these functions.

Resistance Media in South Africa

Opposition publications in South Africa historically have flourished in periods of mass protests, such as in the 1920s and then in the 1940s and 1950s.[2] The Industrial and Commercial Workers' Union's *Workers' Herald*, published between 1923 and 1928, was an early example of the important role a paper could play in disseminating a movement's politics and campaigns.[3] In the 1940s and 1950s, the resistance publication landscape was dominated by left-wing organizations, reflecting the influence of Marxism among intellectuals and political activists.[4] The *Guardian*, which was closely associated with the ANC and the Communist Party of South Africa (CPSA), registered remarkable success in this period, reaching at its height an impressive weekly circulation of fifty-five thousand.[5] At the same time, communist/socialist organizations produced their own publications: the CPSA's *Inkululeko*, the Workers' Party of South Africa's *Spark*, and the Non-European Unity Movement's *Torch*.[6] Although differing substantially in the Marxism they espoused, these papers—all published openly in South Africa but facing differing levels of censorship and repression—shared common objectives of criticizing capitalism and imperialism and advocating for socialism. State repression in the aftermath of the Sharpeville massacre in 1960 dealt a crippling blow to opposition publications, forcing them to either close down or operate underground. The *African Communist* (South African Communist Party, launched in 1959), *Sechaba* (ANC), and the Pan Africanist Congress's *Azania News* and *Azania Combat* were published in exile and disseminated clandestinely in the country, as was *Inqaba ya basebenzi* in the 1980s.

The emergence in the early 1970s of the Black Consciousness Movement (BCM) and the independent trade unions signaled the rebirth of the anti-apartheid movement and triggered a revival of resistance publications produced by social movements, trade unions, community organizations, cultural and religious groups, clandestine parties, and sympathetic academics. By the mid-1980s the alternative press was in the throes of unprecedented expansion, including the publication of more Black newspapers and a new generation of progressive commercial publications.[7] More pertinent was the proliferation of what Keyan Tomaselli referred to as the left-wing presses whose "central motor force . . . was *organization* and not the desire to produce newspapers."[8] These papers were organically linked to and espoused core values of emancipatory movements, such as operating on a nonprofit basis and engendering participatory and dialogic practices in their production.[9] They published strident critiques of apartheid; reported on deteriorating conditions and struggles in Black residential areas and workplaces; engaged in lively debates on liberation theories, strategies, and tactics; and generally propagated ideas of freedom.[10] In the 1970s the BCM published *Black Review*, *SASO Newsletter*, and *SASO Bulletin*, while *Workers' Unity*, *FOSATU Worker News*, and *South African Labor Bulletin* emanated from different parts of the labor movement. As community-based struggles intensified in the 1980s, activists produced local papers to augment their campaigns and organizational efforts. *Grassroots*, a Western Cape paper launched in 1980, was the most successful community newspaper, reaching a circulation of twenty-thousand in 1982.[11] Other notable community papers were *Saamstaan*, *Ilizwi LaseRhini/Grahamstown Voice*, and *Izwi lase Township*. The latter was produced by a group of young socialists from Alexandra township, called Ditshwantsho tsa Rhona, which campaigned on issues facing the local community and simultaneously cohered into a clearly defined political group.[12]

The alternative or resistance press of this period has received considerable scholarly attention highlighting its contributions to the liberation struggle and transformation of the media landscape.[13] Almost absent from this body of research are the less well-known collection of revolutionary papers published by socialist/communist organizations. Of these, the exiled South African Communist Party (SACP) was the most influential with a network of underground members in the country who used the *African Communist* for political work. Independent socialist organizations, broadly defined by their Trotskyist leanings, also produced publications: Cape Action League (*Solidarity*), Action Youth (*Arise/Vukani*), Workers' Organisation for Socialist Action (*Workers' Voice*), Workers' International League of South Africa (*Worker Tenant*), and Comrades for a Workers' Government (*Qina msebenzi*). *Congress Militant* and *Inqaba ya basebenzi* formed part of this flowering of revolutionary publications in the 1980s and early 1990s. The proliferation of socialist publications reflected the widespread influence of Marxism, particularly in trade unions and youth/student movements. Revolutionary papers of the non-Stalinist Left operated independently of each other and rarely featured debates about the others' political positions. In the case of the Tendency, polemics were usually aimed at the SACP and ANC leaders. While sharing socialist politics, especially the Trotskyism of other independent socialist papers, *Inqaba ya basebenzi* and *Congress Militant* were also distinguished by their connection to a particular international network of revolutionary papers. They were probably also more successful in terms of regularity of publication and the period of their existence: *Inqaba ya basebenzi* was published between 1981 and 1990 (twenty-eight editions) and *Congress Militant* between 1989 and 1996, which reflected the growth of the Tendency inside the country.[14]

My own association with the Tendency began in 1985, when a number of youth activists in Cape Town held discussions with the exiled group and decided to join. By then I had been involved in the school boycotts of 1980s and at the end of 1982 joined Zackie Achmat and a few other activists to establish the Bo-Kaap Youth Movement (BKYM), one of several youth organizations created across the Cape Peninsula in the early 1980s. BKYM later became a branch of the Cape Youth Congress, an affiliate of the United Democratic Front (UDF), signaling our orientation to the Congress Movement. I began working full time for the Tendency in 1988 after my contract as a teacher was terminated for political activity. At the end of 1990 I moved to Johannesburg to be part of a new leadership collective, which also involved serving on the editorial committee of *Congress Militant*, and I remained actively involved in its production and distribution until 1996.

What's in a Name?

The name *Congress Militant* encapsulated the salient strategic and political positions of the Tendency. "Militant" referred to the Tendency's close association with the Militant Tendency in Britain, whose founder, Ted Grant, left South Africa in the 1930s out of frustration with the stranglehold of Stalinism on the CPSA.[15] Under his leadership, a small group of Trotskyist activists in October 1964 launched the *Militant* newspaper to propagate its Marxist program in the British Labor Party and the Trade Union Congress. According to Peter Taaffe, the first editor of the paper, the title aimed to establish a historic connection to the newspaper of the American Socialist Workers' Party, which was closely associated with Leon Trotsky in the 1930s. The name also expressed the organization's intention to win "in the first instance, the most conscious, combative, fighting, i.e. *militant* sections of the working class."[16] By the early 1990s, the Militant Tendency had become a formidable force on the Left in Britain, especially among the Labor Party Young Socialists and trade unions. Published weekly, the *Militant* newspaper was a key tool of political intervention in working-class struggles such as the miners' strike, in campaigns against racism, privatization, and the poll tax, and in elections.[17]

In so doing, it created a template for the political work of fellow activists across the globe, who convened under the auspices of the Committee for a Workers' International (CWI), one of several Trotskyist groups aiming to create a viable international organization in opposition to the Stalinist Comintern. The CWI represented a particular tradition of Trotskyism, mostly defined by its tactical orientation to the traditional parties of the working class, called entryism, which involved operating in such parties with the aim of transforming them into worker-led socialist organizations. Differences with other Trotskyist groups on questions such as the character of the Soviet Union, participation in elections, the national and colonial questions, guerrilla warfare, and on perspectives for capitalism also contributed to its self-definition. Where conditions permitted, national sections produced their own newspapers (and sometimes theoretical journals) modeled on the *Militant*. These included the *Militant Irish Monthly*, *Xekinima* (Greece), *Struggle* (Pakistan), and *El militante* (Spain).

"Congress" in the title *Congress Militant* expressed the Tendency's pivotal tactical orientation to the Congress Movement, led by the ANC. In the late 1970s several activists in exile who were involved in the ANC, the independent trade unions, and the Black Consciousness Movement converged to constitute an explicitly Trotskyist tendency in the ANC.[18] Drawing on histories of traditional organizations of the working class internationally, they argued that the ANC, despite its political and organizational shortcomings, would emerge as the preeminent organization behind which the Black majority would unite in its quest for national liberation.[19] Subsequent events confirmed the validity of this perspective. As the struggle inside the country gained momentum, members of the Tendency were involved in student, youth, civic, and women's movements aligned from 1983 to the United Democratic Front (UDF), as well as in trade unions, especially the Federation of South African Trade Union and later the Congress of South African Trade Unions (COSATU). In 1979 four of its leading members (Rob Petersen, Martin Legassick, Paula Ensor, and Dave Hemson), who were active in South African Congress of Trade Unions (SACTU) in exile, were suspended by the ANC; this move, according to Legassick, was driven by the SACP in order to marginalize alternative socialist politics in the Congress Movement.[20]

The suspension came after Petersen, who was the editor of SACTU's newspaper, *Workers' Unity*, penned a memorandum challenging the SACTU leadership's opposition to the independent trade unions that had emerged inside the country in the wake of the 1973 Durban strike wave. Stephen Dlamini, SACTU's president, accused these formations of being "yellow unions," historically defined as unions that are close to the employers, arguing that independent democratic unions could not exist in a fascist country.[21] The suspended group also criticized the ANC for holding discussions with Gatsha Buthelezi, the leader of Inkatha, who was also the chief minister of the KwaZulu Bantustan.[22] Over time the Tendency formulated sharp critiques of the ANC-SACP political program, particularly the two-stage theory, which had been the central plank of the SACP's politics since the late 1920s. In this model, socialists should defer a revolutionary transformation of South Africa until after the achievement of a national democratic revolution. The tasks of national liberation, it was argued by the Tendency, could not be achieved by middle-class nationalists but only through working-class power.[23] Other important differences centered on the characterization of the Soviet Union (whereas the SACP was a loyal defender, the Tendency defined it as a degenerated workers' state) and guerrilla warfare, which the Tendency deemed as inappropriate in an industrial country such as South Africa.[24] *Inqaba ya basebenzi* regularly featured critiques of the ANC-SACP theories and political programs not only to expose how their loyalty to Stalinism distorted Marxism but also to demonstrate the deleterious effects of their politics on mass movements in South Africa. The Tendency articulated its alternative analysis of the South African capitalist crisis and the tasks for revolution in the 1982 special publication *South Africa's Impending Socialist Revolution*, which constituted the framework for subsequent elaborations of its perspectives.[25]

Inqaba ya basebenzi (Fortress of the Workers)

Produced in exile, the journal's overarching objective was to articulate a distinctive political identity for the Tendency through Marxist analyses of apartheid capitalism and by contributing to debates on political programs, strategies, and tactics in mass movements. The inaugural issue of *Inqaba ya basebenzi* in 1981 established a template for future editions with an editorial entitled "Forward to Freedom—Unite under Workers' Leadership." Reflecting on struggles in 1980 by organized workers and youth/students, the editorial explained how an escalation in class struggle would compel workers "to develop more and more their organizations of combat."[26] Emblazoned across the pages of this issue was the defining slogan of the Tendency—"Build a mass ANC on a socialist program"—which appeared in most subsequent issues. It succinctly conveyed the strategic task of transforming the ANC into a mass organization of the working class to prosecute radical struggles against apartheid capitalism. Achieving that objective, the journal argued, also required activists to embrace Marxist ideas against the prevailing Stalinist and nationalist views of the Congress leadership. Workers and youth especially were exhorted to join "in waging the crucial struggle for Marxist policies in the ANC" (fig. 1).[27]

Political education, aimed at developing an activist cadre armed with Marxist theory, was thus regarded as a priority for the Tendency. An early initiative in pursuit of this objective was the establishment of the Southern African Labor Education Project, which produced and disseminated education material among workers and youth in southern Africa.[28] *Inqaba ya basebenzi* was, however, the principal vehicle for education of activists. It emphasized teaching the basic principles of Marxism by publishing articles on dialectical and historical materialism and special supplements titled "Principles of Communism" and "The Wages System."[29] Trade unionists especially were encouraged to reproduce these publications and to use them in reading groups and other education programs.

Internationalism was a central plank in *Inqaba ya basebenzi*'s political education program, based on the conviction that the global system of capitalism could only effectively be challenged through the concerted efforts of the international working class. By regularly publishing articles on struggles from across the world, the journal sought to expand the horizons of South African activists beyond their preoccupation with local politics and thus engender internationalist perspectives and solidarity. Articles on political struggles in various African countries (Namibia, Zimbabwe, Botswana, Mozambique, Zambia, Swaziland, Ghana, Nigeria, and Ethiopia) were standard features. Zimbabwe received prominence due to its recent

Figure 1. From the mid-1980s the theoretical journal carried more articles by members involved in movements inside the country.

liberation from British colonialism, proximity to South Africa, and the role of CWI comrades (including Dave Hemson) in that country's trade union and student movements. A special issue dedicated to Zimbabwe offered critical assessments of the postcolonial state and highlighted the growing contestations at workplaces that pitted the nascent trade unions against employers and the new ruling party.[30] While acknowledging the importance of national struggles for emancipation in the region, the journal advocated for a "Socialist Southern Africa."[31] Reports and analyses of popular struggles by socialist activists belonging to the CWI in, among others, India, Pakistan, Sri Lanka, the Middle East (especially the oppression of Palestinians), Argentina, Chile, Northern Ireland, and Britain underscored the internationalist character of the journal.

     Histories of working-class struggles, especially revolutions, were regarded as foundational in the education of activists. The Russian Revolution and anticolonial movements were celebrated and critically analyzed to highlight both their significance in global struggles against imperialism and to warn against the compromising influence of Stalinism on these historic achievements.[32] Key moments of mass struggles in South Africa also received similar interrogation. One of the most influential special editions, entitled "Lessons of the 1950s," examined the national defiance campaigns of that decade during which the ANC was transformed into a mass movement and established its position as the leading organization of national liberation. Written by Martin Legassick (under the pseudonym Richard Monroe), it criticized the Congress leadership's reformism and the constraints it placed on the nascent workers' movement, including on the campaigns of the SACTU.[33] An article by Basil Hendrickse (Weizmann Hamilton's pseudonym) on the student uprising of 1976 extolled the heroism of students and the important role of Black consciousness in transcending apartheid's racial divisions, but criticized its aversion to a class-based approach.[34]

While the editorial committee operated as a collective, which involved lengthy and detailed deliberations about the overall content and the main political articles in each edition, Paul Storey (the pseudonym of Rob Petersen) and Richard Monroe (Martin Legassick) were the driving forces behind the journal. *Inqaba ya basebenzi* built a reputation in South Africa as an insightful publication of independent socialist politics and garnered a relatively small but influential readership. It was posted from the UK and clandestinely circulated, particularly in the main urban areas. Anecdotally, it seemed to have been widely circulated among activists, but state repression and the cost of reproduction limited its potential reach.[35] In the early 1980s its dissemination and use occurred mostly through sympathetic individuals, but from the mid-1980s the Tendency's organization in the country became the main sites of reporting, reading, and circulation of the journal. The articles published in *Inqaba ya basebenzi*—Marxist theory, analyses of the deepening crisis of the apartheid state and capitalism, the unfolding rebellion against the system, histories of revolutions and contemporary international struggles, and polemics on political strategies—constituted an impressive body of political writing that distinguished the Tendency from other left organizations.

The Launch of *Congress Militant*

As the tempo of protests in the mid-1980s increased, the types of articles appearing in *Inqaba ya basebenzi* changed accordingly. A case in point was issue 18/19 of February 1986, published two months after the launch of COSATU. It contained an unprecedented number of articles, several of which were relatively short firsthand reports of strikes and community campaigns, plus commentaries on strategies and tactics in movements, including a polemic with "UDF Militants" and debates on the attacks on whites and the efficacy of sanctions.[36] Articles based on the experiences and insights of activists in movements had been appearing regularly but now occupied more space in the journal, such as those by Nkululeko Nomji (Madoda Cuphe), Susan van Wyk (Shafika Isaacs), Brenda Adams (Josie Abrahams), Bernard Fortuin

(Zackie Achmat), and Yusuf Gamiet (Noor Nieftagodien). *Inqaba ya basebenzi* was clearly under pressure to report on and analyze struggles as they were unfolding, a task for which a quarterly journal, published in exile and distributed clandestinely, was ill suited.

   With a steady increase from the mid-1980s in the Tendency's membership in the country, there was an urgent need for a revolutionary paper that could be more responsive to current political developments and better reflect the interventions of activists at the coalface of various struggles. Thus *Congress Militant* was launched in 1989 as a pivotal organizing tool alongside *Inqaba ya basebenzi*. The timing was fortuitous, considering the profound transformation of the political landscape with new waves of mass defiance, general strikes, the unbanning of liberation organizations, the commencement of negotiations, and a surge in political violence. The demands of this new context, which required coordinating campaigns, formulating demands, and advising on strategies and tactics, led to the suspension of the theoretical journal in order to focus on the publication of the more regular *Congress Militant*. An editorial committee based in London was responsible for the production of the journal and also constituted the leadership of the Tendency, although from the mid-1980s it had some representation from inside the country. From 1991, a new editorial committee, now an amalgam of the exile leadership and internal activists who joined the Tendency in the 1980s, operated inside the country and was concentrated in Johannesburg. A broader collective, including Rob Petersen, Victor Mhlongo, Weizmann Hamilton, Mark Heywood, Madoda Cuphe, Sharon Ekambaram, Leon Kaplan, and myself, was largely responsible for the production of the paper. Political support for this work also came from Cape Town and Durban, where Martin Legassick and Dave Hemson had respectively settled after returning from exile.

   Congress Militant emulated other papers in the CWI fold, especially the British *Militant*, which it resembled in form, style, and political content. While political analyses continued to feature, agitational pieces became more common. Front pages typically focused on key struggles at the time and articulated the Tendency's position in large, declaratory slogans such as "Smash the LRAA!," "Workers and Youth Unite in Congress!," "Workers' Power for Peace and Freedom!," "The Majority Must Rule!," and so forth. Editorials, crafted by the political leadership, usually appeared on the second page and presented the Tendency's line on key political issues, which in the 1990s invariably were dedicated to the negotiations process. The two center pages comprised lengthy analyses of crucial matters related to national and international politics.[37] The rest of the paper consisted of reports and commentary on local community and workplace struggles from across the country, generally written by activists involved in them. Following in the tradition of *Inqaba ya basebenzi*, *Congress Militant* carried articles in a number of local languages and occasionally published entire special issues in one or other language, depending on the intended regional audiences. From 1991 comrades began to publish in their own names, although, for security reasons, some continued to write under pseudonyms. This was especially the case where activists operated in areas affected by political violence or were in danger of being expelled from their organizations if their association with the Tendency became public.

Party Organizer

By the time *Congress Militant* was launched, the Tendency had established a national network of branches, based primarily in the industrial heartland of the PWV (Gauteng), Western Cape, and Natal (KwaZulu-Natal). Membership in the early 1990s reached a few hundred and the organization ran a campaign to reach a thousand members. A cohort of between fifteen and twenty full-timers was responsible for the day-to-day activities of the organization, including political education, campaigns, recruitment, dissemination of literature, and internal communication. The Tendency's organizational architecture was typical of a revolutionary party, comprising branches, regional committees, a national committee, and an executive. Branches were the primary spaces of political activity and convened weekly in residential areas to engage in political discussions, to receive reports of the organization's work nationally and internationally, and to plan political interventions in various struggles. The entire cycle of producing the paper—from writing to editing and dissemination—was integrally woven into the structure and the activities of the organization.

Writing for *Congress Militant* was regarded as one of the basic responsibilities of Tendency members. Under the best circumstances, reports on campaigns were sourced from branches, with the intention of foregrounding voices from local struggles. However, the process of collecting such articles faced numerous challenges, not least the low literacy levels of many activists who even struggled to write in their home languages. They were also overwhelmed by daily struggles (of politics and survival) and simply did not have time to engage in writing and editing. To mitigate these challenges, a standing practice was developed to assist these comrades to write about their experiences, including interviewing them. Nonetheless, a significant proportion of articles, especially longer and more analytical pieces, were written by full-timers and/or those with formal writing skills. The editorial committee, responsible for the production of the paper, took decisions about the relevance of pieces for particular issues and participated directly in editing articles, usually in consultation with authors. It was here that the detailed discussions about the editorial line, the focus of political analyses, and the content and tone of propaganda took place.

Distributing the paper was another core task assigned to all comrades. When *Congress Militant* was launched, its circulation was primarily a clandestine affair because it was still illegal to openly propagate the ideas of the Tendency, not least the clarion call to build the ANC on a socialist program. The unbanning in 1990 of liberation movements enabled branches to organize public sales of the paper, which generally took place at factories, hostels, transport hubs (railway stations, taxi ranks, and bus stops), education institutions, on marches and pickets, and at political rallies and meetings of mass movements. In this way it was hoped to spread the ideas of the Tendency especially among workers and youth, who were the main audiences of the paper. Sales at factory gates, typically at the change of shifts, and at transport hubs during peak hours were part of the routine activities of members. Paper sales generated varied responses from people. Many welcomed the presence of activists, and some became regular buyers of the papers. Others were bemused by the small groups of enthusiastic paper sellers and chose either to ignore them or buy a paper before rushing off. These activities aimed to establish contact with political sympathizers, which could result in their recruitment to the organization and/or support for campaigns.

But Tendency activists also encountered hostility in their political activities. Workers associated with *Congress Militant* came under close scrutiny by the bosses and, in a few cases, were suspended. In Natal and PWV townships, public sales of the paper were often curtailed to protect comrades from potential attacks by Inkatha, the Zulu nationalist organization led by Buthelezi, whose armed gangs regularly attacked anti-apartheid activists. Many ANC and UDF leaders were also vociferously opposed to the Tendency and campaigned to have them expelled from the party, which required the dissemination of the paper to be handled with circumspection. *Congress Militant* was sold at a modest price of fifty cents in 1990, which doubled to R1 by 1994, with requests for more generous solidarity donations. Again, this drew on the example of the *Militant* paper and was not always popular among potential readers, who were accustomed to receiving political material free of charge. Nonetheless, a principle was established that the paper should be self-financing and that such funds should be raised from workers and youth. Based on personal experience and reports received from regions, it was an approach that earned the respect of most people.

Among the most important roles of the paper was the development of a community of revolutionary cadres who shared their experiences of struggle and expression of political ideas in its pages. Thus articles on local struggles allowed textile workers in Bellville or Epping in the Cape to identify their fellow comrades nationally, such as youth defending their communities against Inkatha in the townships of Natal (now the province of KwaZulu Natal) or civic activists in Alexandra township in Johannesburg. Reports in *Congress Militant* were supplemented with more detailed accounts in branch meetings, sometimes by participants from different regions of South Africa. Sharing information of struggles not only engendered political awareness but was also the basis of solidarity. In this way Tendency members could also engage in discussions about local and national political developments and participate in critical assessments of campaigns. Such educational conversations extended to international political developments (e.g., the demise of the Soviet Union, the invasion of Iraq and the anti–poll tax campaign in Britain). Reading groups convened to study in more detail a wide range of political development as well as theoretical questions. The journal and paper were the main sources for reading material, in addition to major texts by Marx, Engels, Lenin, and Trotsky.

The paper appeared regularly until at least 1994, with several special editions focused on urgent matters, such as the 1993 assassination of Chris Hani, the 1992 Bisho massacre of ANC partisans in the Ciskei Bantustan, and strikes by different unions. Success of sales depended on the political situation, the focus of the paper, and the capacity of branches to organize sales. Records of sales do not exist, but anything between a few hundred and two to three thousand copies per edition were printed. According to one published report, 2,700 copies of Issue 9 and 1,000 of a special issue on struggles in Khayelitsha were sold.[38] In 1990, no fewer than eleven editions of *Congress Militant* were issued, including several special issues, reflecting the exciting and rapidly changing politics of the time. These were likely high points of sales but they indicate the reach of the paper, which probably enjoyed wider circulation than actual sales.

On the Union Front

The first issues of both *Inqaba ya basebenzi* and *Congress Militant* emphasized the centrality of organized labor in the struggle against apartheid and capitalism. COSATU's launch in 1985 was heralded as a historic achievement that confirmed the power of the organized Black working class and its leading role in the struggle. Thereafter the federation led mass campaigns and strikes and openly endorsed socialism. *Congress Militant* enthusiastically supported radical trade unions and regularly published articles highlighting precarious conditions in workplaces, on workers' struggles, and on national campaigns by COSATU and its affiliates. A special issue of the paper in 1989 called on workers to reject and "smash" the proposed Labor Relations Amendment Act, a piece of legislation aimed at ensnaring trade unions in unfriendly bureaucratic procedures.[39] Similar support was given to the federation's national strikes against goods and services tax and value-added tax, and the paper was used to mobilize workers and youth behind these actions. Special issues of *Congress Militant* were produced on industrial action, particularly where the Tendency was involved, such as the strikes by Western Cape hospital workers for a living wage of R1500 a month,[40] by transport workers against the use of corrosive chemicals at Transnet,[41] and by bus drivers against the planned retrenchment at the bus company, PUTCO.[42] In the late 1980s, *Inqaba ya basebenzi* explained the importance of a campaign for national minimum wage, and in the early 1990s *Congress Militant* made the specific demand of R250 for a forty-hour week a central part of its agitational work in the trade unions.[43]

While enthusiastic support for workers' struggles was the norm, the Tendency also regularly criticized union leaders for their perceived role in constraining worker militancy. A case in point was the 1987 miners' strike, which the journal described as "the most important strike in the history of the black workers' movement." However, the decision by the union leadership to send workers home at the beginning of the strike was interpreted as a tactical blunder that undermined the collective power of workers.[44] Miners who supported the Tendency distributed a pamphlet along these lines in the union but had little effect on the course pursued by the union leaders or the outcome of the strike.

From the mid-1980s, the Tendency built a modest presence in a number of trade unions affiliated to COSATU (e.g., National Union of Metalworkers of South Africa, National Union of Mineworkers, Transport and General Workers' Unions, and the South African Clothing and Textile Workers' Union [SACTWU]), mostly among ordinary workers and shop stewards whose activities focused on local shop-floor issues, with occasional interventions in union conferences. Occasionally, members and supporters in particular unions were sufficiently numerous and organized to coordinate broader campaigns, such as in SACTWU. From the late 1980s, several textile workers, especially shop stewards, in Cape Town and Durban joined the Tendency. Faced with large-scale retrenchments in the sector and low wages, there was a groundswell of anger against employers. When, in 1990, the union leaders settled for wages lower than workers' expectations, it generated considerable disappointment among union members. At this point, shop stewards who belonged to the Tendency sharply criticized the perceived conservatism of the union leaders and launched the Campaign for a Militant SACTWU to garner support for its views in the union.[45] A new publication, *SACTWU Militant,* was launched to popularize demands for a minimum wage, an end to retrenchments, the right to recall union leaders, and for the latter to be paid no more than the average wage of a skilled worker.[46] Although independent socialist groups existed in other unions, it was the first time that such a political current published its own paper and publicly mobilized to transform the union. Employers and union leaders reacted by accusing the leaders of the campaign of disrupting both industry and the union. The former suspended shop stewards and the latter accused them for wanting to split the union, which had the effect of weakening the campaign.[47] Despite these setbacks, *Congress Militant* and *SACTWU Militant* for a very short time were rallying points of left opposition in the union.

Negotiations and Violence

The Tendency did not anticipate the unbanning of liberation organizations and the rapid commencement of formal negotiations between the National Party and the ANC. An *Inqaba ya basebenzi* editorial in 1985 dedicated to the question of a negotiated settlement insisted "there is no route to democracy, therefore, except through disarming and dismantling this state—and replacing it by a democratic workers' state. Only a revolution can achieve this." The piece concluded that "it is the implacable hostility of the whole South African ruling class to democracy, enforced through its ruthless state machine, which rules out the possibility of a peaceful negotiated settlement."[48] This line was maintained until 1990. It was, as Legassick explained, a crucial error emanating from not fully appreciating the extent to which the collapse of the Soviet Union and the restoration of capitalism changed the balance of forces globally.[49]

Congress Militant acknowledged this mistake and over the course of the early 1990s effected important adjustments to its position on negotiations. A special issue published in the Western Cape a few days before the historic announcement by F. W. De Klerk to unban liberation organizations demanded Nelson Mandela's release but cautioned the ANC leader not to negotiate with the head of the apartheid government, who was a renowned conservative and opponent of majority rule.[50] A couple of weeks later *Congress Militant* welcomed the release of Mandela and in an "Open Letter" urged him to lead the building of a mass ANC to overthrow the government.[51] These views still corresponded with the position articulated in the mid-1980s. By the end of 1990, however, formal negotiations between the ANC and the apartheid government had commenced, and within a year it was evident that a settlement between the major parties was a distinct possibility. The violence engulfing Natal and the PWV also generated a groundswell of support for peace, which was reflected in an article in the paper with the opening lines, "We share the desire of the masses of the people for peace." Another piece in the same edition called for "workers' power for peace and freedom against the state's iron fist."[52] As the negotiations gained momentum, *Congress Militant* argued in favor of convening a Constituent Assembly to ensure the voices of the majority would prevail against the efforts of the government and its conservative allies to strike deals behind closed doors to protect minority rights.[53] It warned that ANC leaders might be prepared to make concessions, including on the pivotal issue of majority rule. When the National Party in 1992 attempted to introduce a clause requiring a 75 percent majority for the adoption of the interim constitution, the paper called on the ANC to reject it outright. The final issue of that year demanded simply: "The Majority Must Rule!"[54] With elections clearly on the horizon, *Congress Militant* campaigned for mass support for the ANC and urged workers and youth to fill the ranks of the party to ensure a big electoral majority and to campaign for socialist policies (fig. 2). *Congress Militant* made possible the Tendency's timely response to the ebbs and flows of the negotiation process and its public articulation of political views emanating from intense internal debates about the profound transitions unfolding globally and nationally.

Few issues occupied the Tendency more than the political violence engulfing Black townships in Natal and PWV. In April 1991 *Congress Militant* gave full

Figure 2. *Congress Militant* was able to respond in a timely way to the rapidly changing and complex political context in the early 1990s.

support to the ANC's ultimatum to the government to condemn the violence being orchestrated by the Inkatha Freedom Party (IFP), which had started out as a Zulu cultural organization but from the 1970s became a fierce opponent of liberation movements and defender of capitalism and apartheid separate development.[55] As Inkatha-led violence escalated from the mid-1980s in Natal, with growing support from the apartheid government's security forces, the ANC abandoned the idea of Buthelezi as an ally. *Inqaba ya basebenzi* had published several scathing articles on Inkatha, including about its violence against students and striking Metal and Allied Workers' Union members. Soon after the launch of COSATU, Inkatha established its own pseudo-union, United Workers' Union of South Africa, with the express purpose of undermining the new federation, often through violence.[56] The Tendency described Inkatha as "the spear of counter-revolution," a sharp critique that angered Buthelezi, who demanded that the COSATU and UDF leadership denounce the Tendency, which they acceded to in a full-page statement in newspapers.[57] By this time, the Tendency had numerous supporters in townships around Durban and Pietermaritzburg who were involved in defending their communities against Inkatha warlords. A number of them lost their lives. In the early 1990s, Tendency activists in Alexandra and Dobsonville were similarly involved in life and death struggles in their areas. *Congress Militant* called on trade unions to "Build Workers' Defense Army"[58] and for youth and workers in townships to mobilize self-defense.[59] These were not mere abstract declarations. For example, in Alexandra activists from the Civic Organization and living in the hostels procured arms for their local self-defense unit. One of their leaders and a member of the Tendency, Philemon Mauku, was arrested and sentenced to imprisonment until 1994,[60] which prompted the formation of the Philemon Mauku Defense Campaign. The Tendency's connections to an international network of socialists led to a global campaign to demand Mauku's release, consisting of pickets, petitions, and fundraising to support his legal defense. Alexandra supporters used *Congress Militant* to mobilize support in the township and nationally for Mauku and at the same time launched a campaign for the release of all political prisoners (including members of self-defense units and of liberation organizations), which extended also to supporting the international campaign for the release of Palestinian socialist Mahmoud Masarwa.

Conclusion

Revolutionary papers proliferated across the world, particularly in times of revolution, from the early twentieth century in Russia to anticolonial movements and various struggles against fascism, racism, and wars, generally espousing Marxist ideas and propagating socialism or communism as alternative futures. In the South African context, it has been argued, a distinction is required between the alternative media, which flourished from the 1970s and were broadly opposed to apartheid, and revolutionary papers, which sought to overthrow apartheid and capitalism.

Historically, revolutionary papers have served as organizing tools of Marxist and other radical groups (including loose networks and parties) aiming to influence the politics and actions of liberation movements. The Marxist Workers' Tendency of the ANC was one of the socialist groups to emerge in the politically generative years of the late 1970s and early 1980s. Both *Congress Militant* and *Inqaba ya basebenzi* propagated a Marxist political program, created a community of cadres, and intervened in struggles. They established a distinctive public profile for the Tendency and contributed to its growth in the 1980s. Compared to mass movements of this period, the Tendency's membership was very modest, but its supporters made important contributions to building organizations and mobilizing campaigns in communities and workplaces in various parts of the country.

Arguably, however, the Tendency's main legacy was the production of a body of political ideas (theories, programs, and perspectives) that offered insightful analyses of the unfolding crisis of apartheid capitalism and the state of working-class movements. In its trenchant critiques of the political programs of the ANC-SACP, it forewarned about the likely consequences of the application of the Stalinist two-stage theory, particularly the primacy given to the development of a Black bourgeoisie and compromises with capital. In other words, even with the attainment of formal democracy, key aspects of national liberation would remain unfulfilled. It is a perspective that has largely been vindicated. Thirty years after the demise of apartheid, the Black majority, particularly Black women, remain subject to unprecedented high levels of unemployment, landlessness, homelessness, poverty, hunger, and violence.

The demise of the Soviet Union and the ANC's accession to power in 1994 created a serious crisis for revolutionary groups in South Africa, rendering them peripheral to the predominant politics of the democratic era. *Congress Militant* continued to be published as the Tendency attempted, for a short period, to influence the political direction of the ANC government. This proved a futile exercise. In 1996, when the ANC adopted the neoliberal macroeconomic policy of the Growth, Employment and Redistribution framework, the Tendency abandoned its orientation to the ruling party, having concluded that its transformation into a mass party of the working class was no longer possible. That decision led to the cessation of *Congress Militant* and its replacement with a new paper—*Socialist Alternative*.

Congress Militant and *Inqaba ya basebenzi* form a small but important archive not only of the history of one independent socialist group but also of the unfolding revolution against apartheid and the negotiations process. It is possible, as this article has attempted, to reconstruct and critically interrogate aspects of the Tendency's relatively short but productive history using an almost complete archive of its main publications. Although Mark Heywood's archive at Historical Papers Research Archive (University of the Witwatersrand) contains valuable internal documents, they are incomplete, making it difficult to examine in detail the Tendency's internal life as a revolutionary party. Archives of other revolutionary groups are either scattered among former members or nonexistent. Creating archives of these organizations is an urgent task to ensure their histories are not lost and to make them available for contemporary activists involved in developing new critiques of capitalism and building new revolutionary movements.

Noor Nieftagodien is professor and head of the History Workshop at the University of the Witwatersrand (South Africa), where he also lectures in the History Department. His research interests center on aspects of popular insurgent struggles, public history, youth politics, and local history. He is currently investigating the history of the Congress of South African Students, the leading student organization in the struggle against apartheid. He heads the public history initiative the Soweto History and Archives Project.

Notes

1. Lenin, *What Is to Be Done*, 105.
2. Sandwith, *World of Letters*, 14.
3. Johnson and Dee, *"I See You,"* xxx–xxxii.
4. Switzer, "Introduction: South Africa's Resistance Press," 39–40.
5. Zug, *The* Guardian, 2–7.
6. Sandwith, *World of Letters*, 17; Lodge, *Red Road to Freedom*, 233; Soudien, *Cape Radicals*, 136–37.
7. Louw and Tomaselli, "Developments in the Conventional and Alternative Press," 6–12.
8. Tomaselli, "The Progressive Press," 158.
9. Louw and Tomaselli, "Developments in the Conventional and Alternative Press," 7–8.
10. Tomaselli, "The Progressive Press, 155–60.
11. Van Kessel, *Beyond Our Wildest Dreams*, chap. 5; Johnson, "Resistance in Print I," 191.
12. Bonner and Nieftagodien, *Alexandra*, 245–50.
13. For example, see the collections of essays in Tomaselli and Louw, *The Alternative Press in South Africa*; and Switzer and Adhikari, *South Africa's Resistance Press*.
14. Martin Legassick created the most extensive archive of the Tendency, which was donated to University of Cape Town. Tragically, most of this archive was destroyed by fire in 2021. Some of us are attempting to create a new archive based, among others, on Mark Heywood's archive at the Historical Papers Research Archives (Wits) and personal collections. There is a full set of *Inqaba ya basebenzi* but not of *Congress Militant*. I am therefore unable to indicate how many editions of the paper were published.
15. Grant, *Unbroken Thread*, vii–xi.
16. Taaffe, *The Rise of Militant*, 8–9 (my emphasis).
17. Taaffe, *The Rise of Militant*, 8–9.
18. Legassick, *Towards Socialist Democracy*, 1–32.
19. Legassick, *Towards Socialist Democracy*, 394.
20. Legassick, *Towards Socialist Democracy*, 27.
21. Legassick, "Debating the Revival of the Workers' Movement," 261–62.
22. Legassick, *Towards Socialist Democracy*, 29.
23. Legassick, *Towards Socialist Democracy*, chap. 3.
24. Sikhakhane and Monroe (pseudonyms for Victor Mhlongo and Martin Legassick), "Guerilla Struggles and the Workers' Movement," *Inqaba ya basebenzi*, no. 5, January 1982.

25. "South Africa's Impending Socialist Revolution: Perspectives of the Marxist Workers' Tendency of the African National Congress," *Inqaba ya basebenzi*, 1982.

26. "Forward to Freedom—United under Workers Leadership," *Inqaba ya basebenzi*, no. 1, January 1981, 2–3.

27. "Forward to Freedom—United under Workers Leadership," *Inqaba ya basebenzi*, no. 1, January 1981, 2–3.

28. Legassick, *Towards Socialist Democracy*, 410.

29. "Principles of Communism," *Inqaba ya basebenzi*, no. 1, January 1981, supplement no. 1; "The Wages System," *Inqaba ya basebenzi*, no. 2, April 1981, supplement no. 2.

30. "Special Issue on Zimbabwe," *Inqaba ya basebenzi*, no. 22, December 1986.

31. "Unite for a Socialist Southern Africa," *Inqaba ya basebenzi*, no. 2, April 1981.

32. See "Three Concepts of the Russian Revolution," *Inqaba ya basebenzi*, no. 4, October 1981, Supplement no. 4; and "Russian Revolution, 1917," *Inqaba ya basebenzi*, no. 24/25, October 1987.

33. Richard Monroe, "Lessons of the 1950s," *Inqaba ya basebenzi*, no. 13, March–May 1984.

34. Basil Hendrickse, "The Soweto Uprising of 1976: Ten Years of Heroic Struggle," *Inqaba ya basebenzi*, no. 20/21, September 1986.

35. See "Letter from Group of 55," *Inqaba ya basebenzi*, no. 18/19, February 1986.

36. *Inqaba ya basebenzi*, no. 18/19, February 1986.

37. For example, "Yugoslavia's Bloody Disintegration," *Congress Militant*, no. 10, November–December 1992; "Vote ANC for Jobs, Peace, and Freedom," *Congress Militant*, no. 15, February–March 1994; "De Klerk's Hostage Demand Freedom Now," *Congress Militant*, no. 12, 1993.

38. "Raise R4500 for a Regular Congress Militant," *Congress Militant*, no. 10, November–December 1992.

39. "For mass defiance of all apartheid laws," *Congress Militant*, special edition, September 20, 1989.

40. "Forward to Victory for Hospital Workers," *Congress Militant*, special edition, March 13, 1990.

41. "Ban CCA," *Congress Militant*, special edition, May 1, 1991.

42. "PUTCO lies to hide profits," *Congress Militant*, special edition on PUTCO strike, May 3, 1990.

43. "For a National Minimum Wage," *Congress Militant*, special edition on a national minimum wage, November 28, 1990.

44. "The 1987 Mine Strike: Could the Mineworkers Have Won?" *Inqaba ya basebenzi*, no. 24/25, October 1987.

45. Karel Swart (member of the Tendency and former leading shop steward at Table Bay Spinners in Belville), interview with author, September 2, 2022, Cape Town.

46. "Away with VAT," *SACTWU Militant*, no. 1, August 1991.

47. Karel Swart, interview, September 2, 2022; Andre Kriel (former organizer and current general secretary of SACTWU), interview with author, July 5, 2023, Cape Town.

48. Editorial board statement, "Can Negotiations Bring Majority Rule?" *Inqaba ya basebenzi*, no. 16/17, January–June 1985.

49. Legassick, *Towards Socialist Democracy*, 428–34.

50. "We Demand De Klerk Must Announce the Immediate Release of Nelson Mandela and the Scrapping of Apartheid Education," *Congress Militant*, special edition, February 1990.

51. *Congress Militant*, "Open Letter to Nelson Mandela," February 1990.
52. "Workers' Power for Peace and Freedom," *Congress Militant*, no. 5, October 1990.
53. "ANC Congress: Some Draft Resolutions for Discussion," *Congress Militant*, May 8, 1991.
54. "The majority must rule!" *Congress Militant*, no. 10, November–December, 1992.
55. "Stand firm by ultimatum," *Congress Militant*, special edition, April 11, 1991.
56. "How to fight UWUSA," *Inqaba ya basebenzi*, no. 24/25, October 1987.
57. Paul Storey, "Inkatha—This Spear of Counter-Revolution Must Be Broken," *Inqaba ya basebenzi*, no. 18/19, February 1986; Legassick, *Towards Socialist Democracy*, 396–97.
58. "Workers' Power for Peace and Freedom," *Congress Militant*, no. 5, October 1990.
59. "Organise Mass Self-defence," *Congress Militant*, October 10, 1991, special pamphlet on self-defense.
60. "The Majority Must Rule," *Congress Militant*, no. 10, November–December 1992.

References

Bonner, Phil, and Noor Nieftagodien. *Alexandra: A History*. Johannesburg: Wits University Press, 2012.

Grant, Ted. *The Unbroken Thread: The Development of Trotskyism over 40 Years*. London: Fortress Books, 1989.

Johnson, David, and Henry Dee. *"I See You": The Industrial and Commercial Workers' Union of Africa, 1919–1930*. Cape Town: Historical Publications Southern Africa, 2022.

Johnson, Shaun. "Resistance in Print I: Grassroots and Alternative Publishing, 1980–1984." In Tomaselli and Louw, *Alternative Press in South Africa*, 191–206.

Legassick, Martin. "Debating the Revival of the Workers' Movement in the 1970s: The South African Democracy Education Trust and Post-apartheid Patriotic History." *Kronos* 34, no. 1 (2008): 240–66.

Legassick, Martin. *Towards Socialist Democracy*. Durban: University of KwaZulu-Natal Press, 2017.

Lenin, Vladimir. "Declaration of the Editorial Board of *Iskra*." September 1900. Marxist Internet Archive. https://www.marxists.org/archive/lenin/works/1900/sep/iskra.htm.

Lenin, Vladimir. *What Is to Be Done*. https://www.marxists.org/archive/lenin/works/download/what-itd.pdf.

Lodge, Tom. *Red Road to Freedom: A History of the South African Communist Party, 1921–2021*. Johannesburg: Jacana Media, 2021.

Louw, P. Eric, and Keyan G. Tomaselli. "Developments in the Conventional and Alternative Press, 1980–1989." In Tomaselli and Louw, *The Alternative Press in South Africa*, 5–14.

Sandwith, Corinne. *World of Letters: Reading Communities and Cultural Debates in Early Apartheid South Africa*. Durban: University of KwaZulu-Natal Press, 2014.

Soudien, Crain. *Cape Radicals: Intellectual and Political Thought of the New Era Fellowship, 1930s–1960s*. Johannesburg: Wits University Press, 2019.

Switzer, Les. "Introduction: South Africa's Resistance Press under Apartheid." In Switzer and Adhikari, *South Africa's Resistance Press*, 1–75.

Switzer, Les, and Mohamed Adhikari, eds. *South Africa's Resistance Press: Alternative Voices in the Last Generation under Apartheid*. Athens: Ohio University Press, 2000.

Taaffe, Peter. *The Rise of Militant: Militant's Thirty Years*. London: Militant Publications, 1995.

Tomaselli, Keyan. "The Progressive Press: Extending the Struggle, 1980–1986." In Tomaselli and Louw, *The Alternative Press in South Africa*, 155–74.

Tomaselli, Keyan, and P. Eric Louw, eds. *The Alternative Press in South Africa*. Bellville: Anthropos, 1991.

Van Kessel, Ineke. *Beyond Our Wildest Dreams: The United Democratic Front and the Transformation of South Africa*. Charlottesville: University Press of Virginia, 2000.

Zug, James. *The* Guardian*: The History of South Africa's Extraordinary Anti-Apartheid Newspaper*. Pretoria: Unisa Press, 2007.

"Ka Aina No Ka Poe o Hawaii"

Kokua Hawaii's *Huli* Newspaper, 1971–73

Aaron Katzeman and Drew Kahu'āina Broderick

From 1971 to 1973, the nascent grassroots political organization known as Kokua Hawaii independently published and distributed *Huli*, a semiregular newspaper featuring radical economic analysis, community news, organizing strategies, political education, social documentary photography, and illustrated agitprop graphics.[1] Kokua Hawaii, based on O'ahu and active across the islands, was influenced by legacies of militant labor unions in Hawai'i;[2] Black, Indigenous, Puerto Rican, and Chicano struggles in the continental United States; and ongoing Third World national liberation movements abroad. The organization amplified and merged these varying emancipatory traditions to thoroughly analyze local material conditions, taking a decidedly class-conscious and anticolonial approach to fighting for Hawai'i's sovereignty and self-determination. With a political line forged through cadre study of Marx, Lenin, and Mao and tested by ideological strife, such convictions make *Huli*, the mouthpiece of Kokua Hawaii, an invaluable resource for contemplating historical contradictions of Hawai'i in relation to contemporary aspirations for abolition, decolonization, demilitarization, deoccupation, and independence.

In 'ōlelo Hawai'i, Hawaiian language, the word *huli* contains multiple kaona (contextually dependent meanings) and thus evokes many layered interpretations and political overtones.[3] In their coauthored *Hawaiian Dictionary*, the scholar and composer Mary Kawena Pukui and the linguist Samuel H. Elbert recorded the following definitions of *huli*: "To turn, reverse; to curl over, as a breaker; to change, as an

Radical History Review
Issue 150 (October 2024)   DOI 10.1215/01636545-11257434
© 2024 by MARHO: The Radical Historians' Organization, Inc.

opinion or manner of living. To look for, search, explore, seek, study. Section, as of a town, place, or house. Taro top, as used for planting."[4] More pointedly, the prominent Hawaiian sovereignty leader, anti-imperialist activist, poet, and political science scholar Haunani-Kay Trask described *huli* as the desire to "overturn," or "the need to transform the current political and economic system to construct a new order, not merely soften up the existing one."[5] Alluding to these interdependent meanings of knowledge, agriculture, and revolution, *Huli* the periodical encouraged the people of Hawai'i to commit to shared class struggle across racial, ethnic, and cultural backgrounds in opposition to intensifying capital investment and military entrenchment in Ka Pae 'Āina o Hawai'i, the Hawaiian archipelago, following US "statehood" in 1959.[6]

Although this period, the early to mid-1970s, in Hawai'i's radical politics and the burgeoning Hawaiian sovereignty movement is well-known within Native/non-Native activist communities, scholarship has yet to situate *Huli* as a primary source document.[7] Reading through the surviving issues of *Huli* available in institutional archives, we consider the variety of perspectives promoted within its pages to position Kokua Hawaii in relation to international understandings of anticolonial liberatory politics of the Global South, broadly speaking. Revisiting prominent critiques of Kokua Hawaii, we argue that insights provided by *Huli* trouble lasting understandings of the organization, underscoring the periodical's relevance for navigating rising waves of political struggle in Hawai'i today. Moreover, as researchers of lesser-known stories of art, we contend that *Huli*—itself a timely revival of Hawai'i's politically engaged print culture that flourished during the nineteenth century[8]—offers one foundation for constructing a counterhegemonic lineage of socially concerned artists and cultural workers in Hawai'i. Through an analysis of *Huli*'s content, imagery, and context of production, we use the name of the periodical and its call to "huli" as a means of tracking the influence of Kokua Hawaii's politics and aesthetics into the present, with *Huli* acting as a medium for insurgent inspiration.

Huli as Addendum: Layouts of Solidarity

Huli was published directly following the crucial onset of what Haunani-Kay Trask has deemed the "birth of the modern Hawaiian movement." In her influential 1987 essay, Trask describes the organizing efforts of Kokua Hawaii (originally known as Kokua Kalama Committee) against evictions in Kalama Valley on the island of O'ahu from 1970 to 1971 as the pivotal moment when political awareness across Ka Pae 'Āina o Hawai'i began to swell, leading to a reawakening of Kanaka 'Ōiwi (Native Hawaiian) consciousness, increased demands for sovereignty and self-determination, and widespread direct action against US empire.[9] Given the comprehensiveness with which Kokua Hawaii's legacy has already been historicized between Trask's essay and more recent projects, including the journalist

Gary Kubota's *Hawaii Stories of Change: Kokua Hawaii Oral History Project* and the literary scholar Gary Pak's documentary film *Huli! Kokua Hawaii and the Beginning of the Revolutionary Movement in Hawai'i*, our intent in this section is to use *Huli* for novel insights into the organization, examining how the periodical's editorial and design decisions corresponded to and exemplified its political tendencies.[10] If Kokua Hawaii's interventions in Kalama Valley signaled the birth of the modern Hawaiian movement in terms of praxis, *Huli* offers the theory that spurred Kokua Hawaii toward action and, as such, has implicitly shaped struggle in Hawai'i ever since, albeit through ideological influences and international solidarities often underacknowledged.

Published just days after thirty-two Kokua Hawaii members and other Kalama Valley residents were arrested for resisting the destruction of the Portuguese pig farmer George Santos's house on May 11, 1971, the cover of *Huli's* first issue featured a photograph of protestors/protectors overlaid with a handwritten statement in all capitals, "HAWAIIANS ARRESTED FOR 'TRESPASSING' ON HAWAIIAN LAND" (fig. 1).[11] While singular in its focus on Kalama Valley, the issue addressed the complex political issues at hand throughout Hawai'i. At Kalama Valley, land owned by the Bernice Pauahi Bishop Estate—a trust originally designated to support Native Hawaiian children through education and now the largest private landowner in Hawai'i—was set to be newly developed into a suburb and subsumed into the recently constructed upper-class neighborhood of Hawai'i Kai. The agricultural land in Kalama Valley had long been leased to farmers before its speculative value became too great for Bishop to refuse. "The trustees of Bishop Estate are a perfect example of those who help themselves at the expense of our people," an anonymous editorial in *Huli* explained, emphasizing the class discrepancies at play. "While they are reaping the excessive economic benefits of being a trustee, they are using every economic excuse to justify their action of evicting our people from the land without letting them enjoy the fruits of their labor."[12]

This first issue of *Huli* explained how Kalama Valley had become the headquarters of what Kokua Hawaii then called the "Local Movement" (more on this framing in the following section), centering Hawaiian and Chinese, Japanese, Korean, Portuguese, Filipino, Puerto Rican, and Samoan concerns against bosses, trustees, and landowners—primarily haole settlers, but also others—whose class interests clashed with that of the majority of Hawai'i's working population, be they Hawaiian or not. "In Kalama Valley," the first issue of *Huli* explained plainly in Pidgin (Hawai'i Creole), "we learned that we can beat them if we stick together. That means you too bruda. We need some da kine Power for us kine Local People."[13] Another anonymous member, writing about the threat Kokua Hawaii posed in Kalama Valley and the reason for being arrested, said, "We are in jail today because we have the guts to stand up and fight back. We have tried to bring our Local People together and the haole bosses are scared."[14] While all residents in the valley were

Figure 1. Front (*right*) and back (*left*) pages of *Huli* 1, no. 1 (May 1971).

eventually evicted, the conflict continued during the trial of the "Kalama 32," which Kokua Hawaii members used to further agitate and organize. More important, the experiences and knowledge gained from Kalama Valley became crucial guidance for struggles to come—the back cover of *Huli*'s first issue loudly declared, again in all capitals, "WE WILL REMEMBER KALAMA VALLEY—THIS CANNOT CONTINUE" (fig. 1).

Ideological popularization and political education, though, would be imperative for building the mass movement Kokua Hawaii envisioned. Having obtained substantial media reportage in the local and national press about the prolonged activist occupation and series of arrests in Kalama—the group received letters of support from Fidel Castro and Mao Zedong—Kokua Hawaii aimed to advance its newfound reputation by controlling its own production and dissemination of ideas.[15] Through the Kalama struggle, Kokua Hawaii had already gained experience manipulating the mainstream media for its benefit. Before the arrests, for example, Kokua Hawaii prompted white supporters to leave Kalama Valley to clearly insist to the press that the movement was spearheaded by Hawaiians and others descended from sugar and pineapple plantation workers. "We wanted everyone to know that us Locals could do things for ourselves and in our own ways," an editorial in *Huli* reasoned.[16] Although the decision was controversial even among Kokua Hawaii members, documentary photographs of the occupation and arrests have remained inspirational images for generations of activists and artists in Hawai'i, particularly because they represented a newfound form of Hawaiian resistance, one with deeper cultural resonances than mainstream haole environmentalism of the day.

Deploying different tactics to bolster larger strategies, Kokua Hawaii would directly use bourgeois newspapers to draw people into its program and drive interest toward *Huli*. In a full-page ad in the June 13, 1971, issue of the *Honolulu Advertiser*, one of the two largest newspapers in Hawai'i at the time,[17] Kokua Hawaii published its six-point People's Land Program:

1. We must save our farm lands to grow food on. We must stop the developers who want to pour concrete over everything.
2. We must stop people from moving here until we can first take care of our own local people's needs.
3. We must take care of our air, land and water. If we kill nature, nature will kill us.
4. We must get back our land from the few big landholders that have almost all of it. It was stolen from us in the first place.
5. We must use our land to house and feed our people and learn to rely on ourselves to do it—not on the mainland.
6. As a start, we demand that Kalama Valley be saved for the local people and that the tourist and high-income development planned by Bishop Estate and Hawaii-Kai be stopped.

Whereas Kokua Hawaii could afford to have its relatively short People's Land Program printed in mass media (in an ad paid for by the then recently founded Hawaii People's Coalition for Peace and Justice), it was vastly limited by both advertising costs and the risk of censorship. Also published in the first issue of *Huli*, the People's Land Program was further elucidated in the fourth issue, with Kokua Hawaii extrapolating upon the need to "save our land and return it to the people" and positioning the People's Land Program within the political reality of how "[the big Estates, the State, the military and a handful of private landlords] are responsible for the destructive direction of today's Hawaii."[18] It was this need to clarify the People's Land Program and place Kalama Valley within a more historical and globally comparative context that prompted Kokua Hawaii to develop *Huli* as an effective means of shaping broader social consciousness through a venue not tinted or constrained by the interests of colonial-capitalist newspapers.

The first issues of *Huli* were published by *Hawaii Hochi*, a Japanese-language newspaper founded in 1912.[19] Kokua Hawaii was soon able to procure an office headquarters and printing press of its own, opening Moose Lui Print Shop—named after a Hawaiian resident evicted from Kalama Valley—on Pālama Street in the Honolulu working-class neighborhood of Kalihi. Members had differing and fluctuating roles: Ray Catania ran the shop as the pressman, Lucy Witek did the typesetting, and Kalani Ohelo and Gary Kubota were at one point editors. Claire Shimabukuro distributed the paper to housing projects as part of her volunteer work with a co-op delivering milk and eggs.[20] Issues were sold locally, shipped nationally and internationally, and stocked at bookstores, community centers, and sympathetic businesses across Oʻahu, New York, and San Francisco. Different copies we came across in the archives were addressed to Venceremos, a revolutionary Chicano organization based in Palo Alto, California; the *Workers' Power* office in Michigan, a newspaper of the Trotskyist organization International Socialists; and Liberation News Service, an alternative leftist news agency based in New York City.

Having secured the means of print production—and with Kalama Valley becoming an entry point into larger ideological questions—Kokua Hawaii began to expand the scope of *Huli*'s content to be more historically informed, presently engaged, and forward thinking. Future issues continued to update readers on what had happened in Kalama Valley but also extended into Hawaiʻi "people's history" lessons to counter legacies of the Americanized Standard English public school system in Hawaiʻi. One such write-up focused on the Hawaiian Royalist Robert Wilcox, who helped lead the armed Counter-Revolution of 1895 in support of deposed Queen Liliʻuokalani following the overthrow of the internationally recognized Hawaiian Kingdom on January 17, 1893, an armed coup d'état by the Committee of Safety, a group of white pro-American businessmen, with the support of 162 United States Marines.[21] Even by its second issue, published on June 5, 1971, *Huli* broached topics that we would now classify under multispecies justice and food sovereignty. An article discussed the inhumane treatment that George Santos's pigs had suffered from his eviction, being "driven across town [Honolulu] in the hot sun with no cover on the trucks" and with babies separated from their mothers, resulting in twenty-nine pigs dying.[22] In another, Black Richards, a Hawaiian resident of Kalama Valley, recapped the broader importance of Kalama in terms of agriculture and anti-imperialism: "If we're dependent upon the mainland economically, if we're dependent upon them in the way that food comes in here, then they will control everything that happens here, because a person that controls the foods you eat and the clothes you wear is your master and you his slave and we won't have that anymore."[23]

Various issues of *Huli* linked this racial colonial capitalist system in Hawaiʻi to the oppressive social function of prisons. The October 1972 issue included a full page titled, "ALL POOR PEOPLE ARE PRISONERS." An analysis by the Paʻahao Committee, described as "a group working to change the inhumane conditions for prisoners and felons," reasoned, "Prisoners are victims of the society they live in. Most of the people in jail are guilty of only one crime: Poverty."[24] The page also included an interview with a local brother who was incarcerated in Lompoc Prison in California, as well as a poem, illustrated graphics of chained fists and bound prisoners, and a photograph of Kokua Hawaii members visiting imprisoned comrades. Other features in issues of *Huli* reinforced the need to understand the political, economic, and racial structural underpinnings of prison ("Defend Our Rights—Protect our People," May 1972) and spotlighted the incarcerated "Hawaii Sons" in Lompoc (August 1972). In an article addressing both sexism and racism, Claire Shimabukuro plainly stated, "Almost all of the prisoners in O.P. [O'ahu Prison] are local. This is racism."[25] Although not using the term *abolition*, Kokua Hawaii clearly delineated the interdependent root causes of crime (poverty) and policing (racial capitalism) and advanced a politics in *Huli* that attempted to holistically confront each issue as part of a larger system.

Huli most prominently highlighted the rights of dock, refuse, healthcare, and other workers in Hawai'i and aided tenants organizations against capitalist development that arose on O'ahu (in Hālawa, Waiāhole-Waikāne, Salt Lake, Ota Camp in Waipahu, Kahalu'u, Census Tract 57 in Kapālama, and Honolulu's Chinatown), on Hawai'i Island (in Kona), and on Kauai (in Niumalu-Nāwiliwili), among others elsewhere. Some places had more specific ethnic characteristics than others but Kokua Hawaii always stressed that they were interconnected. Kokua Hawaii often collaborated with groups already established within their local communities, such as KEY Project in Kahalu'u, The Hawaiians in Waimānalo, and Third Arm in Chinatown, in addition to contributing to the fight to maintain the ethnic studies program at the University of Hawai'i at Mānoa under the banner "Our History, Our Way!"[26]

This breadth of overlapping efforts morphed *Huli* into a forum of popular discontent; the periodical's content and design conveyed an immersive visual experience that itself prompted and encouraged the selfless solidarity Kokua Hawaii was attempting to cultivate among its readership. Flipping through *Huli*'s pages, readers would encounter polemical position statements, updates on struggles across the islands, and international news presented through Kokua Hawaii's radical lens, accompanied by mostly unattributed photographs, hand-drawn headings, illustrations, and comics. Kokua Hawaii member Gwen Kim described *Huli* as "a very agitational format—lots of pictures with information that hit the spot about what was happening and what we were doing in different communities."[27] In a spread in the June 19, 1971, issue, for example, a plethora of voices from a community meeting resisting development in Hālawa were reproduced with each granted a stand-alone text box; the effect of the layout was to produce a cacophony of voices that represented *Huli*'s belief in popular power.

Hawai'i was far from immune to the global rebellious fervor emanating during the 1960s, but the cause of social unrest in Hawai'i was inextricably tied to changes in local circumstances. The Kalama Valley conflict, precursor to the countless struggles that would follow, began just over a decade after Hawai'i's US statehood in 1959 and was prompted in large part by what this newfound status meant for federal (military) and commercial (tourism) spending in the islands. "Statehood decisively incorporated Hawai'i within the U.S. political system," the ethnic studies scholar Davianna Pōmaika'i McGregor explained, "assuring a stability that bolstered confidence in the economy and made it attractive to U.S. investors."[28] While it primarily emerged in response to the recent wholesale integration of Hawai'i into the US political sphere, *Huli* went to great lengths to clarify that pressing issues in Hawai'i and in places like Vietnam were inseparable, given the sweeping motivations of US empire. As an article by Faith Okabe of the Catholic Action Group spelled out,

Those who benefit from the war [in Vietnam] are the same kinds of people who dream up Hawaii Kai and Kalama Valleys. They think about profits, not the people of Hawaii, not the people of Vietnam. The struggles in Vietnam and Kalama Valley are just two aspects of revolutionary struggle for political sovereignty and self-determination; a revolutionary struggle that is beginning to change people's values and directions.[29]

A full-page spread in the June 1972 issue, also courtesy of the Catholic Action Group, went beyond rhetorically linking Hawai'i and Vietnam, using an ironic "scenic" map of O'ahu to pinpoint exactly how US military presence on the island made it the "home staging-ground for the war in Indochina."[30]

Further expanding this internationalist understanding, Kokua Hawaii designated Hawai'i as a "sister colony" of Puerto Rico, Cuba, Micronesia (likely referring to Guam specifically), the Philippines—all of which were brought under US colonial control in 1898, the same year the United States illegally subsumed Hawai'i without a treaty of annexation—and Okinawa. Discerning Hawai'i as but one location subjected to US imperialism, *Huli*'s articles attempted to apply to Hawai'i lessons learned from anti-imperialist struggles in China ("New China: A Productive and Free Society," December 1972), Vietnam ("Self-Determination for Vietnam," November 1972), and the Philippines ("Philippines: The Next Vietnam," November 1972; "Struggle for National Democracy," December 1972), associating the revolutionary communist movements of the Third World to those in the islands who were likewise attempting to liberate themselves from the yoke of colonialism and imperialism.

A spread in the May 1972 issue of *Huli* is acutely revealing in this regard (fig. 2). The left page, labeled the "international news section," features the Kokua Hawaii Central Committee's position on Vietnam, including three points stating: "We Support The Vietnamese People's Struggle Against the u.s. military"; "We Support Local Brothers Who Oppose Serving in the u.s. military"; and "We Support The Democratic Republic of Vietnam and The National Liberation Front (NLF) Fighting For Self-Determination." Images of Vietnamese peoples' armies sandwich a map of Southeast Asia that itself is overlaid with the extractive interests of transnational oil companies. On the right page of the spread, labeled the "communities news section," is a republished press release from Hui Malama Aina o Ko'olau, a group of concerned residents on the windward side of O'ahu questioning the constituencies meant to be served by planned public works projects, accompanied with a statement of support from Kokua Hawaii and complemented by an illustration of

Figure 2. Kokua Hawaii: On Vietnam and Hui Malama Aina o Koʻolau, *Huli* 2, no. 2 (May 1972), 10–11.

the Koʻolau Mountains. Spanning the over six-thousand-mile geographical gap existing across these two pages, Kokua Hawaii stressed the similarities between Vietnamese revolutionaries and Hawaiians. For a radical or conscientious objector opposed to the Vietnam War, the full-page spread insisted they should also support Hawaiians and their fight to protect and retain access to and control over their lands. For Hawaiians disturbed by capitalist development, the juxtaposition insisted that the Vietnamese were not their foes but, rather, comrades fighting their common enemy of the United States. The material form of *Huli* thus became a conduit for an internationalist politics of solidarity; within a single spread, the reader was encouraged to think about Vietnam and Oʻahu through the same political framework.

Members of Kokua Hawaii likewise found inspiration from movements of colonized peoples in the belly of the beast on the continental United States, including Indigenous resistance ("Our Native American Brothers and Sisters," June 1972) and organizations like the Black Panthers and Young Lords, with whom Kokua Hawaii members had personal connections. Before returning to Hawaiʻi from the San Francisco Bay Area and becoming the de facto founding spokesperson of Kokua Hawaii, Larry Kamakawiwoʻole had befriended the Black Panther Party cofounder Bobby Seale and participated in the Third World Liberation Front. Moreover, in early 1971, Kokua Hawaii members Kalani Ohelo and Moanikeala Akaka, both Native Hawaiian leaders, traveled to a Black Panther convention in Washington,

DC, visited members of the Young Lords in New York, and met with I Wor Kuen and the Red Guard Party in San Francisco, while others had previously visited Cuba. The resonances of such connections were expressed in the April 1972 issue of *Huli*, which recapped a visit to Hawai'i by women members of the Young Lords, I Wor Kuen, the Black Workers Congress, and Rising Up Angry. Summarizing the event, Kokua Hawaii member Val Piamonte stated, "The most common of all our experiences is our struggle for national liberation."[31]

In many ways, *Huli* was intended to be the Hawai'i version of the *Black Panther* (1967–80) and the Young Lords' *Palante* (1970–76) newspapers. The impetus to self-publish was clearly inspired by those and other concurrent periodicals of revolutionary organizations. In its Library for the People, Kokua Hawaii offered issues of *Palante*; *New Dawn*, published by the Marxist-Leninist J-Town Collective in San Francisco's Japan Town; *Getting Together*, published by I Wor Kuen; the *Peking Review*, published by the Communist Party of China; and *Working Together*, published by the Honolulu Chinatown organization Third Arm, as well as books such as Frantz Fanon's *The Wretched of the Earth*.[32] *Huli* also advertised subscriptions to the short-lived *Hawaii Pono Journal* (1970–72). The breadth and tone of these publications made available by Kokua Hawaii spoke to its insistence on and belief in the need for making radical political education widely available, ideals evident in the very existence of *Huli*.

These ardent years of study and struggle culminated in Kokua Hawaii's fifteen-point program and platform, which reads much like the Black Panthers' 1966 ten-point program and the Young Lords' 1969 thirteen-point program (fig. 3). First published in *Huli*'s April 1972 issue and reprinted in later issues, Kokua Hawaii's program outlined its position as "a revolutionary organization dedicated to the liberation of our people and our land," including points to "fight for the respect and equality of woman [*sic*]," "develop a[n] economic system that serves people's needs," advocate for "quality health care" and "decent housing," "support land reform," "demand freedom for all political prisoners," and proclaimed the organization's members as "internationalists" in solidarity with "the people of the Third World in Africa, Asia, Latin America and Oceania who are fighting for their liberation" against "u.s." imperialism. Kokua Hawaii's original focus on land rights in Kalama Valley had thus morphed into *Huli*'s comprehensive analysis of the patriarchal, racial, colonial class structure of Hawai'i, linking Hawai'i to the many modes of exploitation and oppression dictated by capitalism and enforced globally by US military presence.

Between Third and Fourth Worlds: Locating Anticolonial Politics in Hawai'i
The breadth of solidarities expressed in the pages of *Huli* between Hawaiians, across different ethnic and racial communities in Hawai'i, and with peoples struggling against the global leviathan of US empire—be they within the territorial confines

of the United States or not—allows us to complicate some of the ways Kokua Hawaii has been historicized. In this section, building on our outline of Kokua Hawaii's influences and tendencies, we reexamine critical assessments of the organization, arguing that *Huli* offers possibilities of rupture within existing interpretations of Kokua Hawaii's politics. In doing so, we productively challenge both the origins of Asian settler colonial critique and the limitations its proliferation has imposed on solidarity in order to expand revolutionary approaches for a Hawai'i liberated from US imperialism.

In her aforementioned analysis of Kokua Hawaii, Trask discerned an evolution in the focus of political movements in Hawai'i over time, from a "battle for land rights" focusing on "the preservation of agricultural land against resort and subdivision use" (as represented by Kokua Hawaii) to a "larger struggle for native Hawaiian autonomy," with land claims "broadened to cover military-controlled lands and trust lands specifically set aside for Hawaiians by the U.S. Congress but used by non-beneficiaries" (a politics that would come to be most notably characterized during the 1990s by Ka Lāhui Hawai'i, a prominent Native Hawaiian sovereignty group founded in 1987).[33] Further demarcating such differences while still constructing a political lineage from Kalama Valley to movements such as those to stop the US military's bombing of the island of Kaho'olawe and the Nuclear Free and Independent Pacific, Trask continued:

In the beginning of the decade [1970s], the rallying cry was "land for local people, not tourists." By 1976, the language of protest had changed from English to Hawaiian, with emphasis on the native relationship to land. The cultural value of *Aloha 'Āina* (love of the land) was to characterize the demands of protesters into the 1980s. By then, the Movement had branched out politically to link up with American Indian activists on the mainland, anti-nuclear independence struggles throughout the South Pacific, and international networks in Asia and at the United Nations.[34]

As laid out by Trask, these changes suggest a deepening Indigenization (or, in this particular case, 'Ōiwi-ization) of radical politics in Hawai'i.[35] A close reading of *Huli*, however, troubles each of Trask's perceived distinctions between Kokua Hawaii and future movements, which are worth reconsidering in order to allow otherwise foreclosed political alignments to flourish.

From *Huli*'s focus on anti-imperialist struggles in China, Vietnam, and the Philippines—and Third World Marxism more broadly—we can define Kokua Hawaii's ideology as advocating for the national liberation of Hawai'i. The concept of national liberation coalesced from Bolshevik revolutionary Vladimir Lenin's application of Marxism to the national question, imperialism, and the role of the state apparatus,[36] and from the subsequent focus on colonialism at the 1920 Second Congress of the Communist International; this formulation has repeatedly been

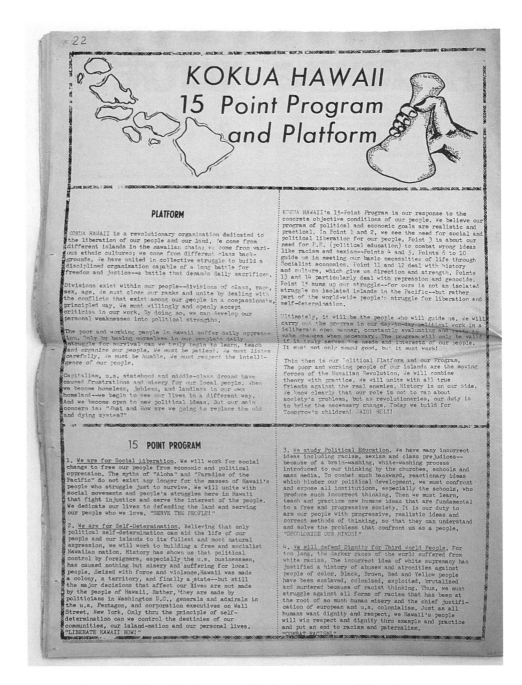

Figure 3. Kokua Hawaii Fifteen-Point Program and Platform, *Huli* 2, no. 4 (July 1972), 22–23.

23

5. We will fight for the Respect and Equality of Woman. Male chauvinism, machismo and sexism are more incorrect ideas that cripple our political development and social practice. It is the whole notion of male supremacy and male dominance, resulting in female passivity and general oppression of the sisters in school, at work, at home and in political organizations. One-half of our nation, the sisters, cannot be kept in a position of suppression and weakness--for we need the full development and all the energies and creativity of our people in the struggle. We aim for liberation not only in politics and economics, but in personal relationships as well. "SISTERS UNITE! "

6. We must develop a Economic System that Serves People's Needs. The present capitalist system is based on profits and not people. Thus it does not benefit the majority of people and promote their interest, but rather causes poverty, hunger, unemployment, high prices and low-standard of life for most people in Hawaii. Historically, Hawaii's economy moved from subsistence to capitalist following the political take-over by haole businessmen in 1893. Hawaii was turned into a u.s. sugar republic, just as Cuba, Puerto Rico and the Philippines. Today, Hawaii's three major industries include sugar, military and tourism--all artificial and unstable--and based on exploitation of Hawaii's workers and their land. So we must have a economic system that serves human needs as it's main purpose. "PEOPLE, NOT PROFITS! "

7. We are for Worker's Control. The profit system of capitalism benefits the bosses, the upper class. The rich get richer, while the poor stay poor. In the past and today, workers in Hawaii have waged militant labor struggles to gain social justice and a better life. While the union movement has won some victories for the workers, the companies keep control and domination thru legal actions, police force and sheer economic power. Many workers who have labored a life time for the industries are cast aside and forgotten once their productivity has ended. We say take care of the old people and treat them with respect, by giving them sufficient pension payments and good retirement benefits. We understand that low wages, heavy unemployment, lay-offs and cutbacks, economic depressions and recessions, boring irrelevant work, and general exploitation of labor will continue until workers gain power of the industry they labor in. "THE ECONOMY BELONGS TO THE WORKERS! "

8. We want Quality Health Care. Good health care and a good diet are necessary to a full and productive life. But there exists today in our society, two kinds of health care and nutrition: one for the rich, and another for the poor. And the present health system is more about profits than curing illness. It is in the economic interest of doctors, hospitals, health insurance companies (i.e. HMSA and Kaiser Health Plan) hospital supply companies and the drug industry to have alot of sick people. For more patients means more profits. We must change that unhealthy system by advocating and practicing preventative and curative health care, the whole idea that you go to the doctor when you're healthy to stay healthy. "HEALTH CARE IS A RIGHT, NOT A PRIVILEGE! "

9. We want Decent Housing. Hawaii has a housing crisis: rents are high, many landlords don't keep up the places, and there just isn't enough housing for the poor and working people. The only kind of buildings going up are luxury homes, vacation houses and hotels. Like food, shelter is one of the basic necessities of life--so we must have it. But lack of housing and existing slums will continue as long as the land/housing monopoly continues. So we want safe, comfortable homes to shelter our families from the elements of nature; environments where we can develop our lives and futures to their fullest extent. "WE WANT HOUSING FIT TO SHELTER HUMAN BEINGS! "

10. We support Land Reform. To Hawaiians, the land belonged to those who toiled it. But today, 35 major land owners control 96% of the land. Land is private property now. The soil is not to produce food with, but rather is something to make huge profits off. We will fight the land rip-off and the abuse, neglect and damage done to the natural resources and beauty of our islands by business and u.s. military operations. Without our sacred, precious land, we are like a people without blood. Land makes life and

freedom possible. The monopoly land control in Hawaii today is increasingly making life impossible for our people as their means of sustenance continues to decrease, and their economic-political dependency and helplessness increases. "KA AINA NO KA POE O HAWAII! "

11. We will learn True History. Hawaii's history is import-ant for us to know. For without knowledge of the historical development of our society and institutions, we cannot possibly understand the present problems. Only by knowing the past can we deal with the present, and plan for the future. True history which is people's history, is not stale or boring. Rather, it is the story of struggle and development of our people. And not only will we learn history, but we intend to make history. History is not kings and queens and presidents--but rather in our history--the common people who work and fight day-to-day are the real heroes and makers of history. "TO LEARN HISTORY IS TO FIND THE ROOTS OF OUR PEOPLE! "

12. We will build a Progressive Culture. Like other coloni-zed people, our culture has been ravaged and destroyed. Our spiritual beliefs and values have mocked. Our language, art, music, dance, religion, chants, our culture has been taken away. The surviving culture has been exploited, especially by the tourist industry. So the spiritual and artistic things in which a people's strength and history are expressed have been destroyed or changed to a point where it all seems lost. But slowly we are regaining some of the lost ethnic heritage, and making links with the past historical development of our people in Hawaii. With the good and positive from the old cultures, we will combine it with the new developing revolutionary culture, that comes as a society struggles to push forward--to build a culture that educates and inspires us to greater under-standing and achievements. "REVOLUTIONARY CULTURE MOVES US FORWARD! "

13. We advocate Self-Defense. In the past, u.s. military force--both u.s. warships and marines--aided the overthrow of the Hawaiian nation. Today, Hawaii has huge u.s. military bases all over the islands for the army, airforce, navy, marines, coast guard and state national guard. They are stationed in the islands for the purpose of not only protect-ing u.s. economic and political interests in Asia and the Pacific, but also as a military security force to put down uprisings of Hawaii's people should they occur. Our principle of self-defense also applies to our local communities, our fellow comrades and ourselves. We will fight off and defend our communities and our comrades from any hostile attack by whatever means necessary. We will not sit by and watch our islands and people be wiped out. Genocide will be resisted. "PROTECT AND DEFEND OUR COMMUNITIES AND OUR PEOPLE! "

14. We demand Freedom for all Political Prisoners. Most of the people in jail are guilty of only one crime: Poverty. The real criminals in our society--politicians, judges, businessmen, bankers, and generals and admirals--are never punished for their crimes against the people. 60% to 70% of the jail population in Hawaii are Hawaiians, who have been imprisoned for acts of survival, after economic opportunities and political power have been denied them. We demand the freedom of these brothers and sisters, some of our finest and bravest fighters, who are political prisoners of an economic system and political state that refuses them the right to exist and live. We also demand the liberty of other political prisoners in the u.s. and throughout the world. "FREE ALL POLITICAL PRISONERS! "

15. We are Internationalists. Historically, Hawaii is a sister colony of Puerto Rico, Cuba, Micronesia and the Philippines as we were militarily invaded during the same period of u.s. expansion in the 19th century. Our destinies are linked to the struggles of progressive peoples in these nations and throughout the world who are fighting our common enemy: u.s. imperialism. We support all Pacific peoples liberation struggles who are fighting for freedom, justice and independence. We support the people of the Third World in Africa, Asia, Latin America and Oceania who are fighting for their liberation. Also, we express solidarity and support to all our Third World brothers and sisters and poor and progressive whites who are fighting within the beast (u.s.) itself to bring u.s. imperialism to an end. Being a small island-nation with a population of less than a million people, we need the inspiration and support of all progressive people in the world in our difficult life-or-death struggle with a powerful and cruel enemy. "POWER TO THE PEOPLE! "

sought by decolonization struggles applying Marxism-Leninism/-Maoism to their respective material conditions of capitalist underdevelopment. For the anticolonial theorist Amílcar Cabral, founder of the African Party for the Independence of Guinea and Cape Verde, "the national liberation of a people is the regaining of the historical personality of that people, its return to history through the destruction of the imperialist domination to which it was subjected." More specifically, Cabral explained that "the basis of national liberation, whatever the formulas adopted on the level of international law, is the inalienable right of every people to have its own history, and the objective of national liberation is to regain this right usurped by imperialism, that is to say, to free the process of development of the national productive forces."[37] National liberation, as Cabral and others such as Frantz Fanon and Walter Rodney have insisted, is not just about gaining independence from colonialism but, rather, the long-term victory over neocolonialism that can only be guaranteed by revolutionary socialism.

Following this genealogy of political theory, Kokua Hawaii, in its own Marxist pursuit for the "birth of a new Hawaiian Nation," was ostensibly in the very beginning stages of becoming a vanguard party—complete with a complementary youth wing, the Huli Youth Organization—and developing a mass line through coordination with labor and tenants unions, farmers, and community and student organizations.[38] Indeed, while Kalani Ohelo confessed in a *Huli* article calling for people of Hawai'i to unite that it is "not easy to build a political party in a colony," he shared his hope that the fifteen-point peoples' program would "within many years . . . come to be adapted by our people to serve as guidelines to constructively change this society for all instead of just a few to share."[39]

Put differently, Kokua Hawaii was not simply interested in protecting disparate sites "against resort and subdivision use," as Trask suggested, but, rather, in coalescing around such struggles with the intent of liberating the entirety of Hawai'i. While *Huli* did provide updates and helped amplify the voices of various communities in Hawai'i organizing against resort and suburban development, it was doing so for an organization attempting to generate a wholesale national liberation struggle. As explained in the Red Nation's revolutionary Indigenous socialist political program, *The Red Deal*, we can think of Kokua Hawaii as strategically addressing "what are commonly thought of as single issues like the protection of sacred sites—which often manifest in specific uprisings or insurrections—as structural in nature, which therefore require a structural (i.e., non-reformist reform) response that has the abolition of capitalism via revolution as its central goal."[40] What Trask perceives as a geographical expansion in later movements was, then, actually a *smaller* focus; it relocated attention away from the outright liberation of Hawai'i and toward, as she explains, "military-controlled lands and trust lands specifically set aside for Hawaiians by the U.S. Congress but used by non-beneficiaries," which do not constitute the entirety of the islands. If Kokua Hawaii's politics challenged the very notion of

Hawai'i's imbrication within the US imperialist system, Trask questioned more the colonial government's continual unjust actions toward Native Hawaiians. It is thus imperative to appraise Trask's interpretation of succeeding movements not necessarily as an "advancement" or betterment of Kokua Hawaii's politics but, rather, as a shift, for doing so allows us to consider what was gained over time but also what might have been lost.

Furthermore, while Trask describes activists' move toward incorporating 'ōlelo Hawai'i in the mid-1970s, it is worth noting how Kokua Hawaii also repeatedly engaged 'ōlelo Hawai'i, not the least being its multifaceted use of "huli" from the outset. Even in the first issue of *Huli*, Kokua Hawaii coined the catchphrase "Ka Aina No Ka Poe o Hawaii" (Land for the People of Hawaii), which would later become the paper's official tagline.[41] Recent scholarship has also suggested that Kokua Hawaii collectively nurtured relations and epistemologies to land through na'au (gut) reactions to the injustices of colonization and the use of mele aloha 'āina, matriotic songs, particularly "Kaulana Nā Pua."[42] Composed by Eleanor Kekoaohiwaikalani Wright Prendergast in the days and weeks following the overthrow of the Hawaiian Kingdom on January 17, 1893, "Kaulana Nā Pua" defiantly proclaimed that Kānaka would rather "eat stones" than submit to colonial rule.[43] The lyrics of "Kaulana Nā Pua," also known as "Mele 'Ai Pōhaku" ("Stone-Eating Song"), appear in both English and 'ōlelo Hawai'i in the April 1972 issue of *Huli*, printed atop a portrait of an individual resolutely looking upward (fig. 4). To the left of "Kaulana Nā Pua" is a similarly rousing poem by the Kokua Hawaii member Linton Park, affirming:

we are native
we are immigrants
we are all races
we are not american
we are HAWAIIAN
our country HAWAII
. . .
we will fight to liberate our country
we are becoming socialist
our system is for the people
we will fight to liberate our people.

Park's insistent phrase "we are not american" came over twenty years before Trask herself repeatedly declared the same at 'Iolani Palace in 1993 during the centennial observance of the overthrow of the Hawaiian Kingdom.[44] However, while Trask's call was directed toward Kānaka, Park and Kokua Hawaii extended the option of disidentifying with the United States to "immigrants" and "all races." By using 'ōlelo Hawai'i to seamlessly place long-standing Hawaiian resistance to the overthrow

Figure 4. Linton Park, "Our Country HAWAII," and "Kaulana Nā Pua" (*right*), *Huli* 2, no. 1 (April 1972), 16–17.

alongside Kokua Hawaii's contemporary resistance to US imperialism, *Huli* implicitly positioned Kānaka at the *forefront* of class struggle in Hawai'i (also evidenced by Park beginning his inclusive poem with "we are native"), while tying the material interests of other working-class communities to an anticolonial politics, too.

To better rally people against the United States and build a movement for national liberation, Kokua Hawaii strategically used the big-tent label of "local" identity. Kokua Hawaii's use of the term had a certain intent that was class based and oppositional rather than strictly ethnic or assimilationist, which was the meaning "local" came to take on in the decades after Kokua Hawaii's presence waned. Trask herself noted how Kokua Hawaii—in establishing a marked difference between "local" and "mainland"—insisted the "local choice was rooted in Hawaiian culture rather than in Asian or Western culture."[45] Nonetheless, the latter appropriation of "local" was what prompted Trask's scathing critique of the term in her 2000 article "Settlers of Color and 'Immigrant' Hegemony: 'Locals' in Hawai'i." Outlining how Asians (primarily Japanese) across the archipelago strategically wielded their identities as "local" to materially advance their class status and uphold the US settler colonial regime in Hawai'i at the direct expense of Hawaiians, Trask summarized, "Simply said, 'locals' want to be 'Americans.'"[46]

Trask's analysis has since formed the foundation for scholarship on Asian settler colonialism,[47] yet neither Trask nor other theorists of Asian settler colonialism have examined how Kokua Hawaii's use of "local" to denote a politics of radical solidarity might otherwise complicate the utility of the forms of allyship to which these critiques have led. This is in part because, as the scholar of race, empire, and settler colonialism Dean Itsuji Saranillio explains, the framework of Asian settler colonialism is primarily responding to "a kind of liberalism, underpinning a multicultural form of settler colonialism."[48] In other words, although Asian settler colonialism as a descriptive tool is often totalizing (i.e., all Asians in Hawai'i are now implicitly contributing to a settler colonial project, no matter when or why their ancestors might have arrived to the islands, even if they were brought as plantation workers before the overthrow of the Hawaiian Kingdom and exploited through colonial processes themselves), Saranillio clarifies that Asian settler colonialism is actually directed toward those of Asian descent who weaponize their identity to provide ideological support for settler colonialism through liberal multiculturalism. Asian settler colonialism is therefore more of a diagnosis of an ideological disease than an outright cure to dismantle its structural roots, embedded as they are within the settler state formation.

Despite the absence of Kokua Hawaii in existing scholarship on Asian settler colonialism, an early theorization of Asian settler colonialism's class- and colonial-collaborationist politics was thoroughly formulated in *Huli* nearly thirty years before Trask helped usher in the concept. Criticizing the nomination of the Japanese businessman Matsuo Takabuki to the Bishop Estate Trustees, Kokua Hawaii member Claire Shimabukuro suggested that "the government and the rich keep ignoring poor local people's needs and are using local stooges to do their dirty work for them." Shimabukuro continued, "Today there are many Japanese people who are trying to become rich and trying to be haole. . . . They now have the kind of greediness that the rich haoles showed the local people how to have. These Japanese should stop and think about their position. Are we going to remain local or become more and more haole?"[49] Shimabukuro, herself of Asian descent, clarifies a difference between a "local" whose politics actively fought against the racial colonial capitalist state and a "local" whose politics sought recognition within it. Half a century later, it is clear that the term *local* ultimately took a reactionary turn, away from being anti-American, as the term was used by Kokua Hawaii in *Huli*, and toward becoming anti-Hawaiian, as posited by Trask, a victory for liberal representation politics at the expense of anticolonial resistance. Applying critiques of Asian settler colonialism to Kokua Hawaii due to its use of *local*, then, would not only diminish the participation of and erase its prominent Kanaka leadership and members who contributed to its efforts over time—including Larry Kamakawiwo'ole, Kalani Ohelo, Moanikeala Akaka, Terrilee Keko'olani, Kehau Lee, Soli Niheu, Joy Ahn, and Pete Thompson, among many others[50]—but also unproductively denigrate the synthesis of anticolonial Marxism that Kokua Hawaii espoused and promulgated to a wider audience through *Huli*.[51] It was this tradition of anticolonial Marxism that allowed

Shimabukuro to both diagnose the workings of Asian settler colonialism *and* assume a politics of national liberation that worked toward dismantling such structural relations.

Although in no way forgiving to US settler colonialism or military occupation, the politics held by Kokua Hawaii's Hawaiian members were decidedly not what Trask would later deem as "Hawaiian nationalist," nor were Kokua Hawaii's non-Hawaiian members necessarily upholding the accompanying position of what Candace Fujikane, a Japanese settler ally and literary scholar, would consider as "fore-grounding Native nationalisms."[52] As understood through Trask's repeated endorse-ment of the 1995 Ka Lāhui Hawai'i Master Plan for Hawaiian Self-Government (including in her article "Settlers of Color and 'Immigrant' Hegemony"), her concep-tion of sovereignty focused on forming a Native Hawaiian nation comprising the nearly two million noncontiguous acres consisting of Hawaiian Kingdom government trust lands that were "ceded" following the overthrow and Hawaiian Home Lands established and held by the United States.[53] Boosting this brand of Native Hawaiian nationalism, understandings of allyship building on Trask's critique of settlers of color paradoxically encouraged those of non-Hawaiian descent to renounce the settler colo-nial project of the United States while limiting their political kuleana (responsibility) to offering support for piecemeal decolonization.[54] Such a position begins from already conceded (or, quite literally, stolen) ground and would lead to a "two-state solution" that all but guarantees continued colonial aggression.

This tactical misstep is in part due to Trask's own slippage in terminology. While rightfully equating Hawai'i to the anticolonial national liberation struggles of the "Irish of Northern Ireland" and the "Palestinians of occupied Palestine," Trask specified that her idea of Hawaiian nationalism was "a *kind* of national liber-ation" (emphasis added).[55] The differences implicit to this "kind" of national liber-ation are significant, yet they have been glossed over by scholars affirmatively citing Trask's comparison. Unlike Irish and Palestinian resistance to the presence of any colonial entity (British or Zionist, respectively) in their historic national territories, Trask pivoted to advocating for a sovereign nation for Native Hawaiians within the US state of Hawai'i. While this was presumed to be a strategic measure toward the eventual usurpation of US colonial presence in Hawai'i, to believe so would require ignoring how Native American nations on the continent (the motivating model for Ka Lāhui Hawai'i[56]) remain constrained by the US government and—rather than being granted additional sovereignty to their traditional territories over time—are geographically confined to reservations, or what the Kul Wicasa scholar of American Indian studies Nick Estes reminds us are the continuation of prisoner-of-war camps.[57]

Differing from Trask's "nation-to-nation" or "nation-within-a-nation" solu-tion, Kokua Hawaii's approach to the national question in Hawai'i was that of national liberation à la Cabral, in which a nation in its entire territorial configuration must be fully liberated from imperialist domination for it to be "true national liberation." Kokua Hawaii was pursuing a Hawai'i completely free from the depredations of US influence, beyond the scope of Trask's Hawaiian nationalism and decades before the terrain of struggle turned toward international courts in an effort to compel deoccupation through a recognition of the continued existence of the Hawaiian Kingdom. This legal effort has sometimes consolidated alongside capitalist and conservative social values as a result of being conducted in a primarily bureaucratic manner, divorced from the verve of mass movements and devoid of class analysis on both a local and global scale.[58] On the contrary, both recalling the multiethnic citizenship that existed before the overthrow and relying on a coalitional solidarity that breaks from a liberal politics of patronizing individualism, Linton Park summarized Kokua Hawaii's egalitarian hopes for a "new Hawaiian nation" in *Huli* as follows: "A Hawaii where people are equal regardless of color. A Hawaii where all the people own and use the land, where people's needs come first. A Hawaii without rich and poor but one united people working together for the good of everyone."[59]

Finally, completing our reassessment of Trask's summary that opened this section, Kokua Hawaii's members were clearly involved in meaningful conversation with various international struggles, although the branching out to other movements and activists did take on a more regional and trans-Indigenous dimension upon entering the 1980s. Partially as a result of the shift described by Trask, Hawai'i is now primarily discussed in conversation with Pan-Pacific social movements and Indigenous struggles in Australia, Aotearoa New Zealand, Oceania, Canada, and the United States—what the Secwépemc political leader George Manuel would deem the Fourth World, or still-colonized Indigenous peoples existing *within* otherwise independent states.[60] But Hawai'i is seldom situated in relation to national liberation movements of the Third World (Palestine being a key exception, in no small part due to the settler colonial nature of the Zionist entity and its military occupation) or anti-imperialist states in the Global South.[61]

These distinctions between Third and Fourth World are imperative for clarifying the position in which one locates oneself and for linking solidarities across specific contexts. An ideological identification with either Third or Fourth World politics, though, can result in different tacks, emphases, and focuses, thereby delineating one's horizon of struggle. Historically, Third World national liberation struggles have been approached through a Marxist-Leninist/-Maoist framework, aiming to overthrow an existing state to establish a revolutionary state. Alternatively, understandings of the Fourth World lend themselves to seeking recognition as a nation within an existing state without overthrowing said state or—when the Fourth World label becomes a signifier of difference from all forms of Westphalian sovereignty—through anti-statist Indigenous anarchist traditions, in which the procedural scaffolding for eventual wholesale liberation against imperialism is less clearly outlined. Responding to similar anti-statist positions that hesitate to thoroughly address the complexity of the national question as dictated by US settler colonialism, the historian Roxanne Dunbar-Ortiz reasons, "It seems that a valuable theoretical tool is abandoned by not dealing with the dialectic of the workers or masses of citizens in the colonial state and their potential for revolution and the Indigenous peoples and other nationalities that are colonised by that state."[62] As *Huli* reveals, Kokua Hawaii refused to disavow such a possibility.

In this sense, it is useful to understand Trask's portrayal of Kokua Hawaii's politics as being caught between Third and Fourth World struggles. Kokua Hawaii distinctly positioned itself as a Third World movement for an independent Hawaiʻi that was, as Trask's later analysis suggests, too little infused with what would come to be understood as Fourth World struggle, or what we can consider to be concerns specific to Kānaka.[63] Kokua Hawaii's political commitments thus represent the inverse of what Glen Sean Coulthard, a scholar of Indigenous politics, has elsewhere deemed "Third World currents in Fourth World anti-colonialism."[64] Per Trask's critiques, the Fourth World—or, in this case, Kānaka ʻŌiwi—currents within Kokua Hawaii's Third World anticolonialism were insufficient. Trask's own politics therefore veered toward a Fourth World lens, articulated through her support for Ka Lāhui Hawaiʻi.

To be forthright, we concur with Trask's insistence on the importance of foregrounding Kanaka ʻŌiwi historical claims and cultural values and the absolute necessity of understanding how non-Natives (and Natives) are complicit in upholding settler colonialism, so long as it does not lead to a rejection of Kokua Hawaii's political approach toward national liberation. As our analysis of *Huli* demonstrates, these positions are not incompatible; rather, they are each indispensable and must continue to inform each other, developing relationally and evolving dialectically.[65] Imagine what a political framework would entail that borrows from both Kokua Hawaii's fifteen-point program and Ka Lāhui Hawaiʻi's master plan—a consolidation between the Hawaiian internationalism of Ohelo and the Hawaiian nationalism of Trask. Might a multiethnic, multiracial national liberation movement organized along class lines best help reconstitute an independent Hawaiʻi and, in turn, provide the mechanisms for the very forms of self-determination Kānaka desire? How could a Hawaiʻi led by a revolutionary party conduct large-scale agrarian reform across the islands, benefiting all working residents through a planned reintegration of Indigenous forms of land management and sustainable food systems while also redistributing lands to dispossessed Kānaka and for those in the diaspora to return? These are but a few of the countless questions of utmost importance that this close reading of *Huli* prompts. By continuing to unravel such intricacies, a more informed theory for liberatory movements in Hawaiʻi can be advanced. As Cabral forewarned, "Nobody has yet made a successful revolution without a revolutionary theory."[66]

Huli Aesthetics: Revolutionary Art and Visual Culture

In an internal organizational document from August 1972, Kokua Hawaii addressed the "future role and form" of *Huli*, which the group understood to be "a powerful revolutionary weapon for uniting and educating our people and for attacking and destroying our enemies."[67] One point in a list of guiding principles for the paper remarked, "Revolutionary newspapers as well as revolutionary art and literature must reflect the struggle and heroic efforts of our people." Further in the document, it becomes clear that these views are based on two included references from *Quotations from Chairman Mao Tse-tung*, themselves excerpted from Mao's 1942 "Talks at the Yan'an Forum on Literature and Art." Within *Huli*'s broader educational purposes, Kokua Hawaii thus recognized the unique importance of revolutionary art and visual culture for achieving its aims. *Huli* once promoted an art exhibition at a University of Hawai'i at Mānoa ethnic studies symposium, explaining the need "to give local artists some exposure as well as establish the basis of and general need for a local based progressive art movement which is relevant specifically to Hawaii, her history, her children, and their heritage and most of all the present situation of our people."[68] Having already detailed how *Huli*'s graphic design and overall visual experience represented its politics to its readers, here we trace a "Huli aesthetics" as initiated by Kokua Hawaii, expressed within *Huli*, and extended beyond its pages. In doing so, we posit *Huli* as one foundational forum for constructing a politically and socially engaged contemporary story of art in US-occupied Hawai'i.

The origins of "Huli aesthetics" can be located before *Huli* began. On March 31, 1971, Kokua Hawaii co-organized a rally at the Hawai'i State Capitol with the environmental group Save Our Surf (SOS) to raise awareness about Kalama Valley and other destructive development projects impacting O'ahu.[69] Demonstrators marched with a massive handmade banner reading "PEOPLE NOT PROFIT$— HULI!!," while Kalani Ohelo and other Kokua Hawaii members—adorned with brown berets adopted from the Young Lords, who themselves adopted the headwear from the Black Panthers—gave speeches before a sign reading "HULI," in a photo by esteemed photographer and self-identified haole ally Ed Greevy (fig. 5).[70] *Huli* would later present similar social documentary images and other depictions of community struggle, including some by Greevy and others by members of Kokua Hawaii such as James Kimo Ng. At this and subsequent rallies, Trask noted that "Huli" was "emblazoned on every banner and leaflet" in addition to becoming an exclamation regularly called out during marches and sit-ins.[71] A later report in *Huli* from a demonstration on Kona on the island of Hawai'i stated, "'Huli' wrang [*sic*] from the audience, 'Huli' again with the tutus joining in—the love and power and comradeship grew—food arrived from somewhere and we continued to rejoice, we weren't alone."[72]

Kokua Hawaii also produced a toolkit of graphic symbols for *Huli* meant to represent and uplift the colonized proletariat, understood to be a continuation of the

Figure 5. Save Our Surf (SOS) and Kokua Hawaii demonstration for Kalama Valley, Hawai'i State Capitol, 1971. Photograph by Ed Greevy.

Figure 6. kekahi wahi (Sancia Miala Shiba Nash and Drew K. Broderick), *no ke kai ka hoi ua aina*, 2022. Video still.

maka'āinana (commoners, landless workers, or people of the land) from Hawaiian society before the Hawaiian Kingdom was overthrown. This was most evident in Kokua Hawaii's logo, which featured a raised fist holding a pōhaku ku'i 'ai, the stone tool used to pound kalo (taro) into poi, a staple food of the Hawaiian diet. Offering Hawai'i-specific imagery to an established leftist visual lexicon, the logo purposefully linked the organization's goals of continual growth to kalo farmer's use of the "huli," the cutting of the stem from the corm, from which new taro plants sprout when replanted. In some uses of the logo, the fist and pounder were depicted not only as a sign of vitality and connection to the land but also as a symbol of righteous destruction. In an illustration featured in the November 1972 issue of *Huli* above a poem by the Vietnamese revolutionary Hồ Chí Minh, the fist and pounder emerge from Ka Hae Hawai'i, the Hawaiian flag, to crush an airplane, freeway, highrise building, and cruise ship. This same graphic had previously been used for Kokua Hawaii's annual Huli Kakou concert series, a gathering to develop political consciousness through music, support Hawaiian musicians, and raise money for Kokua Hawaii's various initiatives, including *Huli*, which repeatedly advertised the concert in full-page ads.[73] *Huli*'s August 1972 issue included a write-up of that year's event, which featured an anticolonial historical theater skit covering early Hawaiian society through the present moment, ending with workers of different ethnicities coming together in a people's revolution to liberate Hawai'i from its various overlords.[74] The sensibility of "Huli aesthetics," then, had quickly transitioned from handmade demonstration banners to documentary photography, from the pages of the periodical to concert stages, and from illustrative graphics into performance.

While these changes in medium continued to give voice to the politics brought to the fore by Kokua Hawaii and the periodical *Huli*, other artists have more directly summoned the sensibilities of the word *huli*, moving from prose into poetry. In 1979, several years after *Huli*'s cessation, the Kanaka poet, translator, journalist, and educator Wayne Kaumualii Westlake created an unassuming concrete poem by printing "HULI" with a hand stamp in black ink on paper.[75] Consistent with his playful and often mischievous approach, Westlake presented the word flipped upside down and reversed. A "simple and unsettling gesture," the one-word poem literalizes the transformational potential of *huli*, "allowing its meaning to be sensed, if not necessarily understood, by all readers."[76]

Like Westlake, 'Īmaikalani Kalāhele, a Kanaka poet, artist, musician, activist, and pillar within the Hawaiian and local literary and visual arts communities, has also channeled the energies of the word *huli* into his creative output. In the poem "Huli" from 1993, composed one hundred years after the overthrow of the Hawaiian Kingdom, Kalāhele examines the ever-lingering nature of the word as he repeatedly poses the question, "Can you hear it?" Moving across registers, Kalāhele differentiates between the sounds of "History singing its sad song," "The cries of a people," "The howl of the Imperialist beast," and the "SONG OF SOVEREIGNTY," ending the combative poem where he began with the timely exhortation, "HULI."[77] In another poem, titled "Make a Fist," Kalāhele evokes the revolutionary and regenerative interpretations of *huli* through its connection to kalo, calling on readers loyal to Hawai'i to take matters into their own hands:

Make a fist
hold it high.

Plant the resistance
deep.

Kanu! Kanu!
Kanu now.
Hoʻoulu hou.
Hoʻoulu hou.
Hoʻoulu hou.

Huli.[78]

Responding to intensifying US military desecration, tourist intrusion, and racial violence, *huli* has lately reemerged in crucial efforts that have affirmed underacknowledged legacies of artistic defiance in Hawai'i, such as *Down on the Sidewalk in Waikīkī* (2019), a narrative short film by the Kanaka director and filmmaker Justyn Ah Chong. Departing from a collection of poems of the same name that Westlake wrote while working as a janitor in Waikīkī from 1972 to 1973,[79] the film follows a soft-spoken janitor named Keali'i, played by the Kanaka director and screenwriter 'Āina Paikai, as he works through the frustrations of cleaning up after an endless parade of tourists with no regard for the land they are visiting, nor for its caretakers. As Keali'i tries to make sense of this far-from-idyllic situation, he stumbles on a corpse in a restroom and a handwritten journal full of poetry. After scrubbing the scene, Keali'i turns his attention to the journal. On one of its pages is scrawled "HULI," written upside down and reversed like Westlake's original concrete poem. Engrossed in this finding, Keali'i's introspective reading is suddenly interrupted by an obnoxiously drunk businessman on vacation just as he starts to flip the journal, as if undoing the poem's intended antagonistic effect transported himself back into reality. Over the course of the film, Keali'i comes to understand the significance of this and other poems haunting his nightmarish dreamscapes, guided by the lingering ghost of their author, an overlooked old Hawaiian man played by 'Īmaikalani Kalāhele. When inspirational clarity finally comes to Keali'i, the camera flips, suggesting that "huli" is an embodied attitude and state of enlightenment one can realize through the combination of personal experience and internal reflection.

In the immediate wake of the COVID-19 pandemic, the collapse of the tourism industry in Hawai'i, and the Black Lives Matter movement in 2020, the Honolulu-based forum Tropic Zine and numerous collaborators also returned to prior expressions of *huli*, pushing back against the "Imperialist beast" and holding space down on the sidewalks of Waikīkī. In residence at the community venue Aupuni Space in the Kakaʻako neighborhood of Honolulu, Tropic Zine converted the gallery into a movement space to discuss individual and collective concerns, agree on a unified plan of action, and make signs, banners, and T-shirts in parallel to participating in marches, demonstrations, and public interventions.[80] Among the material crafted for such endeavors was a handmade cutout sign on recycled cardboard in homage to Westlake's 1979 "Huli (concrete poem)," a reproduction of which appears as one of four double-sided folded posters originating from the forum's residency at Aupuni Space that together comprise the experimental publication *Tropic Zine Issue 3*.[81]

Another cardboard sign similarly emblazoned with Westlake's "HULI" and held during a Black Lives Matter demonstration on Oʻahu makes an appearance in *no ke kai ka hoi ua aina* (2022), an experimental short film by grassroots film initiative kekahi wahi that presents a postmortem portrait of Waikīkī in 2020. This "HULI" sign, though, is not waved by a group of human demonstrators but by a digitally generated bootleg animation of Experiment 626, or "Stitch" as he is more commonly known, the genetically engineered, extraterrestrial life form from Disney's *Lilo and Stitch* franchise (fig. 6). While the original 2002 film remains controversial for Disney's stereotyped (mis)representations and capitalization of Hawaiian culture, Stitch's fugitivity, avoidance of capture, and eventual refuge also make him a suitable allegory for abolition. Standing in solidarity amid a group amassed in front of the Duke Paoa Kahanamoku statue in Waikīkī, Stitch's protesting presence in *no ke kai ka hoi ua aina* suggests a possible commandeering of his innate destructive tendencies toward a decolonial impulse, a reinterpretation of Stitch's character that would compel him to "huli" the infrastructures of racial injustice rather than be placated by his new environs. Like Kealiʻi in *Down on the Sidewalk in Waikīkī*, the figure of Stitch in *no ke kai ka hoi ua aina* refuses to quietly assimilate into a world with inverted priorities.

Most recently, Westlake's "HULI," along with some of his other concrete poems, featured prominently as vinyl wall and floor treatments in an expansive installation of printed matter, *In Memoriam Wayne Kaumualii Westlake (1947–1984)*, at the Hawaiʻi State Art Museum during Hawaiʻi Triennial 2022: *Pacific Century—E Hoʻomau no Moananuiākea* (fig. 7).[82] Serving as a commemoration of various collaborative artistic afterlives, this inclusion in a locally rooted periodic exhibition of global contemporary art also latently renewed both Kokua Hawaii's initial belief in agitational publishing and *Huli*'s internationalist outlook. Through these increasingly enlarged and widely distributed presentations on screen, in the streets, and in museums, the potentialities of the word *huli* and its underlying meanings, as envisioned in Kokua Hawaii's *Huli*, continues to be activated by new generations fifty years after the periodical ceased.

Figure 7. 'Elepaio Press (Richard and Mark Hamasaki), *In Memoriam Wayne Kaumualii Westlake (1947–1984)*, 2022, Hawai'i State Art Museum, Hawai'i Triennial 2022: *Pacific Century—E Ho'omau no Moananuiākea*, curated by Drew Kahu'āina Broderick, Miwako Tezuka, and Melissa Chiu. Installation view. Photograph by Drew Kahu'āina Broderick.

Conclusion: Educate to Liberate

On the back page of *Huli*'s December 1972 issue, a boy stands shirtless behind cinder block and stone, his eyes directed downward toward an open spread of the October 1972 issue held in his hands (fig. 8). Above him in capital letters reads the galvanizing phrase, "EDUCATE TO LIBERATE." This prophetic image, referencing a previous issue of the same paper in which it was published, demonstrates the impetus of *Huli*'s very existence, that being the political education and radicalization of ka po'e o Hawai'i, the people of Hawai'i, through the dissemination and propagation of generational knowledge. Much like this self-referential page implies, our analysis of *Huli* has insisted that its production, design, and materiality internalized the politics it tried to imbue as a means of externalizing its impact. As a learning tool for activists and artists alike, *Huli* thus retains a timely relevance.

In preparing to write this article, we successfully obtained copies of every issue of *Huli* except for the very last, published in April 1973. This final issue likely exists in someone's personal collection, potentially stashed away in a box with other ephemera of past struggles. There is something fortuitous about us not having access to the last issue, though, which might have hinted toward internal reasons for both *Huli*'s end of publication and Kokua Hawaii's eventual dissolution. Without

Figure 8. Educate to Liberate, back page of *Huli* 2, no. 7 (December 1972).

knowing the specifics of how it ended, we can think of the next issue as being still in production. This lack of a definitive conclusion—supplemented by the ongoing US occupation of Hawaiʻi—also leaves the future of "huli" as a politics ultimately undetermined. With growing right-wing sentiment throughout Hawaiʻi masquerading as anti-establishment freedom fighting, "huli" is at increasing risk of being wholly misappropriated, weaponized by those who, despite feigning self-determination and claims to "huli" otherwise, uphold reactionary politics that would only reinforce cis-hetero patriarchal prejudice, racial colonial capitalism, and the hegemony of US imperialism.[83]

Given the drastic worsening of the same conditions Kokua Hawaii correctly assessed over five decades ago, our reclaiming of *Huli* is therefore imperative for combatting such sloganeering contrarianism and empty rhetoric.[84] Perhaps this text, cowritten by a white, non-Native scholar with familial ties to Maui (Katzeman) and a Kanaka ʻŌiwi artist from Oʻahu (Broderick), is one small part of carrying *Huli*'s intentions into the present, toward more just futures for Hawaiʻi in which our racial, ethnic, and cultural differences inform and strengthen how we unify around shared values and political aspirations.[85] For, if Kokua Hawaii were around to #HuliDaSystem today, it would entail an anticolonial national liberation struggle to construct an independent Hawaiʻi rooted within Kanaka ʻŌiwi ways of being, shaped by scientific socialist study, and in alignment with liberatory freedom movements of the oppressed around the world. To defend against further material dispossession and theoretical dilution, then, not only must settler colonial institutions and the means of production—from agribusiness plots to military bases, transnational hotel chains to museums, and, above all else, ʻāina (that which sustains)—be seized for revolutionary means, but so, too, should "huli."

PAIO! HULI!

Drew Kahuʻāina Broderick is an artist, curator, and educator from Mōkapu, a peninsula on the windward side of Oʻahu. Currently, he serves as director of Koa Gallery at Kapiʻolani Community College and as a member of kekahi wahi (2020–), a grassroots film initiative documenting stories of transformation across Moananui, the Pacific. Recently, he cocurated *ʻAi Pōhaku, Stone Eaters* (2023) with Josh Tengan and Noelle M. K. Y. Kahanu; Hawaiʻi Triennial 2022: *Pacific Century—E Hoʻomau no Moananuiākea*, with Melissa Chiu and Miwako Tezuka; and *Mai hoʻohuli i ka lima i luna* (2020), with Kapulani Landgraf and Kaili Chun.

Aaron Katzeman is an art historian, curator, and postdoctoral fellow at the Getty Research Institute. He received his PhD in visual studies at the University of California, Irvine, and was previously a Landhaus Fellow at the Rachel Carson Center for Environment and Society. His research focuses on contemporary art and visual culture produced alongside resistance to military occupation, social movements for agrarian reform, and anticolonial national liberation struggles. His writing has appeared in *Third Text*, *caa.reviews*, *Pacific Arts*, and *Antipode: A Radical Journal of Geography*.

Notes

Mahalo to the librarians and archivists at the University of Hawai'i at Mānoa, University of Connecticut, University of Kansas, University of Michigan, and Amherst College who assisted our requests. Mahalo also to Ray Catania and Gary Pak for sharing insights and documents with us, respectively.

1. Throughout this article, we have opted to write the name of the organization Kōkua Hawai'i without diacritics in keeping with the way it was spelled at the time. Elsewhere, we retain kahakō (macrons) and 'okina (glottal stops), following the writing conventions of today. In support of, and in attempt not to other, 'ōlelo Hawai'i, we do not italicize words in the Hawaiian language.

2. See Horne, *Fighting in Paradise*; *Cane Fire* (dir. Anthony Banua-Simon, United States, 2020).

3. For more on kaona, see Arista, "Navigating Uncharted Oceans of Meaning"; McDougall, *Finding Meaning.*

4. See Pukui and Elbert, *Hawaiian Dictionary*, s.v. "huli."

5. Trask, "Birth of the Modern Hawaiian Movement," 146.

6. Following the illegality of Hawai'i's incorporation into the US in 1898 through the Newlands Resolution passed in the US Congress rather than a treaty of annexation, the process that resulted in Hawai'i becoming the fiftieth US state in 1959 was similarly questionable. Hawai'i was included on the United Nations List of Non-Self-Governing Territories in 1946 but, at the request of the United States, was removed from the list following the statehood plebiscite in 1959. In 1953, the UN General Assembly passed Resolution 742 outlining explicit stipulations that must be followed for a non-self-governing territory to be removed from the list, including the right to pursue the option of independence from its "administering agent," that being the United States in the case of Hawai'i. However, there was no option for independence during the statehood plebiscite, with voters only able to choose between Hawai'i remaining a US territory or becoming a US state (there are also questions about *who* should have been able to vote, as all current residents including US military personnel were allowed to participate). For these reasons and more, it is common for activists to refer to the current entity known as the State of Hawai'i as the "fake state." See Lopez-Reyes, "Re-inscription of Hawaii"; Trask, "Hawai'i and the United Nations."

7. See McGregor-Alegado, "Hawaiians: Organizing in the 1970s." The existing scholarship on *Huli* is scarce. For references to *Huli* in discussions about Kokua Hawaii, see Chapin, *Shaping History*, 341; and Najita, *Decolonizing Cultures in the Pacific*, 132, 137, 144, 148, 150–51.

8. See Silva, *Aloha Betrayed*.

9. Kalama Valley was the catalyst for the formation of Kokua Hawaii, which prior to the struggle was a loosely affiliated and undefined group of like-minded students and young adults who had been meeting in various political groups, including Students for a Democratic Society (SDS) and the antiwar Hawai'i Resistance. In May 1970 another organization, Youth Action, hosted a Youth Congress in Hawai'i, which called for the secession of Hawai'i from the United States. Aware of what was happening in Kalama Valley and wanting to maximize this fermenting social unrest, the community advocate Lawrence "Larry" Kamakawiwo'ole organized radicalized Hawaiians and others into forming the Kokua Kalama Committee. The group later changed its name to reflect larger ambitions and focus beyond Kalama Valley.

10. Trask, "Birth of the Modern Hawaiian Movement"; Kubota, *Hawaii Stories of Change*; *Huli! Kokua Hawaii and the Beginning of the Revolutionary Movement in Hawai'i* (dir. Gary Pak, Hawai'i, 2019).

11. In response to a final threat of eviction after some farmers had already been forced to move from their farms, a handful of Kalama Valley residents decided they would stay put and fight against relocation. In solidarity with those taking a stand, members of Kokua Hawaii slowly began to establish relationships with residents, temporarily relocating themselves to the valley to assist with everyday farm duties and bring the strength in numbers necessary to attempt to stop the bulldozing of homes and removal of residents.

12. "Open Letter to Bishop Estate," *Huli* 1, no. 1 (May 1971), 4.

13. *Huli* 1, no. 1 (May 1971), 3.

14. "From Jail," *Huli* 1, no. 1 (May 1971), 5.

15. Larry Kamakawiwo'ole mentioned the letters from Mao and Castro in Pak's documentary *Huli!* For more on the breadth of press coverage Kalama Valley garnered, see Kubota, *Hawaii Stories of Change*, 138–39.

16. *Huli* 1, no. 1 (May 1971), 3.

17. Along with the *Honolulu Star-Bulletin*, both newspapers had deep ties to figures who either endorsed or were directly involved in the overthrow of the Hawaiian Kingdom in 1893, attempts to annex Hawai'i to the United States, and the later promotion of tourism. The two newspapers merged in 2010, becoming the *Honolulu Star-Advertiser*.

18. "Land for the People," *Huli* 1, no. 4 (July 3, 1971), 7.

19. Kubota, *Hawaii Stories of Change*, 288.

20. Kubota, *Hawaii Stories of Change*, 265.

21. Ray Catania, "Robert Wilikoki Wilcox: Independence Fighter and Hawaiian Patriot," *Huli* 2, no. 2 (May 1972), 20.

22. "29 Pigs Dead," *Huli* 1, no. 2 (June 5, 1971), 8.

23. Black Richards, "Kalama Bust," *Huli* 1, no. 2 (June 5, 1971), 6. Richards's words precede those of Thomas Sankara, the Marxist-Leninist and pan-African president of Burkina Faso, who in 1986 similarly explained, "Where is imperialism? Look at your plates when you eat. The imported rice, maize, and millet—that is imperialism."

24. Pa'ahao Committee, "All Poor People Are Prisoners," *Huli* 2, no. 5 (October 1972), 9.

25. Claire Shimabukuro, "Sexism and Racism: Two Wrong Ideas Which Divide Our People," *Huli* 2, no. 3 (June 1972), 23. For a more recent analysis of prison abolitionism in Hawai'i, see Jenkins, "Pu'uhonua Not Prisons."

26. See *Huli* 2, no. 1 (April 1972). For more on ethnic studies at the University of Hawai'i at Mānoa, see McGregor and Aoudé, "'Our History, Our Way!'"

27. Kubota, *Hawaii Stories of Change*, 288.

28. McGregor, "Statehood," 311. See also Saranillio, *Unsustainable Empire*.

29. Faith Okabe, "Vietnam–Kalama," *Huli* 2, no. 3 (June 1972), 17.

30. Catholic Action of Hawaii, "Welcome to Hawaii," *Huli* 2, no. 3 (June 1972), 12–13.

31. Val Piamonte, "Solidarity in Struggle," *Huli* 2, no. 1 (April 1972), 8.

32. The contents of Kokua Hawaii's Library for the People were published in *Huli* 2, no. 7 (December 1972), 14.

33. Trask, "Birth of the Modern Hawaiian Movement," 126.

34. Trask, "Birth of the Modern Hawaiian Movement," 126–27.

35. For additional analysis of these very distinctions by Trask, see Goodyear-Ka'ōpua, "Introduction."

36. Lenin addressed these various issues in *The Right of Nations to Self-Determination* (1914); *Imperialism, The Highest Stage of Capitalism* (1916); and *The State and Revolution* (1917).

37. Cabral, "Weapon of Theory."

38. Linton Park, "Kalama Valley: Birth of a New Hawaiian Nation," *Huli* 1, no. 4 (July 3, 1971), 3. The Huli Youth Organization is discussed in *Huli* 2, no. 1 (April 1972), 12–13; and *Huli* 2, no. 2 (May 1972), 18–19.

39. Kalani Ohelo, "Lokahi People of Hawaii," *Huli* 2, no. 1 (April 1972), 3.

40. Red Nation, *Red Deal*, 21.

41. *Huli*'s tagline shifted from "Local People's News" to "Ka Aina No Ka Poe o Hawaii" beginning with the April 1972 issue.

42. Okuda et al., "'You Gotta Be Responsible.'"

43. When the new provisional government issued a mandate for all government workers to sign an oath of loyalty, many resisted the order and stood in steadfast support of their deposed queen and country. Among those who objected were members of the Royal Hawaiian Band, who were famously memorialized in this mele. One of the only two band members who signed the loyalty oath was the Royal Hawaiian bandmaster himself, Henri Berger, who notoriously expelled his intransigent colleagues with the words, "a mahope ai pohaku no," or "later you will eat stones." Berger's cautionary comment, meant to mock and belittle the band members, instead became a desirable quality of resistance. For additional context, see Nordyke and Noyes, "'Kaulana Nā Pua'"; and Stillman, "'Aloha Aina.'"

44. For more on the lasting resonances of Trask's declaration, see the forthcoming "'We Are Not American' Still," special issue of *American Quarterly*, edited by Maile Arvin, Hiʻilei Julia Hobart, Bryan Kamaoli Kuwada, Brandy Nālani McDougall, and Lani Teves.

45. Trask, "Birth of the Modern Hawaiian Movement," 146.

46. Trask, "Settlers of Color," 20. The ideas in this essay were first presented by Trask in a keynote address at the 1997 conference of the Society for the Study of the Multi-Ethnic Literature of the United States (MELUS).

47. Trask's 2000 essay, for instance, was reprinted in Fujikane and Okamura, *Asian Settler Colonialism.*

48. Saranillio, "Why Asian Settler Colonialism Matters," 281. This article thoroughly addresses Nandita Sharma's critical book review of *Asian Settler Colonialism.* See Sharma, "Book Reviews."

49. Claire Shimabukuro, "The Takabuki Disease," *Huli* 1, no. 4 (July 3, 1971), 6.

50. For more on Moanikeala Akaka's and Terrilee Kekoʻolani's participation in Kokua Hawaii-related and other struggles, see Goodyear-Kāʻopua, *Nā Wāhine Koa.*

51. For an overview of Marxism's anticolonial attributes that correlate with Kokua Hawaii's application, see Rodney, "Marxism as Third World Ideology."

52. See Fujikane, "Foregrounding Native Nationalisms."

53. See Trask, *"Hoʻokupu a Ka Lāhui Hawaiʻi."*

54. Trask's critique of settlers of color and her related ideas about the limits of solidarity has led to a body of scholarship theorizing different forms of allyship for non-Natives that have gradually departed from her views. See Trask, "Coalition-Building." Most prominent of these has been the concept of settler aloha ʻāina, which asserts settlers can care for and love the lands on which they reside but should also support and uplift Indigenous relations to said lands. See Goodyear-Kaʻōpua, *Seeds We Planted*, 149–55; and Fujikane,

Mapping Abundance, 12–16. For additional ways in which individual positionalities have been productively challenged for purposes of solidarity in Hawai'i, see Saranillio, "Haunani-Kay Trask"; and Arvin, "Indigenous Feminist Notes." Recently, scholars have begun theorizing hoa (comrade) and hoaʻāina (caretaker of the land) as terms that further emphasize relational actions more than identitarian differences, without completely collapsing them. See Aikau, "From Malihini to Hoaʻāina"; Tengan, "Hoa."

55.   Trask, "Settlers of Color," 6.

56.   The limits of this kind of model were later made starkly evident through debates regarding the Akaka Bill, which likewise proposed federal recognition for Native Hawaiians, albeit through a state-driven rather than grassroots initiative. See Kauanui, "Precarious Positions"; Kauanui, "Resisting the Akaka Bill."

57.   Estes, *Our History Is the Future*.

58.   Kokua Hawaii's approach to the national question drastically differed from those whom the Kanaka scholar J. Kēhaulani Kauanui labels "kingdom nationalists." See Kauanui, *Paradoxes of Hawaiian Sovereignty*. For additional critiques of how some expressions of Hawaiian nationalism reinforce cis-hetero patriarchy, see Osorio, *Remembering Our Intimacies*.

59.   Linton Park, "Kalama Valley: Birth of a New Hawaiian Nation," *Huli* 1, no. 4 (July 3, 1971), 3.

60.   See Trask, "Politics in the Pacific Islands"; Manuel and Posluns, *Fourth World*.

61.   For more on the origins of Zionism's settler colonial nature, see Sayegh, *Zionist Colonialism in Palestine*. For more on Palestine in relation to Native and Indigenous studies, see Salaita, *Inter/Nationalism*.

62.   Dunbar-Ortiz, "Relationship between Marxism and Indigenous Struggles," 82.

63.   This is despite Trask herself noting that "the specifics of Hawaiian history coupled with the universals of Third World history places the Hawaiians and other locals in a similar category" ("Birth of the Modern Hawaiian Movement," 147).

64.   See Coulthard, "Once Were Maoists."

65.   For more on how these positions once came to a head between Kokua Hawaii and the Protect Kahoʻolawe ʻOhana, see Niheu, "Huli." For recent attempts to navigate beyond this impasse, see Hui Aloha ʻĀina o Honolulu's participation in the event "Ka Paio Hookahi: The Crossroads of Indigenous and Working Class Struggles" on October 8, 2022, later published as an episode of the *Red Nation Podcast*.

66.   Cabral, "Weapon of Theory."

67.   This document was shared with the authors by Gary Pak.

68.   *Huli* 2, no. 2 (May 1972), 16. For more on institutional critique of the University of Hawaiʻi at Mānoa, specifically its Department of Art and Art History, see Dudoit, "Carving a Hawaiian Aesthetic"; Kosasa, "Pedagogical Sights/Sites"; Clark, "Hānau Kahikikū me Kahikimoe"; and Broderick, Tengan, and Kahanu, *ʻAi Pōhaku*.

69.   Save Our Surf (SOS), a grassroots community organization founded in the mid-1960s by the lifelong activists John and Marion Kelly, was initially concerned with protecting surf spots and shorelines of Hawaiʻi threatened by commercial development but soon began supporting other issues including tenants rights and land struggles. At this event, Save Our Surf was rallying to stop proposed tourist development along Sandy Beach, near Kalama Valley. The graphic identity John Kelly established in SOS's leaflets would later influence Kokua Hawaii's own visuals.

70.   Greevy began documenting the political and environmental movements of Hawaiʻi in 1970. After meeting John and Marion Kelly at an SOS meeting held at their home,

Greevy quickly became an instrumental member of the organization. Encouraged by the Kellys to document the events taking place in Kalama Valley during 1971, Greevy was forever changed by the experience. Newly radicalized, he repeatedly turned his camera to numerous land struggles in the decades that followed. See Trask and Greevy, *Kū'ē*.

71. Trask, "Birth of the Modern Hawaiian Movement," 146.
72. Dixon Enos and Jackie Enos, "Kona Rises in Struggle," *Huli* 2, no. 5 (October 1972), 3.
73. For more linking Kalama Valley to the resurgence of Hawaiian music, see Milner, "Home, Homelessness, and Homeland."
74. In its leftist political orientation and audience engagement, such a skit closely relates to the Brazilian theater practitioner Augusto Boal's concept Theater of the Oppressed.
75. Westlake, *Westlake*, 130.
76. This description of Westlake's work comes from a text written by Drew Kahu'āina Broderick and Josh Tengan for *Notes for Tomorrow*, a traveling exhibition conceived by Independent Curators International.
77. Kalāhele, *Kalahele*, 47–51.
78. Kalāhele, *Kalahele*, 1. For more on Kalāhele, see the short film *Ho'oulu Hou* (dir. kekahi wahi, 2023).
79. See Westlake, *Westlake*, 138–69.
80. For more on Tropic Zine's residency, see Katzeman, "Burning the American Flag."
81. Emi, *Tropic Zine Issue 3*.
82. For more on the Hawai'i Triennial 2022, see Broderick, "E Ho'omau no Moananuiākea."
83. Such sentiments were prevalent in the former mixed martial arts fighter BJ Penn's unsuccessful campaign to win the Republican Party nomination for governor of Hawai'i in 2022. Frantz Fanon diagnosed a similar kind of commandeering as "the pitfalls of national consciousness," or when the struggle for sovereignty is overtaken by the class of colonized bourgeoisie who have no material inclination to successfully stave off neocolonial exploitation after independence, nor to advocate for the needs of the most marginalized. See Fanon, "Pitfalls of National Consciousness."
84. The Hawai'i Unity and Liberation Institute (HULI), formed in 2017, has also reclaimed *huli*, reworking the fist and pounder logo of Kokua Hawaii for its own. HULI provides social movement aid and advocates kapu aloha (nonviolent direct action), which has been a key component practiced by kia'i (protectors) in the preventing the construction of the Thirty Meter Telescope atop Mauna a Wākea.
85. Positionality statements often come at the beginning of texts to disclose or situate the author's identity in relation to their research. In putting ours at the end, we intend to embody the ideals of Kokua Hawaii, starting from a place of cohesion rather than division and allowing our respective positionalities to be subsequently suffused through the collaborative writing process.

References

Aikau, Hōkūlani K. "From Malihini to Hoa'āina: Reconnecting People, Places, and Practices." In *The Past before Us: Mo'okū'auhau as Methodology*, edited by Nālani Wilson-Hokowhitu, 81–93. Honolulu: University of Hawai'i Press, 2019.

Arista, Noelani. "Navigating Uncharted Oceans of Meaning: *Kaona* as Historical and Interpretive Method." *PMLA* 125, no. 3 (2010): 663–69.

Arvin, Maile. "Indigenous Feminist Notes on Embodying Alliance against Settler Colonialism." *Meridians* 18, no. 2 (2019): 335–57.

Broderick, Drew Kahuʻāina. "E Hoʻomau no Moananuiākea: Native/Non-Native Artist Collaborations against U.S. Empire in Hawaiʻi." In *Hawaiʻi Triennial 2022: Pacific Century—Hoʻomau no Moananuiākea*, edited by Melissa Chiu, Miwako Tezuka, and Drew Kahuʻāina Broderick, 37–57. Honolulu: University of Hawaiʻi Press, 2022.

Broderick, Drew Kahuʻāina, Josh Tengan, and Noelle M. K. Y. Kahanu, eds. *ʻAi Pōhaku, Stone Eaters*. Honolulu: Puʻuhonua Society, 2024.

Cabral, Amílcar. "The Weapon of Theory: Address delivered to the first Tricontinental Conference of the Peoples of Asia, Africa and Latin America held in Havana in January, 1966." Marxists Internet Archive. https://www.marxists.org/subject/africa/cabral/1966 /weapon-theory.htm (accessed November 28, 2023).

Chapin, Helen Geracimos. *Shaping History: The Role of Newspapers in Hawaiʻi*. Honolulu: University of Hawaiʻi Press, 1996.

Clark, Herman Piʻikea. "Hānau Kahikikū me Kahikimoe: A Call for the Development of a Theory for Kanaka Maoli Visual Culture Education." *Educational Perspectives* 37, no. 1 (2004): 23–30.

Coulthard, Glen Sean. "Once Were Maoists: Third World Currents in Fourth World Anti-colonialism, Vancouver, 1967–1975." In *Routledge Handbook of Critical Indigenous Studies*, edited by Brendan Hokowhitu, Aileen Moreton-Robinson, Linda Tuhiwai-Smith, Chris Andersen, and Steve Larkin, 378–91. London: Routledge, 2020.

Dudoit, D. Māhealani. "Carving a Hawaiian Aesthetic." *ʻŌiwi: A Native Hawaiian Journal* 1 (1998): 20–26.

Dunbar-Ortiz, Roxanne. "The Relationship between Marxism and Indigenous Struggles and Implications of the Theoretical Framework for International Indigenous Struggles." *Historical Materialism* 24, no. 3 (2016): 76–91.

Emi, Marika, ed. *Tropic Zine Issue 3*. Honolulu: Tropic Editions, 2020.

Estes, Nick. *Our History Is the Future: Standing Rock versus the Dakota Access Pipeline, and the Long Tradition of Indigenous Resistance*. New York: Verso, 2019.

Fanon, Frantz. "The Pitfalls of National Consciousness." In *The Wretched of the Earth*, translated by Constance Farrington, 148–205. New York: Grove Press, 1963.

Fujikane, Candace. "Foregrounding Native Nationalisms: A Critique of Antinationalist Sentiment in Asian American Studies." In *Asian American Studies after Critical Mass*, edited by Kent A. Ono, 73–97. Malden, MA: Blackwell, 2005.

Fujikane, Candace. *Mapping Abundance for a Planetary Future: Kanaka Maoli and Critical Settler Cartographies in Hawaiʻi*. Durham, NC: Duke University Press, 2021.

Fujikane, Candace, and Jonathan Y. Okamura, eds. *Asian Settler Colonialism: From Local Governance to the Habits of Everyday Life in Hawaiʻi*. Honolulu: University of Hawaiʻi Press, 2008.

Goodyear-Kaʻōpua, Noelani. "Introduction." In *A Nation Rising: Hawaiian Movements for Life, Land, and Sovereignty*, edited by Noelani Goodyear-Kaʻōpua, Ikaika Hussey, and Erin Kahunawaikaʻala Wright, 1–33. Durham, NC: Duke University Press, 2014.

Goodyear-Kāʻopua, Noelani, ed. *Nā Wāhine Koa: Hawaiian Women for Sovereignty and Demilitarization*. Honolulu: University of Hawaiʻi Press, 2018.

Goodyear-Kaʻōpua, Noelani. *The Seeds We Planted: Portraits of a Native Hawaiian Charter School*. Minneapolis: University of Minnesota Press, 2013.

Horne, Gerald. *Fighting in Paradise: Labor Unions, Racism, and Communists in the Making of Modern Hawaiʻi*. Honolulu: University of Hawaiʻi Press, 2011.

Jenkins, Jen. "Puʻuhonua Not Prisons, a Manifesto." *Harbinger* 46, special issue, "Movements for Freedom: Scholarship from the Inside." https://socialchangenyu.com/harbinger/puuhonua-not-prisons-a-manifesto/.

Kalāhele, ʻĪmaikalani. *Kalahele*. Honolulu: Kalamakū Press, 2002.

Katzeman, Aaron. "Burning the American Flag Before the World: Ecologies of Abolition and Demilitarisation in Hawaiʻi." *Third Text* 36, no. 6 (2022): 603–29.

Kauanui, J. Kēhaulani. *Paradoxes of Hawaiian Sovereignty: Land, Sex, and the Colonial Politics of State Nationalism*. Durham, NC: Duke University Press, 2018.

Kauanui, J. Kēhaulani. "Precarious Positions: Native Hawaiians and US Federal Recognition." *Contemporary Pacific* 17, no. 1 (2005): 1–27.

Kauanui, J. Kēhaulani. "Resisting the Akaka Bill." In *A Nation Rising: Hawaiian Movements for Life, Land, and Sovereignty*, edited by Noelani Goodyear-Kaʻōpua, Ikaika Hussey, and Erin Kahunawaikaʻala Wright, 312–30. Durham, NC: Duke University Press, 2014.

Kosasa, Karen K. "Pedagogical Sights/Sites: Producing Colonialism and Practicing Art in the Pacific." *Art Journal* 57, no. 3 (1998): 46–54.

Kubota, Gary T., ed. *Hawaii Stories of Change: Kokua Hawaii Oral History Project*. Honolulu: Hawaiʻi Council for the Humanities, 2018.

Lopez-Reyes, Ramon. "The Re-inscription of Hawaii on the United Nations' List of Non-Self-Governing Territories." *Peace Research* 28, no. 3 (1996): 71–96.

Manuel, George, and Michael Posluns. *The Fourth World: An Indian Reality*. Minneapolis: University of Minnesota Press, 2019.

McDougall, Brandy Nālani. *Finding Meaning: Kaona and Contemporary Hawaiian Literature*. Tucson: University of Arizona Press, 2016.

McGregor, Davianna Pōmaikaʻi. "Statehood: Catalyst of the Twentieth-Century Kanaka ʻŌiwi Cultural Renaissance and Sovereignty Movement." *Journal of Asian American Studies* 13, no. 3 (2010): 311–26.

McGregor, Davianna Pōmaikaʻi, and Ibrahim Aoudé. "'Our History, Our Way!' Ethnic Studies for Hawaiʻi's People." In *A Nation Rising: Hawaiian Movements for Life, Land, and Sovereignty*, edited by Noelani Goodyear-Kaʻōpua, Ikaika Hussey, and Erin Kahunawaikaʻala Wright, 66–77. Durham, NC: Duke University Press, 2014.

McGregor-Alegado, Davianna. "Hawaiians: Organizing in the 1970s." *Amerasia Journal* 7, no. 2 (1980): 29–55.

Milner, Neal. "Home, Homelessness, and Homeland in the Kalama Valley: Re-imagining a Hawaiian Nation through a Property Dispute." *Hawaiian Journal of History* 40 (2006): 149–76.

Najita, Susan Y. *Decolonizing Cultures in the Pacific: Reading History and Trauma in Contemporary Fiction*. New York: Routledge, 2006.

Niheu, Soli. "Huli: Community Struggles and Ethnic Studies." *Social Process in Hawaiʻi* 39 (1999): 43–59.

Nordyke, Eleanor C., and Martha H. Noyes. "'Kaulana Nā Pua': A Voice for Sovereignty." *Hawaiian Journal of History* 27 (1993): 27–42.

Okuda, Leiʻala, Alicia Nani Reyes, Ethan Chang, Gwen Kim, and Raymond Catania. "'You Gotta Be Responsible': How Kokua Hawaii Fostered Kuleana for the Land and People of Hawaiʻi." *Review of Education, Pedagogy, and Cultural Studies* 45, no. 4 (2023): 337–58.

Osorio, Jamaica Heolimeleikalani. *Remembering Our Intimacies: Moʻolelo, Aloha ʻĀina, and Ea*. Minneapolis: University of Minnesota Press, 2021.

Pukui, Mary Kawena, and Samuel H. Elbert. *Hawaiian Dictionary*. Honolulu: University of Hawaiʻi Press, 1986.

Red Nation. *The Red Deal: Indigenous Action to Save Our Earth*. Brooklyn: Common Notions, 2021.

Rodney, Walter. "Marxism as Third World Ideology." In *Decolonial Marxism: Essays from the Pan-African Revolution*, edited by Asha Rodney, Patricia Rodney, Ben Mabie, and Jesse Benjamin, 52–73. New York: Verso, 2022.

Salaita, Steven. *Inter/Nationalism: Decolonizing Native America and Palestine*. Minneapolis: University of Minnesota Press, 2016.

Saranillio, Dean Itsuji. "Haunani-Kay Trask and Settler Colonial and Relational Critique: Alternatives to Binary Analyses of Power." *Verge: Studies in Global Asias* 4, no. 2 (2018): 36–44.

Saranillio, Dean Itsuji. *Unsustainable Empire: Alternative Histories of Hawaiʻi Statehood*. Durham, NC: Duke University Press, 2018.

Saranillio, Dean Itsuji. "Why Asian Settler Colonialism Matters: A Thought Piece on Critiques, Debates, and Indigenous Difference." *Settler Colonial Studies* 3, nos. 3–4 (2013): 280–94.

Sayegh, Fayez A. *Zionist Colonialism in Palestine*. Beirut: Palestine Liberation Organization, Palestine Research Center, 1965.

Sharma, Nandita. "Book Reviews." Review of *Asian Settler Colonialism: From Local Governance to the Habits of Everyday Life in Hawaiʻi*, edited by Candace Fujikane and Jonathan Y. Okamura. *Hawaiian Journal of History* 44 (2010): 107–10.

Silva, Noenoe K. *Aloha Betrayed: Native Hawaiian Resistance to American Colonialism*. Durham, NC: Duke University Press, 2004.

Stillman, Amy Kuʻuleialoha. "'Aloha Aina': New Perspectives on 'Kaulana Nā Pua.'" *Hawaiian Journal of History* 33 (1999): 83–99.

Tengan, Ty P. Kāwika. "Hoa: On Being and Binding Relations." *Amerasia Journal* 46, no. 3 (2020): 280–83.

Trask, Haunani-Kay. "The Birth of the Modern Hawaiian Movement: Kalama Valley, Oʻahu." *Hawaiian Journal of History* 21 (1987): 126–53.

Trask, Haunani-Kay. "Coalition-Building between Natives and Non-Natives." *Stanford Law Review* 43, no. 6 (1991): 1197–1213.

Trask, Haunani-Kay. "*Hoʻokupu a Ka Lāhui Hawaiʻi*: The Master Plan 1995." In *From a Native Daughter: Colonialism and Sovereignty in Hawaiʻi*, 2nd ed., 211–36. Honolulu: University of Hawaiʻi Press, 1999.

Trask, Haunani-Kay. "Politics in the Pacific Islands: Imperialism and Native Self-Determination." In *From a Native Daughter: Colonialism and Sovereignty in Hawaiʻi*, 2nd ed., 41–55. Honolulu: University of Hawaiʻi Press, 1999.

Trask, Haunani-Kay. "Settlers of Color and 'Immigrant' Hegemony: 'Locals' in Hawaiʻi." *Amerasia Journal* 26, no. 2 (2000): 1–24.

Trask, Haunani-Kay, and Ed Greevy. *Kūʻē: Thirty Years of Land Struggle in Hawaiʻi*. Honolulu: Mutual Publishing, 2004.

Trask, Mililani B. "Hawaiʻi and the United Nations." In Fujikane and Okamura, *Asian Settler Colonialism*, 67–70.

Westlake, Wayne Kaumualii. *Westlake: Poems by Wayne Kaumualii Westlake (1947–1984)*, edited by Mei-Li M. Siy and Richard Hamasaki. Honolulu: University of Hawaiʻi Press, 2009.

Clandestine Issues

Tracing US Imperialism across Ethiopian Revolutionary Papers

Amsale Alemu

Anti-imperial politics were fraught in 1960s Ethiopia. Governed by an emperor, world-famous for having never been colonized by a European power, yet quickly emerging as a client state of the United States, Ethiopia presented interlocking, at times conflicting imperialisms. Yet anti-imperialism was a pillar of revolutionary Ethiopian rhetoric, signifying issues ranging from Emperor Haile Selassie's rule, Ethiopian territorial claims to Eritrea, and the question of nationalities to "world imperialism."[1] Take one photograph from a spice-processing workers strike in Addis Ababa featured in a demonstration poster by Ethiopian activists in Amsterdam in 1978 (fig. 1). Workers held a sign declaring, "Let imperialism, feudalism, and bureaucratic capitalism be destroyed" (impériyālizm fawdālizmna birokrātik kāpitālizm yewdamu አ.ምፔሪያሊዝም ፈውዳሊዝምና ቢሮክራቲክ ካፒታሊዝም ይውደሙ).[2] *Imperialism* here was directly transcribed as *'impériyālizm*, where other terms, like *qeñ gezāt* ቅኝ ግዛት (lit. colonialism), might have worked.[3] Through transliteration, *'impériyālizm* signified its quality of being both mediated and from elsewhere, marked by its material and cognitive externality. This article will present a genealogy of anti-*'impériyālizm*, one of many forms of Ethiopian anti-imperialism, across a selection of Ethiopian revolutionary papers in the 1960s and 1970s. It pursues a particular but significant Ethiopian anti-imperial argument: US imperialism in Ethiopia.

Radical History Review

Issue 150 (October 2024)   DOI 10.1215/01636545-11257447

© 2024 by MARHO: The Radical Historians' Organization, Inc.

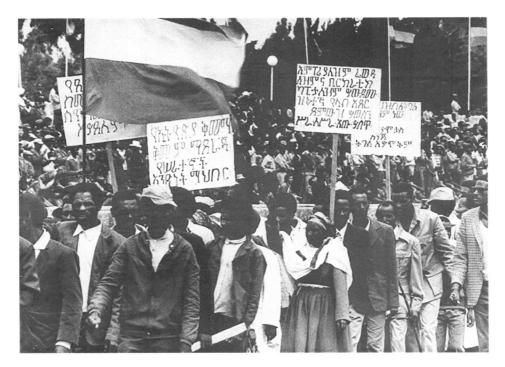

Figure 1. Detail of "Ethiopië Manifestatie," demonstration poster (1978), International Institute of Social History.

By tracing significations of US imperialism in Ethiopia, this article constructs a genealogy of a document that was a crucial text of Ethiopian revolutionary thought but no longer exists: a paper from the late 1960s that was transcribed by hand in Addis Ababa, bearing the title, "US Imperialism in Ethiopia." We know it once existed from oral history. Speaking at a conference of former student activists convened by Bahru Zewde in 2005, Hailu Ayele remembered being arrested in 1968 and asked to write the word *imperialism* on a piece of paper.[4] The colonels investigating him were attempting to match Hailu's handwriting to a document that had been circulating among radical students in Addis Ababa. Hailu was eventually acquitted, but the investigation signaled the potency of a single word: "The moment he had uttered the word 'Imperialism' I had gotten the message, for I knew what he was getting at," that the use of the term would mark the document as political contraband.[5] It remains uncertain precisely what Hailu was accused of transcribing, and the original paper has since been destroyed, but the censorship that "US Imperialism in Ethiopia" attracted evidences the radical status of its argumentation. Its use of *imperialism* could be said to have been a counterpolitical vocabulary, an anticolonial concept trialed over many revolutionary papers that attempted to establish Ethiopia's need for anticolonial transformation. Being destroyed, we do not know the contours of the document's argumentation, evidence, and circulation, but we can still trace the instances of its formulation of imperialism in Ethiopian revolutionary papers.[6]

This article has assembled papers that trialed novel analyses of growing US imperialism in Ethiopia, presenting a possible genealogy of the destroyed document Hailu Ayele was accused of transcribing. Doing so will animate a pillar of Ethiopian revolutionary argumentation that prefigures the movement's turn to Marxist-Leninism and gives nuance to Ethiopia's status as a regional imperial power. Naming imperialism, let alone anti-imperialism, was a complex task in mid-century Ethiopia, itself an empire that negotiated client relationships among nation-states navigating their own neoimperial ambitions after World War II. Was an Ethiopian empire-state exclusively symbolic of the strength of Black African sovereignty, as popularly imagined? Or, as Dessalegn Rahmato suggested in a 1967 review of Kwame Nkrumah's *Neo-colonialism: The Last Stage of Imperialism*, could its ruling class also be the "umbilical cord which feeds and sustains neo-colonialism"?[7]

Reading Revolutionary Papers as Media

After discussing the stakes of tracing "US Imperialism in Ethiopia" toward an Ethiopian anti-imperial politics and introducing the materials, this article will examine four moments in the progression of naming US imperialism across a selection of Ethiopian revolutionary papers in the 1960s and 1970s. To assemble these documents, I read revolutionary papers as media networks in two senses. The first acknowledges the transnational dispersion of revolutionary publications in the 1960s and 1970s as a product of the very imperial entanglements their authors sought to repudiate. What use, I ask, did such a network—its circulation within but also attenuating distance from Addis Ababa—afford these periodicals? With an interest in a genealogy that predates the proliferation of popular papers in the postrevolutionary era,[8] I argue that reading these earlier journals as media networks was complicated; their locations were inscribed by empire yet offered new evidence, proximity to both US and Ethiopian government records, and means to circulate iterated concepts. Periodicals distributed in North America and Europe also faced relatively less censorship, a fact that still recognizes the surveillance apparatuses employed against activists abroad or the agility of underground communications in Addis.

The second use of reading revolutionary papers as media networks is to hold attention to the myriad forms of revolutionary papers, including serial journals, stand-alone pamphlets, ephemeral treatises, and recycled materials. It would mean regarding the format of less discussed periodicals like the *Patriot* of the Ethiopian People's Movement Council (*ya'ityopya hezbāwi neqnaqé mameriyā* የኢትዮጵያ ሕዝባዊ ንቅናቄ መምሪያ) as a canvas for trialing revolutionary arguments in the form of curation and assemblage. To think with Ethiopian revolutionary papers as networked is to hold this expansive terrain of writing, reprinting, and furtive reproduction as not only instrumental to the final product of Ethiopian revolutionary writing but as itself a revolutionary praxis, one particularly adapted to the analytical problem of drawing evidence around US imperialism in Ethiopia.

This method takes inspiration from Cajetan Iheka's formulation in *African Ecomedia*.[9] Building a cohort of materials that enter African studies into both environmental and media studies, Iheka examines his archive with attention to ecomedia's representational, destructive, and critical possibilities. If media infrastructures work by "invisibilities and forgetting" of their materiality, ecomedia can, but does not always, wage critique by holding its production and reproducibility as an object of study.[10] My reading of Ethiopian revolutionary papers draws from the study of African ecomedia in recognition that the archive's contours are shaped along the very lines of the neoimperialism its authors struggled to name and repudiate. Waging critique and leveraging the primary materials (e.g., government reports, academic texts, newspaper clippings) available from Euro-America, they assembled what Adalaine Holton has called *counterarchives*, a term used to describe Arthur Schomburg's collecting and curatorial practice of Afro-diasporic history and culture.[11] That said, the assembled, clandestine issue was not only a site for archival recovery and political clarification. The very networks that facilitated generative debate were also channels for misinformation. The "transnational," in this sense, was a stage for not only connection and articulation but indeterminacy, ambivalence, and fission.

This effort endeavors to contribute to critical histories of Ethiopian revolutionary thought and practice while recognizing the seminal work of Bahru Zewde and Randi Balsvik—scholarship that remains all the more significant as we celebrate the revolution's fiftieth anniversary in September 2024.[12] Continued work is required of us to think within the problem spaces of Ethiopian revolutionary thought so we are not enjoined to exclusively condone or exalt its founding thinkers, as well as to widen the scope of pre-1974 revolutionary thought to include not only students but other organizational actors. It means to think with both historical contingency and archival inheritance so we may trace the shifting debates that motivated the movement's turn to leftism, which have elsewhere been attributed to cultural dislocations, Eurocentric assimilation, and leftist sabotage.[13] It is to think with the historian and former activist Tesfaye Demmellash in a line of questioning that remains to be seriously taken up: How did Ethiopian transnational organizations both theorize revolutionary transformation and make political space where they were?[14] What evidentiary use could there have been for these papers being so widely dispersed, and what were the pitfalls and spaces for sabotage made possible by the geographical vastness of this media network?

"Trojan Horse of American Imperialism": Ethiopia and US Clientelism at Mid-century

Following the Italian occupation, after Haile Selassie was returned to the throne in 1941, he was confronted with two diplomatic priorities. The first was to neutralize Britain, which had begun insinuating itself into Ethiopia's administration after assisting in the removal of the Italian occupying forces.[15] The second was to enact his vision of modernization, which would entail capital, goodwill, and technical assistance. The solution to both, Haile Selassie strategized, was to recruit widely from many foreign powers; soon, however, US economic and military advisors replaced British advisors, US loans replaced British subsidies, and the dollar replaced the pound as the backing of Ethiopia's national currency.[16] Haile Selassie calculated that the United States was a relatively benign superpower that, technically, had no African colonizing legacy.[17] In 1945 Ethiopia signed a contract granting Sinclair Oil fifty years of exclusive oil development rights in the country. In 1953 Ethiopia and the United States signed the Mutual Defense Assistance Agreement, pledging military arms, training, and capital as well as American personnel who would administer the agreement from Addis Ababa. Last, a former Italian colonial radio station in Asmara, Eritrea, was leased to the United States by Ethiopia on a twenty-five-year contract in 1953. The station was called Kagnew Station after the cohort of Ethiopian soldiers sent by Haile Selassie to fight for the US in the Korean War. Located on the point closest to the equator and Red Sea for its elevation in the world, the station had unsurpassed access to intercepting and relaying radio transmissions, making it a benchmark in US Cold War intelligence programs for nearly three decades. The United States had vested economic, military, and diplomatic interests in protecting Haile Selassie, who set "the price of good relations" of maintaining a strategic client state: by the late 1960s over 60 percent of US military aid to Africa.[18]

By September 1974 Haile Selassie would be escorted out of his palace grounds by what would become a socialist military regime, commonly referred to as the Derg. This ouster of the oldest Christian emperor in the world would mark the Ethiopian Revolution. Before 1974 other attempts had been made to overthrow the emperor. The closest to succeed among them was in 1960, a coup attempt planned by two brothers, Germame and Mengistu Neway. It is rather ironic, if unsurprising, that the United States intervened to silence this coup and that later revolutionaries would claim political descendance from the Neway brothers. An avowed reformist, Germame Neway had studied at Wisconsin and Columbia, writing a master's thesis on settler colonialism in Kenya with an appreciative invocation of the Federalist Papers. In Germame's words, "the subsequent achievement of Americans in establishing a free government and in building up a prosperous nation has fired the hearts of those still under colonial rule."[19] While the 1960 coup can be seen as a first attempt at political transformation that the sixties generation would call revolution, its aspirations were reformist and its thought leader pro-American. The revolutionaries of the ensuing decade would eventually mobilize a much more radical revolutionary politics, one that would require an anticolonial argument about the entanglement of Ethiopian monarchical power with US imperialism. In less than ten years Ethiopian political dissidence shifted from associating the United States with "free government" and a "prosperous nation," to burning President Lyndon Johnson in effigy and declaring the abolition of "Yankee imperialism."[20] Theorizing Ethiopian imperialism in two senses—as the Ethiopian imperial state and the entanglements of US clientelism—was crucial for an Ethiopian revolutionary program.[21]

Meanwhile, mounting liberation movements for Eritrean independence alleged that Eritrea was a colonial holding of Ethiopia. In 1950 the United Nations had voted to federate Eritrea to Ethiopia, to go into effect after two years of transitional British administration.[22] Over the next ten years Haile Selassie exerted increased territorial and political power, which would incite resistance movements for Eritrean liberation.[23] In 1962, after conflicts initiated by these early critics of Ethiopian federal rule, Ethiopia staged a vote among Eritrean representatives, who unanimously agreed to Ethiopia's annexation of Eritrea.[24] Annexation occasioned harsher reprisals against dissidents (described by Haile Selassie as "traitors, alien puppets and hypocrites"), who had begun to organize the beginning of what would be a decades-long struggle for independence.[25]

A more in-depth discussion of Eritrean revolutionary politics is beyond the scope of this article, though I will discuss an image created and distributed by an Eritrean activist organization in the United States as an effective illustration of US imperialism in Ethiopia. Literally projecting Haile Selassie as the shadow of Richard Nixon onto Eritrea, the cartoon demonstrated the ways Ethiopian *'impériyālizm* could elucidate nested, interimperial militarization in the region. After all, one year after Eritrea was federated to Ethiopia, the US signed the twenty-five-year lease on Kagnew Station in Asmara with Haile Selassie. At the same time, fissions among solidarity movements debated the prioritization of national independence for Eritrea, the revolutionary class question, or the still-contentious Ethiopian question of nationalities.[26]

Critical work on Ethiopian political thought has sought to think prior to the 1974 revolution's ideological consolidation and to sit with the revolution's contingent questions instead of diagnosing its successes and failures. This is work taken up in Elleni Zeleke's examination of the status of the social sciences among key debates of the 1960s student movement, Elizabeth Wolde Giorgis's history of artistic and political modernism in twentieth-century Ethiopia, and Netsanet Gebremichael's ongoing work on the status of the women's question in Ethiopian revolutionary writing.[27] Semeneh Ayalew Asfaw recently made an exciting contribution to *Revolutionary Papers*, examining *Revolutionary Forum* (*'abyotāwi madrak*

አብዮታዊ መድረክ), an opinion column in *Addis Zemen*, as a space for debating the path of indigenized versus "scientific" or antirevisionist socialism in postrevolutionary Ethiopia.[28] Acknowledging his call for us to think with Ethiopian revolutionary thought beyond the student movement, I read both student unions and other Ethiopian revolutionary organizations, like the Ethiopian People's Movement Council. Well before 1974, and even before the revolution would avow Marxist-Leninism, Ethiopian revolutionary thought required an anticolonial argument, precisely to make the case for the world-historical problematic of what they alleged was Ethiopian feudo-capitalism.[29] The problem-space of this anticolonial argument, I argue, was a product of neoimperialism, one that required iterative investigations published across multiple serial journals.

Media Networks Traversing Neo-empire

Ethiopian revolutionary papers of the 1960s circulated along pathways structured by the very relationships its editorials alleged were neo-imperial. Smuggled across university campuses, printed and distributed both in Addis Ababa and in metropoles across North America and Europe, and reprinted in outlets including Liberation News Service and *Tricontinental*, some of the most decisive papers of this revolutionary intellectual space were as much enabled by as they were cautious of Ethiopia's growing reliance on US foreign aid.[30] This article assembles and reads journals, stand-alone pamphlets, and reprinted issues created and distributed among organizations based in Addis Ababa, North America, and Europe. The papers are housed in several archives, including Addis Ababa University, the International Institute of Social History, and dozens of university library and special collections in the United States. They have also been personally compiled and republished by former participants, memoirists, and historians such as Ayalew Yimam.[31]

The selected materials were produced and distributed by the Ethiopian Student Union in North America (ESUNA), Ethiopian Students Union in Europe (ESUE), Ethiopian People's Movement Council (EPMC), and Eritreans for Liberation in North America (EFLNA). ESUNA and ESUE were student unions that rose to prominence in the 1960s with growing populations of university students abroad. Major chapters of ESUNA were based in Boston; New York; Washington, DC; Madison; and Oakland. ESUE had chapters in Berlin, Paris, Vienna, and London; this article will discuss a publication of a union in Benelux. Together, ESUNA and ESUE would boast over a thousand active members by the late 1960s.[32]

This article also centers the writing of an organization that is often overlooked in genealogies of Ethiopian revolutionary thought because it was not a student organization. Information about the Ethiopian People's Movement Council (EPMC) is scattered, though it was likely formed by Getachew Garedew, a participant in the 1960 coup attempt who then sought protection in Mogadishu.[33] According to Dawit Shifaw, Getachew Garedew produced Amharic-language shows for

Radio Mogadishu, which became anti-imperial media that was consumed by a grow-ing opposition population in Addis Ababa.[34] From its editorial centers of Moga-dishu, and later Amsterdam and Brussels, the EPMC operated as both a purveyor of original information and an amplifier and self-fashioned advisor of the growing student struggle, in its words, "to examine and expose the burning questions of our revolution."[35] The *Patriot* and the Amharic-language journal of the same name, *Arbegnaw* አርበኛው, had post office boxes under the names of Michel Bakafa and Theodros Dashan.[36] The EPMC also staged and sponsored direct actions in Addis Ababa, signing correspondences and producing papers that were occasion-ally reprinted in the *Patriot*. This article will cover selected EPMC publications that speak to an intellectual genealogy of "US Imperialism in Ethiopia"; I welcome readers with any additional information about the EPMC or its participants to be in touch.

Last, Eritreans for Liberation in North America (EFLNA) was formed as the ideological arm of the Eritrean People's Liberation Front (EPLF), both in the early 1970s.[37] Composed of many former members of ESUNA, the EFLNA published a monthly journal that reprinted EPLF materials and produced original editorials and multimedia, one of which will be discussed at the end of this article.

In the following sections I examine four nodes of anticolonial argument cen-tering US imperialism in Ethiopia: satirical renditions of new consumerisms afforded by "Coca Cola culture"; comparisons of US militarization in Ethiopia to Vietnam; critiques of US technical assistance as reifying a feudal monarchy; and sources compiled to reveal US imperial entanglements in Ethiopian culture and education. The materials include a piece published in an early student journal that would become *Challenge*; editorials in *Arbegnaw* and the *Patriot*, journals of the EPMC; two pamphlets produced by the EPMC, *Facts Accuse Ethiopian Autocracy* and *Political Developments in Ethiopia*; and *Imperialism in Ethiopia*, a special issue of ESUNA's *Challenge*, featuring articles that were reprinted in *Ethiopia Uncov-ered* by an Ethiopian student union in Benelux. A political cartoon created by the EFLNA will also be discussed. Holding intergenerational portrayals of US imperi-alism in tension, I argue that building the case for US imperialism in Ethiopia was a necessary step to clarify and link the Ethiopian revolutionary struggle to anticolo-nialism. I will conclude with remarks on the clandestine issue's use in uncovering US imperialism in Ethiopia, offering "the clandestine" as an analytic for reading revo-lutionary papers beyond this study.

Satirizing "Coca-Cola Culture"

In the early sixties, Ethiopian print culture made veiled critique of the markings of US consumer culture that were associated with new developments in Ethiopian for-eign relations. The "Yankee Dolla'" and "Coca-Cola culture," "hollow hearts and jazz minds"—such were wry sketches of the US consumerism that was indicative of modernization, if not yet explicitly understood as a vector of Ethiopian underdevelopment or dependency.[38] The "pocket" became a synecdoche of the assimilation of Western fashion, as in Tsegaye Gabre-Medhin's "Also of Ethiopics," published in *Présence africaine*: "with pocketed hands that refuse / To touch the earth our mothers bent to till."[39] To this early commentary on Ethiopian Americanization, we can add early revolutionary student writing. Before it was called *Challenge*, the journal of ESUNA was more innocuously titled *Journal of the Ethiopian Students in North America*. The publications of the journal were a space for intellectual introspection, reflecting on the problem of Ethiopian development with often detached cynicism.

Exemplary of satire's ability to indict, if shallowly, US consumerism was Kebebe Bellehu's "Ethiopian Bread Baker."[40] It adopted the tone of a magazine advertisement:

This household appliance is a compact, 4' high and 1½" diameter, cylinder with beautiful exterior finish. Completely automatic, guaranteed to operate silently, it assures unbelievable convenience and economy of operation. Provided with adjustable speed of baking and remote control without at the same time destroying the true taste of Ethiopian bread (*injera*) we believe this appliance is a tremendous revolution the Ethiopian housewife is requested to face.[41]

With intentionally nonsensical, jargon-riddled language, Kebebe described the working of electricity, gadgets, and gizmos that made the bread baker function through "the conventional way of changing electrical energy into mechanical energy by relays and magnifying motions by lever actions."[42] The process was designed to take "an Injera minute," involving air-conditioned storage compartments and remote-controlled operation.[43] Kebebe even included two full-page diagrams ("for those who wish to follow it")—playful if plausible renditions of what the process of making the daily staple of injera might look like if it were "revolutionized" with modern technology (fig. 2).[44] A note added at the end of the piece played on the circuitry of technical aid's claims to its own authority: "In case of questions concerning article or sketches please refer to their numbers."[45] From the perspective of the author, possibly studying mechanical or applied sciences at the time, the piece was a wry, if exasperated joke.

Another article from the same issue, "The Age of Exchange," was signed by Assefa Liban. In it, Assefa sarcastically lamented the influx of "yeoman farmers" into the capital in search of economic opportunity. Since these new arrivals to the capital had nearly "ruined" several city-dwelling families, Assefa offered a surprising remedy to those trying to stave off distant relatives seeking material support: "Anyhow, whether you believe me or not, the remedy is Melotti or St. George Beer!"[46] The "country guests" who had come seeking hospitality, expecting quality *talla*, or homemade beer, would be stunned by the new factory-manufactured beers. Assefa

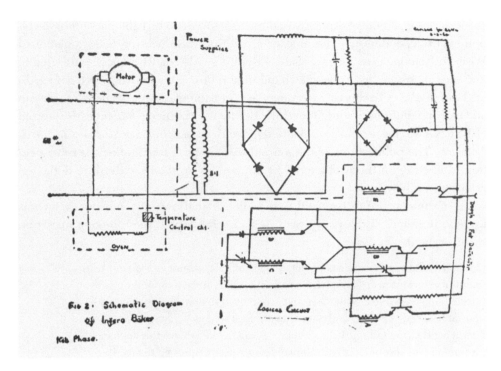

Figure 2. Kebebe Bellehu, "Fig. 2. Schematic Diagram of Injera Baker," from "Ethiopian Bread-Baker," August 1960.

described their reaction in detail: "They will frown, shrug their shoulders, close their eyes, and finally say with amazement: 'Did you give us medicine or what!'"[47] Coyly, Assefa wondered, "I am not informed yet how these discriminating, stout, and exacting peasants reacted to the latest citizen of Ethiopia, Coca-Cola!"[48] Despite its short form and comedic stylings, "The Age of Exchange" was dense with commentary. It expressed dissatisfaction with peasant dispossession, ambivalence about economic opportunities in the city, cynicism about spontaneous visits from needy relatives, and skepticism about "the latest citizen of Ethiopia," US-manufactured imports and factory franchises.

"Ethiopian Bread Baker" and "The Age of Exchange" were flippant and seemingly unbothered but rooted in a deeper critique of modernization's self-justifications, a witty rebuke to futurist promises of consumerism supposedly afforded by importing US manufactured goods. They were in this sense ambivalent; neither rejecting nor desiring American consumer culture, they thrived in ironic detachment. These pieces marked early forays in naming growing US influence in Ethiopian modernization at mid-century. Their witty, if disinterested tone would soon be overwhelmed by more unambiguous positions decrying Americanization as imperialism.

"Another Vietnam"

Revolutionary papers began to frame Ethiopian-US affairs as a figuration of neocolonial clientelism, noting the insinuation of US capital, goods, and manufacture in Ethiopia. They used comparative analogies as analytical attempts to extend and evidence this new line of argument. Vietnam became a site for projecting Ethiopian and Eritrean revolutionary aspirations. While they were far from alone in invoking Vietnam as a limit case of US military interventionism, Ethiopian revolutionaries made the case that Ethiopia, like Vietnam, was uniquely situated to highlight the entanglements of capital, arms, and technical assistance that characterized US neo-imperialism.

The Ethiopian People's Movement Council (EPMC) used its platforms to source widely, omnivorously excerpting and reprinting materials from international news outlets, original editorials, student congresses, travel accounts, and personal dispatches. In a piece published in the tenth issue of *Arbegnaw*, the editors summarized an article from a newspaper of the Democratic Republic of Vietnam, in a piece they titled, "Vietnam, Yankee Grave" (*Viyatnām—yānki maqāber* ቪየትናም—ያንኪ መቃብር).[49] The article presented the People's Army's confidence against "the rebellious Americans" (*āmaṣañoču āmérikānoč* አመጸኞቹ አሜሪካኖች), citing better unity of leadership, greater familiarity with mountainous landscape, determination, and superior fighting methods. The US forces, in contrast, were described as incompetent and "condemned" by the world. When invoking US imperialism, the authors used the transliterated term *'impériyālizm* እምፔሪያሊዝም.[50] Despite the heavy resources of their US opponent, the editorial lauded the People's Army's principled outlook and unbreakable spirit (*yaxawm taktaktalaña hegāwi 'alāmānā yamāybagarnā yamāysebar manfas naw* የኸውም ተከተከለኛና ሕጋዊ ዓላማና የማይበገርና የማይሰበር መንፈስ ነው።).[51] The EPMC paired "Vietnam, Yankee Grave" with an excerpt from the travelogue of the French explorer Henry de Monfreid as counterpoint. Monfreid described an interaction with Haile Selassie, who was hosting a group of foreign journalists. Bestowing gifts and titles, the emperor spoke of Ethiopia as a "model country where all was only virtuous." In an oblique aside, the editors, voicing Monfreid, countered, "This is the bluff that will cost the life of this ancient people" (*C'est ce bluff qui va coûter la vie à ce vieux peuple*).[52]

Another, more explicit comparison to Vietnam was published in the *Patriot*, considering whether Eritrea might be "Another Vietnam."[53] The editorial recounted "two American pilots, accompanied by their Ethiopian interpreter," who disappeared in a region under control by the Eritrean Liberation Front, waging what would be a decades-long guerrilla war for independence from Ethiopia. A few days later, a US rescue aircraft similarly "disappeared" in Agordat, south of Eritrea.[54] Despite the fact that, alleged the writer, "the Ethiopian feudal government until now refused to admit any casualties and even the existence of the Freedom Movement," the presence of US troops, operations to gather "conventional military intelligence," and foreign injured were evidence of the legitimacy and threat of the growing movement.[55] The visible traces of US military intervention built the case for imperialism in Ethiopia, and validated armed Eritrean independence as a liberation movement against Ethiopian imperialism.

Elucidating the Feudal-Imperial Problematic

By the mid-1960s, critics of US imperialism in Ethiopia argued that the "twinned problem" of Ethiopian political economy was feudal land tenure suffused with foreign capital.[56] Land ownership during Haile Selassie's reign could be inherited and bequeathed, often as a royal favor to religious leaders or allies of the court. Some estates came with the ability to exact tribute from tenant farmers, including a tax on a portion of the harvest, seasonal gifts, and personal fealty.[57] In an article that outlined the nature of the "twinned existence of feudalism and imperialism," the ESUNA activist Hagos Gabre Yesus alleged that American technicians had "overrun" the country with promises to "improve the peasant's lot by means of technical and legal measures."[58] He claimed these "mercenaries of the intellect" were brought in to codify extant systems of land tenancy with official-seeming veneers of expertise and summary reports.[59] He cited the 1960 Civil Code, which capped tenant rent at 75 percent of the crop. He argued that codifying a cap on rent so large served only to "devour the crumbs of false hope scattered by the reformers."[60] The code failed to outlaw feudal privileges, including peasants' informal obligations to pay additional tributes above rent, transport crops to market, provide domestic services, and offer gifts for religious and government holidays. Instead of reforming, US technical aid was accused of "preserving (in modern dress) the ancient slave-master relationship" of lord and tenant.[61]

The EPMC would reprint Hagos Gabre Yesus's "Land Reform" as part of a larger project of compiling primary material to indict US involvement in Haile Selassie's regime. Special publications like *Facts Accuse Ethiopian Autocracy* (1965), published in Mogadishu, used news clips, statistics, and first-hand accounts to create what was effectively a primary source packet toward redressing the "syndicated falsehood" of Ethiopia's international reputation.[62] Intended for both Ethiopian reading publics and potential allies, the pamphlet drew from radio, newspapers, case reports, and speeches providing details about Kagnew Station, hypocrisies in the Organization of African Unity, Ethiopia's potential ties to Patrice Lumumba's assassination, Zionism and Portuguese colonialism, and imperial caches of money in Swiss banks.[63] It implicated the Peace Corps, Ethiopian Air Lines as a Trans World Air subsidiary, and NATO bases in Ethiopia, with minimal editorial explication.

A little over a year later, the EPMC would issue *Political Developments in Ethiopia*, which drew on the research consolidated in *Facts Accuse Ethiopian Autocracy* with new materials to examine the relationship between imperialism in Ethiopia and the monarchy. The typewritten pamphlet featured one essay, "The Crisis of

Ethiopian Feudalism."[64] In no uncertain terms it accused the Ethiopian government of being a "Trojan Horse of American Imperialism."[65] It suggested that Haile Selassie, host of the Organization of African Unity, assumed "the role of the Emperor in Pan African Affairs" to facilitate US counterinsurgency operations: "coups d'état, political murders, and other criminal conspiracy against the African Peoples," here likely referencing the recent US-abetted deposing of Kwame Nkrumah.[66] The writers demanded the abolition of Kagnew Station and argued that US imperialism was especially insidious in Ethiopia, given its protected status within the monarchy: "The direct political influence, military and economy controls on our country by the US Imperialism is a luxury that we cannot afford."[67] The pamphlet reported on recent direct actions aimed at the infrastructures of neo-empire, including the bombing of a Mobil Oil reservoir in Massawa port, a city in present-day Eritrea; hijackings of Ethiopian Airlines planes; and a writers' strike of the government publishing house Berhanena Selam (Light and Peace).[68] These actions, the essay argued, were the necessary and inevitable conflicts that would continue to occur at the infrastructural points where US capital articulated with Ethiopian land and economy.[69]

Imperialism in Ethiopia

The arguments advanced by *Facts Accuse Ethiopian Autocracy* and *Political Developments in Ethiopia* were also being rehearsed and researched by revolutionary students in the United States. They leveraged their time, proximity to documentary evidence, and relative freedom of publication to issue a special issue of their journal, *Challenge*, which would be reproduced widely. The Ethiopian Student Union of North America (ESUNA) issued *Imperialism in Ethiopia*, including short essays describing the history of imperial influence in Ethiopia by European powers and the United States.[70] Most of its space was dedicated to "Imperialism in Ethiopia Today," focusing on US imperialism in three sectors: economy; education and culture; and military and politics. The essays were assembled to serve a "step of immediate urgency" to educate "a number of people within the student movement who do not see a clear-cut antagonism between our movement and imperialism."[71] Cautioning against those students who believed they could "hood-wink imperialism into a position of neutralism while we carry on the struggle against the feudal dictatorship," ESUNA insisted "that a revolutionary transformation of Ethiopia can only be attained on an anti-imperialist platform."[72]

What was novel about *Imperialism in Ethiopia* was its marshalling of evidence. It employed materials available to academic and policy circles in the United States. The authors paraphrased and condensed sections of a US Senate Report, "US Foreign Operations in Africa," to compile a list of United States Information Services activities in Ethiopia, including scholarship programs, personnel, radio and film distribution, and motion picture production. *US News and World Report* and State

Department reports evidenced military and defense agreements between Ethiopia and the United States. Ethiopian Ministry of Information and Education documents were made accessible in the United States because of increased US research interests in African politics in the early Cold War; the authors consulted these and complete serial copies of the *Ethiopian Herald* to voice Ethiopian government policy and foreign policy interests. For instance, citing a Ministry of Education census report, the students reported that the majority of high school teachers in 1963–64 (655 out of 1,055) were foreign, and over half of those were Peace Corps volunteers.[73] By 1971, as cited from a *US News and World Report*, "ninety-five per cent of the high school teachers [in Ethiopia] are brought in from abroad."[74] "US Imperialism in Ethiopia" was a revolutionary paper that was as much a product of its proximity to the neo-imperial metropole as it was a clarification of revolutionary arguments about the perniciousness of US imperialism.

A few months later, the Ethiopian Students in Benelux union chapter had published a pamphlet, *Ethiopia Uncovered*, which featured a reprint of ESUNA's "Imperialism in Ethiopia Today."[75] From the document's formatting, the original essay was likely either hand-copied or reproduced from a draft manuscript. While the first section, "Economic Aspects," was largely expanded, with many sections rewritten for clarity, the second and third sections, "Military and Political Aspects" and "Educational and Cultural Aspects," were left largely unchanged.[76] Several new appendices reproduced the Mutual Defense Assistance Agreement between the United States and Ethiopia, including correspondence on aid allotments, training, and facilities.[77] Most significantly, *Ethiopia Uncovered* placed "Imperialism in Ethiopia Today" among other editorials and eyewitness reports: a piece signed by Fanno Tessemara, "Some Highlights on the Eritrean Political Mystery"; an ESUE statement of solidarity with South Africa; and a tribute and extended report on the death of the former president of the University Students Union Addis Ababa, Tilahun Gizaw, who had been assassinated by police forces earlier that year.[78]

This new framing of the ESUNA article more explicitly tied the question of US imperialism in Ethiopia to the colonial question of Eritrea. Some of these arguments were being trialed as early as the late 1950s and early 1960s by the EPMC and would be more forcefully taken up by the early 1970s. For instance, a striking political cartoon would be printed by Eritreans for Liberation in North America (EFLNA) on the back cover of *Harnet* (*Liberation*), its monthly English- and Tigrinya-language journal (fig. 3). The occasion was Haile Selassie's final state visit to the United States in his lifetime, as the guest of Richard Nixon.[79] The cartoon depicted Nixon in a suit of armor, holding a sword and helmet. His shadow, cast onto a map of Eritrea on the wall behind him, takes the shape of Haile Selassie, as both figures look askance at the viewer. The cartoon concisely illustrated a framework of Eritrean coloniality that the EFLNA would advocate—that Ethiopian imperialism was the immediate object of Eritrean struggle, but that it was in essence

Figure 3. Detail of cartoon depicting Haile Selassie as the shadow of Richard Nixon in front of a map of Eritrea. EFLNA, *Liberation* (June–July 1973), back cover.

the projection of a US military apparatus. The suit of armor no doubt also played on the idea of Haile Selassie's medievalism and the "feudal state," tropes used to caricature the emperor and Ethiopia.[80] Addis Ababa students had burned Lyndon Johnson in effigy a few years prior; US-based students iterated a version of this politics in the form of political caricature.[81]

The sign of US empire would not abate, even with Haile Selassie's overthrow. Indeed, the early Derg was targeted by revolutionary critics for receiving US funding for the first few years of the postrevolutionary era, before Mengistu Hailemariam received military aid from the USSR, a move that critics alleged was merely a new client relationship. Meanwhile, newly-publishing organizations of Oromo student unions in North America and Europe, like Tokkuma Bartota Oromo Holland, declared their movement to "not only shake the basis of imperialist-Zionist dominated colonial empire but also crystalize and ignite its structural, class and national contradiction in the colonial empire state of Ethiopia."[82] I offer that a term like "imperialist-Zionist dominated colonial empire" was available to authors posing a postrevolutionary critical history of Ethiopian imperial domination of Oromia because it was now legible in Ethiopian revolutionary print culture, because of the elucidation of US imperialism in Ethiopia decades prior.

Clandestine Issues

If it could be recovered, the document that Hailu Ayele was accused of distributing, "US Imperialism in Ethiopia," would likely live in the archives of Addis Ababa University as "Clandestine Literature." It would join over ten thousand documents catalogued and indexed in the Institute of Ethiopian Studies, carrying the burden of their transgression, now fifty years later. In his recollection, Hailu Ayele used the term *clandestine* to describe the multisited, movable process for editing and reproducing censored texts among activist circles in Addis Ababa:

As it was a clandestine operation, the typing was done in one place by a given group, while it was run off somewhere else by another group. Probably about a month later, several copies of this mimeographed material were discovered in a house. When the paper was discovered, the person who used to reside in that house was in prison on another case.[83]

Bahru Zewde, the director of the catalog project, also uses the term *clandestine* to characterize an archive that was smuggled, containing papers that were often anonymous and illegally produced.[84] *Clandestine*, in this sense, is an index, a descriptive label, for political contraband.

Reflecting on the process of building a prehistory of "US Imperialism in Ethiopia," I would like to think with and extend this archival designation *clandestine*. Not just a descriptive term, the clandestine may present an historical analytic for revolutionary papers beyond this study. Among the papers discussed in this article, the clandestine was not only the condition of their production but also the conspiracy of alleging heretical propositions: in this case, that US imperialism was quickly suffusing Ethiopia's socioeconomy in the 1960s, and that Ethiopia's exceptional legacy of independence was perhaps a means of retrenching its status as US client. This argument emerged from seminal revolutionary periodicals, forged both in the possibility and critique of their location within Ethiopian neo-imperialism. Clandestine issues, in this light, emerge from the furtive act of evidencing, re-archiving, and distributing materials within and just beyond neo-empire's reach. To read the *use* of the clandestine has entailed that we read across and within revolutionary papers. The clandestine issue is not only an archival index but also a site for transcribing lateral exchanges among the inheritors of its history.

Inspired by a likely unrecoverable document, the censored, hand-copied edition of "US Imperialism in Ethiopia" in Addis Ababa in the late 1960s, this article has traced the concept and usage of US imperialism across Ethiopian revolutionary papers of the 1960s and 1970s. Attending to repetition, retranslation, and transformation, it has assembled materials toward a genealogy of "US Imperialism in Ethiopia" that holds Ethiopian revolutionary papers as porous, transferable sites for iterating anticolonial arguments and counterpolitical vocabularies. In the process, I suggest we hold the clandestine issue as a descriptive, archival designation as well as an analytic for the trialing of revolutionary ideas like that of an Ethiopian monarchy operating as a client state of US imperialism. Revolutionary papers become enlivened by the generative force of fugitive thought, mutable yet potent. To offer a genealogy of a text that may no longer exist is to dwell in both the archival ambiguity and deep, contingent, and branching debates of Ethiopian revolutionary thought, now fifty years later.

Amsale Alemu is assistant professor of African Studies at Howard University. She holds a PhD in African and African American studies from Harvard University. Her current book project examines university surveillance and US geopolitics in the Horn of Africa, with attention to relationships among Ethiopian and Eritrean revolutionary activists and anticolonial collaborators in the 1960s and 1970s.

Notes

1. "World imperialism has erected an intricate structure of dependency on the Ethiopian peoples. We consider it the principal task of the Ethiopian peoples to break out of the financial, military, cultural and political ring of imperialism in unity with the rest of oppressed humanity" (ESUNA, 1965). Institute of Ethiopian Studies (IES).
2. "Ethiopië Manifestatie," demonstration poster (1978), International Institute of Social History (IISH). When quoting Amharic text, this article will use transliteration tables approved by the American Library Association and Library of Congress: https://www.loc.gov/catdir/cpso/romanization/amharic.pdf.
3. *Qeñ gezāt* ቅኝ ግዛት is used and defined as the colonial subjugation of one territorial power over another. For instance, in the following title, it is used in the context of the 1896 Battle of Adwa and Ethiopia's famous resistance to Italian colonization: ኤርሚ ያስ ጉልላት, የዓድዋ ጦርነት እና የዓለም ቅኝ ገዛት አሰላለፍ (Addis Ababa: 'Adwā pān 'Afrikā ṭenātenā meremer māʿekal, 2013 E.C.).
4. Zewde, *Documenting the Ethiopian Student Movement*, 41.
5. Zewde, *Documenting the Ethiopian Student Movement*, 41.
6. I proposed this idea in a brief reflection on archival method: Alemu, "U.S. Imperialism in Ethiopia."
7. Rahmato, "Review," IES; Nkrumah, *Neo-Colonialism: The Last Stage of Imperialism*.
8. Not included in this study, for instance, are the later popular newspapers in circulation after 1974 (e.g., *Democracia* or *Ye Sefiew Hizb Dimts*).
9. Iheka, *African Ecomedia*.

10. Iheka, *African Ecomedia*, 6.

11. Holton, "Decolonizing History."

12. Bahru, *Quest*; Balsvik, *Haile Sellassie's Students*; Milkias, *Political Revolution in Ethiopia*; Lemma, "Ethiopian Student Movement"; Demmellash, "On Marxism and Ethiopian Student Radicalism."

13. Emblematic of this popular characterization is Kebede, *Radicalism and Cultural Dislocation in Ethiopia*.

14. Demmellash, "On Marxism and Ethiopian Student Radicalism."

15. As S. A. Haynes reported for the *Afro-American*, five years after Ethiopia restored its independence from Italy, Britain insinuated itself as "still a friend of the unhappy and seething Ethiopians" (July 6, 1946).

16. As Haile Selassie himself explained: "Our dollar-based currency is also there to assure the ready return to the United States of the profit of their investments" (Council on African Affairs, "In Quotation Marks," *Spotlight on Africa*, June 22, 1954).

17. W. E .B. Du Bois: "[Haile Selassie's] plan is to get the capitalistic nations against each other. It's a dangerous game, but he has so far had much success" ("Ethiopia: State Socialism under an Emperor," 170). For more on the fascinating debates among Black internationalists about the vitality of Selassie's rule after the Italian occupation, see Nurhussein, *Black Land*; and Sundiata, *Brothers and Strangers*.

18. Henry A. Kissinger, "Memorandum for the President," July 6, 1969, "Ethiopian Emperor Haile Selassie visit to US, July 7–10, 1969," Richard M. Nixon National Security Files, 1969–1974, NAACP 103974-003-0383, ProQuest.

19. Neway, "White Settlement Policy in Kenya," 3.

20. Neway, "White Settlement Policy in Kenya"; *Sun*, "Students Hang Johnson Effigy."

21. On the idea of anticolonial arguments as generative sites for political theory, see Getachew and Mantena, "Anticolonialism."

22. The decision was made alongside Italy's other former colonies, Libya and Somalia, where trusteeships were intended as a transition to independence. See Iyob, *Eritrean Struggle for Independence*; and Anderson, *Bourgeois Radicals*.

23. Iyob, *Eritrean Struggle for Independence*, 85.

24. Iyob, *Eritrean Struggle for Independence*, 89.

25. *Hartford Courant*, "Eritrea Seen Chafing under Ethiopian Rule."

26. See Simachew Belay and Simachew Belay, "FDRE Constitution"; and Labzaé, "A Past That Doesn't Rest."

27. Zeleke, *Ethiopia in Theory*; Wolde Giorgis, *Modernist Art in Ethiopia*; and for example, Netsanet Gebremichael's curated exhibition "The History of Ethiopian Women's Resistance," Gebre Kristos Desta Modern Art Museum, Addis Ababa University, May–June 2021.

28. Semeneh Ayalew Asfaw, "Abyotawi medrek/Revolutionary Forum," Revolutionary Papers, https://revolutionarypapers.org/journal/abyotawi-medrek-revolutionary-forum/.

29. As expressed in a letter by Ethiopian activists in the United States: "The analysis of Ethiopia's present geo-political position and political economy does not simply rip off the mystique of traditional Ethiopian independence, but also unmasks the real mastery of many a so-called independent state of the underdeveloped world" (ESANA Executive Council, "Letter," May 31, 1966 (New York), Institute of Ethiopian Studies (IES)/2395/03/1.9).

30. For example, Hagos Gabre Yesus's "Land Reform" and the *Challenge* special issue "Imperialism in Ethiopia," discussed later in the article. Both were reprinted across

organizational publications spanning UCAA's *News and Views*, as well as in ESUE's *Ta'teq* and EPMC's *Patriot*.

31. Yimam (Mukhtar), *Ethiopian Student Movement*.

32. See Zewde, *Quest for Socialist Utopia*.

33. Shifaw, *Diary of Terror*, xii.

34. Shifaw, *Diary of Terror*, xii.

35. *Patriot* (September 1965). In another issue, the *Patriot* announces itself as "the first and only free, REVOLUTIONARY, journal in 3,000 years of SSENDRAWKCAB!" (October–November 1965), 12, IISH.

36. EPMC journals are housed in the IISH.

37. See Mehretab Mehari, "Eritreans For Liberation in North America (EFLNA)," July 26, 2007, https://www.marxists.org/history/erol/eritrea/elna-history.pdf.

38. Ethiopian People's Movement Council (EPMC), *Patriot* 6 (December 1965), 1; EPMC, *Patriot* 4–5 (October–November 1965), 8; Gabre-Medhin, "Also of Ethiopics," 327.

39. Gabre-Medhin, "Also of Ethiopics," 328.

40. Kebebe Bellehu, "Ethiopian Bread-Baker," *Journal of the Ethiopian Students in North America* 2, no. 4 (August 1960): 13–15.

41. Bellehu, "Bread-Baker," 13.

42. Bellehu, "Bread-Baker," 13.

43. Bellehu, "Bread-Baker," 13.

44. Bellehu, "Bread-Baker," 14–15.

45. Bellehu, "Bread-Baker," 13.

46. Assefa Liban, "The Age of Exchange," *Journal of the Ethiopian Students in North America* 2, no. 4 (August 1960): 12.

47. Liban, "Age of Exchange," 12.

48. Liban, "Age of Exchange," 12.

49. EPMC, "Vietnam, Yankee Grave" (*Viyatnām—yānki maqāber* ቪየትናም—ያንኪ መቃብር), *Arbegnaw* 10 (*Hidar* 1966 E.C.), 17–18.

50. "Vietnam, Yankee Grave," 17.

51. "Vietnam, Yankee Grave," 18.

52. "Vietnam, Yankee Grave," 18.

53. EPMC, "Another Vietnam," *Patriot* 2 (August 1965), 7.

54. "Another Vietnam," 7.

55. "Another Vietnam," 7.

56. ESUNA Special Publication, January 1974, IES/2395/03/3/12.

57. For more on land tenancy in mid-century Ethiopia, see Gebeyehu, "Land Tenure, Land Reform, and the *Qalad* System"; and Ambaye, *Land Rights and Expropriation*.

58. Hagos Gabre Yesus, "Land Reform, Plus Ça Change?," *Challenge* 5, no. 1 (March 1965), 4.

59. Yesus, "Land Reform," 4.

60. Yesus, "Land Reform," 5.

61. Yesus, "Land Reform," 5.

62. EPMC, *Facts Accuse Ethiopian Autocracy*, vol. 1 (Mogadishu: Ethiopian People's Movement Council, 1965).

63. EPMC, *Facts Accuse*.

64. EPMC, *Political Developments in Ethiopia: 1966* (Amsterdam: May 1967).

65. EPMC, *Political Developments*, 2.

66. EPMC, *Political Developments*, 2.

67. EPMC, *Political Developments*, 9.
68. EPMC, *Political Developments*.
69. EPMC, *Political Developments*, 5.
70. "Imperialism in Ethiopia," *Challenge* 11, no. 1 (January 1971).
71. "Imperialism in Ethiopia."
72. "Imperialism in Ethiopia."
73. ESUNA, "Imperialism in Ethiopia Today."
74. ESUNA, "Imperialism."
75. Ethiopian Students in Benelux, *Ethiopia Uncovered* (Amsterdam: December 28–29, 1971).
76. Ethiopian Students in Benelux, *Ethiopia Uncovered*, 35–36.
77. Ethiopian Students in Benelux, *Ethiopia Uncovered*, Appendix II.
78. "Adolf Haile Sellassie [*sic*] and the Preplanned Student Massacre," in Ethiopian Students in Benelux, *Ethiopia Uncovered*.
79. EFLNA, *Liberation*, 2, no. 5 (June–July 1973): back cover.
80. EFLNA, *Liberation*, back cover.
81. *Sun*, "Students Hang Johnson Effigy."
82. Tokkuma Bartota Oromo Holland (Union of Oromo Students in Holland), "Revolutionary Call in Defense of the Oromo Revolution" (May 1979).
83. Zewde, *Documenting the Ethiopian Student Movement*, 40.
84. Addis Ababa University, *Catalogue of Clandestine Literature*, vii, ix.

References

Addis Ababa University. *A Catalogue of Clandestine Literature on Ethiopia.* Addis Ababa: Institute of Ethiopian Studies, 1995.
Alemu, Amsale. "U.S. Imperialism in Ethiopia: Biography of an Ambiguous Document." *Borderlines*, September 15, 2022. https://borderlines-cssaame.org/posts/2022/9/13/us -imperialism-in-ethiopia-biography-of-an-ambiguous-document.
Ambaye, Daniel W. *Land Rights and Expropriation in Ethiopia*. Cham: Springer International, 2015.
Anderson, Carol. *Bourgeois Radicals: The NAACP and the Struggle for Colonial Liberation, 1941–1960*. New York: Cambridge University Press, 2015.
Balsvik, Randi Rønning. *Haile Sellassie's Students: The Intellectual and Social Background to Revolution, 1952–1977*. East Lansing: Michigan State University Press, 1985.
Council on African Affairs. "In Quotation Marks." *Spotlight on Africa*. June 22, 1954.
Demmellash, Tesfaye. "On Marxism and Ethiopian Student Radicalism in North America." *Monthly Review* 35 (1984): 25–37.
Du Bois, W. E. B. "Ethiopia: State Socialism under an Emperor." In *The World and Africa: An Inquiry into the Part Which Africa Has Played in World History*, rev. ed., 170–71. New York: International Publishers, 1965.
Gabre-Medhin, Tsegaye. "Also of Ethiopics." *Présence africaine*, n.s., no. 57 (1966): 327–29.
Gebeyehu, Temesgen. "Land Tenure, Land Reform, and the *Qalad* System in Ethiopia, 1941–1974." *Journal of Asian and African Studies* 46, no. 6 (2011): 567–77.
Getachew, Adom, and Karuna Mantena. "Anticolonialism and the Decolonization of Political Theory." *Critical Times* 4, no. 3 (2021): 359–88.
Giorgis, Elizabeth Wolde. *Modernist Art in Ethiopia*. Athens: Ohio University Press, 2019.
Hartford Courant. "Eritrea Seen Chafing under Ethiopian Rule." July 17, 1962.

Haynes, S. A. "The Battle for Freedom." *Afro-American*. July 6, 1946.

Holton, Adalaine. "Decolonizing History: Arthur Schomburg's Afrodiasporic Archive." *Journal of African American History* 92, no. 2 (2007): 218–38.

Iheka, Cajetan Nwabueze. *African Ecomedia: Network Forms, Planetary Politics*. Durham, NC: Duke University Press, 2021.

Iyob, Ruth. *The Eritrean Struggle for Independence: Domination, Resistance, Nationalism, 1941–1993*. Cambridge: Cambridge University Press, 1995.

Kebede, Messay. *Radicalism and Cultural Dislocation in Ethiopia, 1960–1974*. Rochester, NY: University of Rochester Press, 2008.

Labzaé, Mehdi. "A Past That Doesn't Rest: Domination, Violence, and the 'Question of Nationalities' in Ethiopia." *African Studies Review* 66, no. 1 (2022): 203–11.

Lemma, Legesse. "The Ethiopian Student Movement 1960–1974: A Challenge to the Monarchy and Imperialism in Ethiopia." *Northeast African Studies* 1, no. 2 (1979): 31–46.

Milkias, Paulos. *Haile Selassie, Western Education, and Political Revolution in Ethiopia*. Youngstown, NY: Cambria Press, 2006.

Neway, Germame. "The Impact of the White Settlement Policy in Kenya." Master's thesis, Columbia University, 1954.

Nkrumah, Kwame. *Neo-colonialism: The Last Stage of Imperialism*. London: Heinemann Educational, 1968.

Nurhussein, Nadia. *Black Land: Imperial Ethiopianism and African America*. Princeton, NJ: Princeton University Press, 2019.

Shifaw, Dawit. *The Diary of Terror: Ethiopia 1974 to 1991*. Bloomington, IN: Trafford Publishing, 2012.

Simachew Belay, Tessema, and Habtamu Simachew Belay. "The Procedure for the Creation of New Regional States under the FDRE Constitution: Some Overlooked Issues." *Mizan Law Review* 13, no. 1 (2019): 91–122. https://doi.org/10.4314/mlr.v13i1.4.

Sun. "Students Hang Johnson Effigy: Ethiopian Demonstration Protests Viet War." January 7, 1968.

Sundiata, Ibrahim. *Brothers and Strangers: Black Zion, Black Slavery, 1914–1940*. Durham, NC: Duke University Press, 2003.

Yimam (Mukhtar), Ayalew. *The Ethiopian Student Movement and the National Question: Theory and Practice, 1950–1980*. Takoma Park, MD: Signature Book Printing, 2013.

Zeleke, Elleni Centime. *Ethiopia in Theory: Revolution and Knowledge Production, 1964–2016*. Boston: Brill, 2019.

Zewde, Bahru. *Documenting the Ethiopian Student Movement: An Exercise in Oral History*. Addis Ababa: Forum for Social Studies (FSS), 2010.

Zewde, Bahru. *The Quest for Socialist Utopia: The Ethiopian Student Movement, c. 1960–1974*. Oxford: James Currey, 2014.

The Periodical as Political Educator

Anticolonial Print and Digital Humanities in the Classroom and Beyond

Sara Kazmi

The night of the sword and the bullet was followed by the morning of the chalk
and the blackboard. The physical violence of the battlefield was followed by the
psychological violence of the classroom.
—Ngũgĩ wa Thiong'o, *Decolonising the Mind*

Twentieth-century revolutionary print was key to organizing struggle, theorizing political subjects, and galvanizing cultures of protest in the Global South. In this essay, "revolutionary print" or "revolutionary papers" collectively refers to diverse forms like the political magazine, pamphlet, cultural journal, and party newspaper. It also encompasses the communities and practices that coalesced around these publications in contexts of anticolonial and Third World struggle. While other essays in this special issue explore how such publications operated as "political organizers" and fora for visual and aesthetic experimentation,[1] this section focuses specifically on how these periodicals constituted a Global South infrastructure for pedagogy and political education. Often embracing a multigeneric form with content ranging from reportage to illustrations, poetry, manifestos, and cultural commentary, revolutionary papers doubled as a teaching library built on historical and ongoing struggles facing colonial and authoritarian repression. As fora for public debate and "movement thought," these publications served as alternative educational

Radical History Review
Issue 150 (October 2024)   DOI 10.1215/01636545-11257460
© 2024 by MARHO: The Radical Historians' Organization, Inc.

institutions in their own right.[2] Revolutionary papers fostered communities of shared inquiry and action to combat the "psychological violence" of the colonial classroom and, indeed, of the colonial condition at large.[3]

Inspired by the pedagogical mission of revolutionary print, this section of the issue explores its relationship with pedagogy through a series of digital "teaching tools" centered on periodicals that resisted colonialism, capitalism, and authoritarianism in the Global South. The Revolutionary Papers teaching tools were conceptualized as interactive digital presentations that could be used in both classroom and organizing settings by scholars, students, and activists to engage and learn about, and with, anticolonial and left periodicals.[4] This essay offers an introduction to these teaching tools. I elaborate the impetus behind creating them and reflect on their use in the classroom through a Revolutionary Papers teaching initiative based in Lahore, Pakistan. This initiative developed an experimental undergraduate syllabus that drew on revolutionary print and digital teaching tools that study its forms and cultures. Along the way, I incorporate insights from students who participated in the course and introduce and discuss the seven teaching tools featured in this special issue, including one contributed by these students. I also discuss the potential posed by Global South revolutionary papers as an alternative curriculum and pedagogical guide for addressing contemporary calls to "decolonize" the university.

Revolutionary Papers as "Pedagogical Infrastructure"

As Katerina Gonzalez Seligmann argues, a lack of "literary infrastructure" in imperialized geographies created the push for periodicals to function as both aesthetic and material resources.[5] "Literary infrastructure" here refers to structures and resources such as "the book industry that includes publishers, editors, and mechanisms of national, regional, and international literary circulation."[6] As I discuss in this essay, Global South print also operated as a pedagogical infrastructure that created an alternative curriculum and fostered critical practices of collective reading, writing, and reflection. As an alternative curriculum, these publications created and disseminated critical knowledge about ongoing struggles, regional languages and their literatures, alternative histories, and global solidarities against the nexus of empire and dominant nationalism. As pedagogical forms, they experimented with both Freirean and vanguardist approaches in engaging their readership, feeding cultures and spaces of political community through debate. They also served as community archives.

For example, the quarterly *Pancham* (*The Fifth*) is a left-leaning Punjabi-language literary journal published in Lahore, Pakistan, that functions as both a literary and pedagogical infrastructure to counter the colonial and post-colonial marginalization of the regional language.[7] It operates as an alternative institution for Punjabi literary culture built around a program of people's language. The magazine publishes original poetry and essays and carries translations of anticolonial, Marxist, and feminist writings. *Pancham*'s office hosts study circles where the magazine's latest issue is read and discussed. Through these study circles, *Pancham* also offers a space for Punjabi language learning where none is provided by formal education, invigorating a culture of reading, writing, and speaking in a language seen as a "vulgar" "rural patois" spoken by the so-called illiterate working masses.[8] *Pancham* is an archive, a public library, and a language school that resists the confines of dominant knowledge in Pakistan. Helmed by the veteran Marxist intellectual Maqsood Saqib, *Pancham* has also provided political education to left-wing cadres across the city.

Thus the struggle for "the means of communal self-definition" against the alienation imposed by colonial/neocolonial education came to rely heavily on media like *Pancham*, that is, on the "little magazines" of the Global South.[9] The pages of these periodicals combated the "exclusionary practices of 'metropolitan publishing houses'" and state censorship.[10] For example, journals like the Afro-Asian literary magazine *Lotus* imparted "non-Eurocentric modes and models of comparatism" through Afro-Asian literary translation to its transnational readership, while magazines like the 1920s Punjabi language monthly *Kirti* (*Worker*) translated and introduced Marxist texts into colonial India.[11] Thus, print forms like political magazines were organizers, institutions, and political educators in their own right. They trained cadre and community alike by coordinating struggle, raising political consciousness, and documenting movement history. They did so by offering an alternative curriculum and accessible resources for a program of people's education.

This pedagogical impulse was a key component of anticolonialism. Revolutionary papers fostered what Daniel J. Elam calls "anticolonial readerly communities" across the Global South.[12] These communities imagined a world "in which the circulation of aesthetic ideas could be made common and egalitarian," instituting "serious engagement with reading and critique as anticolonial practice."[13] Elam's insistence on reading as a revolutionary act locates Global South print culture as a key site for anticolonial politics and theory, expanding debates on decolonization beyond national independence, sovereignty, and statehood. Further, the focus on reading—and especially, on reading *with* others as anticolonial practice—emphasizes the role of revolutionary papers as political educators. In this capacity, revolutionary papers reflected the mobilizational forms of ongoing left and anticolonial movements, innovating pedagogies ranging from vanguardist to Freirean approaches. Periodicals that operated as Freirean "educational projects" tried to forge pedagogy with and not simply for the oppressed, serving as organizational and intellectual tools for liberation.[14] Often, they embodied a form that was collectively authored, multilingual, popular, and noncanonical. For example, the *Congress Militant*, a newspaper published by the Marxist Workers' Tendency of the African National Congress, engaged its working-class readership in its production through collective writing exercises, literacy education, and oral history in an effort to generate "writing from below."[15] In an article in this issue, Noor Nieftagodien describes how the paper developed a practice to interview and assist comrades overwhelmed by daily struggles and hindered by low literary levels in writing about their experiences.[16] Revolutionary papers like the *Congress Militant* challenged what Paolo Freire described as the "fundamentally narrative character" of the "teacher-student" relationship. In the pedagogy of the oppressor, the "teacher" acts as the narrating subject, while the "student" is merely a passive, listening object.[17] Freirean pedagogy seeks to transform teachers and students into "teacher-students" and "student-teachers" that both learn from and teach one another. This approach to education as liberation can be read into the collective institutional form of many revolutionary periodicals.

Conversely, other revolutionary publications embraced a hierarchical editorial and institutional structure rooted in vanguardist approaches. Writing about the iconic Bolshevik publication *Iskra* (*Spark*), Lenin described the vanguardist role of the paper as a "collective propagandist and a collective agitator . . . [and] also a collective organizer."[18] In this capacity, periodicals served as a forum for communication between party members, coordinating and documenting struggle, and helping cadres imagine communities of political action. For example, Sam Longford's study of the journal of the militant wing, UMkhonto weSizwe of the African National Congress (ANC) and the South African Communist Party details how *Dawn* mythologized the contested figure of Chris Hani (1942–93) to inculcate discipline and obedience among MK cadres.[19] Hani, an MK leader who was assassinated by Conservative Party members, became an important symbol of the ANC's struggle for freedom, while for critics of the ANC's post-apartheid project, his figure "haunts . . . and unsettles the ANC's triumphalist narratives."[20] Yet other revolutionary papers were dictated by CIA, Soviet, or authoritarian states, or operated as vanity projects of lone left intellectuals. For example, *Tulu* (*Rise*) was a Soviet-backed Urdu-language periodical published in 1970s Pakistan whose editorial line was closely controlled by Moscow.

While an emphasis on the party line and discipline animated the vanguardist pedagogy of revolutionary publications like *Dawn* and *Tulu*, this did not detract from their collective and popular nature. For one, their circulation and reception in what Mae A. Miller-Likhethe identifies as "lesser-studied sites of print culture"[21] such as study circles, canteens, and family settings exceeded and indeed expanded the leadership's disciplinarian and propagandist visions. Further, in their afterlives such print forms came to function as movement archives that could be critically engaged by broader communities and contemporary activists. For example, in this issue, a teaching tool authored by Koni Benson, Asher Gamedze, and Nashilongweshipwe Mushaandja engages the *Namibian Review* to invigorate cross-border connections and radical political remembering in contemporary South Africa. Namibia, a former German colony then known as South West Africa, was governed by the South African apartheid state between 1915 and 1990. Through the archive of the *Namibian*

Review, a journal published in 1970s southern Africa by anti-apartheid Marxist revolutionaries, the authors construct an alternative curriculum and people's history around one of its editors, Ottilie Abrahams (1937–2018). Abrahams was a Namibian revolutionary whose political life history maps key shifts and developments in revolutionary politics in the region. Her experiences with militant underground reading groups in Cape Town, exile in Zambia and Sweden, and education camps in Tanzania in turn inspire and shape the tool authors' own pedagogical and organizing work in contemporary Cape Town and Windhoek, where renewed calls for decolonization have challenged persisting racial and class-based disparities in the post-apartheid era. Benson, Gamedze, and Mushaandja, present teaching materials like "Radical History Bingo" and an imaginative, interactive timeline of educational history as windows into the Pan-African, anticolonial, socialist, and Black consciousness movements that swept across southern Africa in the twentieth century. Through these materials, they introduce readers to key struggles and organizations including 1960s radical left study groups such as the Yu Chi Chan Club and the South African Committee for Higher Education, which countered segregated education under apartheid.

Through contemporary engagements of this kind, publications like the *Namibian Review* can serve as alternative history and pedagogical guides for educators and activists. Inviting students to learn about the political life of a revolutionary woman of color like Aunty Tilly, whose work spans the supposed pre- and post-apartheid divide, grounds education and inquiry in self-reflexive and community-led methodologies for engaging movement archives. Featured in this issue, the teaching tool on the Ukombozi Library similarly elaborates how anticolonial print cultures continue to serve as pedagogical infrastructure for contemporary political education on the Left. Activist-archivist Kimani Waweru and scholar-organizer Njoki Wamai present an annotated guide to the library and its archives, discussing the magazines, bulletins, and pamphlets published by Kenyan revolutionaries between the 1930s and 1990s. The Ukombozi Library was founded in 2017 by a cluster of political collectives including the Progressive African Library and Information Activists group and the Mau Mau Research Centre. The library houses resources on Marxism and Pan-Africanism alongside a plethora of print emanating from the Kenyan African Union Party in the 1930s and 1940s, the Kenya Land and Freedom Army (Mau Mau, active during the 1960s and 1970s), and Mwakenya, an anti-dictatorship socialist movement in 1980s Kenya. The library collaborates with local communities and political movements to author and archive a people's history of Kenya focused on anticolonial and anti-authoritarian struggle. The Ukombozi Library's practice counters colonial and dominant approaches to archiving, shunning academic notions of "objectivity" and "neutrality" to embrace a collective and creative recordkeeping practice committed to "a socialist world outlook" that can "[liberate] minds from the capitalist and imperialist stranglehold."[22] It highlights the possibilities presented by a movement archive to not just serve as a historical repository but to function as an "agent of political representation" that can transform "distant and passive memory" into an insurrectionary present.[23]

Thus, such revolutionary periodicals constituted a pedagogical infrastructure that countered dominant knowledge and fostered popular cultures of critique and intellectual engagement. They developed curricula for political education as well as social institutions and cultural practices within party formations and beyond. Inspired by these aesthetic, intellectual, and political experiments, the teaching tools featured in this issue take a multimedia and flexible form to capture the variety of the publications they study.

Learning from Anticolonialism in the Digital Age

The Revolutionary Papers teaching tools are a meditated departure from the academic essay form with an eye to a more inclusive, accessible, and creative form for showcasing insights about and archival material around anticolonial and Third World struggles. They emerged from a series of conversations between scholars, activists, and design practitioners exploring the intersection between digital humanities, archiving, and political organizing in Global South contexts. Between 2021 and 2022, the Revolutionary Papers team, comprising Mahvish Ahmad, Koni Benson, Chana Morgenstern, Ben Verghese, and myself, worked with digital humanists Lizzie Malcolm and Daniel Powers to develop a digital interface. The tool design is inspired by and attempts to echo the variety of print forms that accompanied revolutionary movements of the Global South, and draws on interdisciplinary multimedia combining audio, visual, archival, and analytical content. As a teaching aid in the classroom, the tools can be assigned as background reading, deployed as an in-class exercise in close reading or visual analysis, or used to present archival material during a lecture. In community and organizing settings, they can serve as resources for study circles and group discussions. They also function as archival engagements and platforms to house and curate movement archives. In this way, the tools can serve as a digital repository of community memory and movement history, especially in Global South contexts defined by state censorship, underfunding, and erasure.

In terms of form, revolutionary papers made aesthetic choices that rejected fetishized design. They prioritized communication and community access, with artwork and templates often sketched not by professionals, but by designers embedded within movements.[24] Taking their cue from this mode of design, the teaching tools deliberately attempt to diffuse *author-ity*. The result is a dialogic format that draws on scholarly interpretation but resists the subjugation of the archive to the interpreter's voice. Thus, while each tool is presented by a scholar or archivist, the design emphasis on periodical elements like excerpts, images, and table of contents incorporates unmediated access to archival voices. For example, Hana Morgenstern's teaching tool on a Haifa-based, Arabic-language journal offers crucial insights on

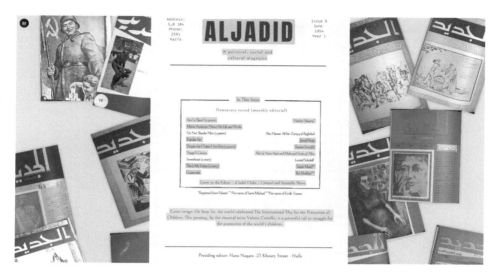

Figure 1. Hana Morgenstern's teaching tool features a translated reproduction of the table of contents of *al-Jadid* (*The New*).

left-wing Palestinian cultural activities in the aftermath of the Nakba, highlighting the role of periodicals in "literary reconstruction" in a landscape of colonial destruction and dispossession.[25] The tool is structured around Morgenstern's selection of a table of contents from a 1954 issue of *al-Jadid* (*The New*), and reproduces the table of contents in its entirety, in both English translation and as the original Arabic archival document. However, on the page, readers can only see the table of contents, with highlights that reveal Morgenstern's annotations only when clicked (fig. 1). Thus, the design privileges the revolutionary archive over academic analysis, reversing the typical form of an academic article in which archival sources are embedded to reinforce the voice and authority of the scholar. In this way, the teaching tools strive to establish a more open and dialogic relationship between scholars, archives, and students. Through their visual and accessible form, they seek to demystify archives as obscure "objects" and footnotes to academic production, inviting both students and teachers to become interpreters and interlocutors for revolutionary papers.

Following a series of conversations between 2020 and 2021, three distinct templates for the teaching tools were created. Dubbed the "linear," "close reading," and "table" models respectively, each template was designed to encourage focused exploration of and reflection on a specific aspect of the revolutionary publication under study. The linear teaching tool emphasizes historical detail, allowing tool authors to explain the context that surrounded the periodical through a range of eclectic materials including but not limited to excerpts, covers, photographs, music, and maps. Each linear tool is divided into "chapters" that allow the presenter

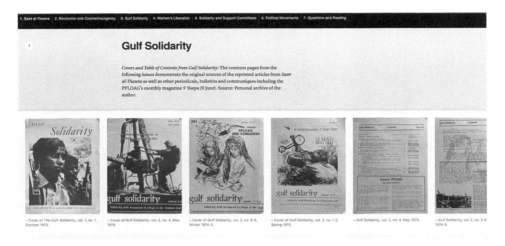

Figure 2. A chapter in Marral Shamshiri-Fard's linear tool presents archival scans of reprinted articles from *Sawt al-Thawra*.

to map the development of movements across longer periods of time. This narrative nature of the linear teaching tool was inspired by the desire to tell untold stories—to contextualize, elaborate, collate, and hence render legible histories buried by state violence, colonial thinking, and bordering logics. In this issue, Marral Shamshiri-Fard's linear teaching tool on *Sawt al-Thawra* (*Voice of the Revolution*) narrates the understudied pan-regional history of Marxist internationalism and armed struggle in Oman and the Arabian Gulf. *Sawt al-Thawra* was a bilingual Arabic and English periodical published by the Marxist-Leninist People's Front for the Liberation of Oman and the Arabian Gulf (PFLOAG) from 1972. *Sawt al-Thawra* addressed a global audience to build internationalist solidarity for Dhufar revolutionaries fighting the British-backed puppet regime of the Omani sultan. As Shamshiri-Fard details, the magazine's linguistic form and political content consciously connected the Dhufar Revolution in Oman with the regional Arab Left and global Marxist networks that ranged as far as Latin America and Vietnam (see fig. 2).

As a teaching tool on left-wing revolutionary politics in the Middle East, Shamshiri-Fard's reading of *Sawt al-Thawra* offers an alternative curriculum for the region. As Taymiya Zaman observes, the region's study in the post–9/11 Global North classroom is often mired in a "self-referential, shifting and urgent present" that focuses on contemporary geostrategy and international relations to the exclusion of alternative and regional histories. These histories face "forms of historical erasure that are central to modern state formation" within the region and beyond, and can contest the frequent flattening of the region's complex history into Orientalist tropes around the Arab world and Islam.[26] By teaching *Sawt al-Thawra* and its resistance against imperialism and regional authoritarianism, educators can hope to unsettle these reductive and essentialist constructions. Offering people the textured and intimate experience of perusing the pages of the magazine as well as letters, photographs, and songs, Shamshiri-Fard's tool on the PFLOAG unearths revolutionary pasts that can shift student perceptions about a widely misunderstood region. Thus linear teaching tools like *Sawt al-Thawra* present scholarship that challenges institutionalized methods in history and archiving by incorporating noncanonical archival sources like political pamphlets, songs, and interviews with activists.

The second model for teaching tools discussed in this issue is designed to facilitate close reading. Compared to the linear model, which emphasizes the historical development of struggles and organizations, a close-reading teaching tool encourages intimate engagement with movement texts. It is structured to center multilingual, noncanonical Global South texts as key sites for political concepts and alternative vocabularies. Furthermore, by spotlighting key formal elements of revolutionary papers such as tables of contents, editorials, and published poems, the close-reading tool digitally reproduces the material experience of perusing the pages of a magazine. The tool design works with a limited, excerpted text that is annotated to provide translations, context, and commentary on periodicals and their contexts. As a methodology inspired by literary criticism, the close-reading digital tool embodies sustained attention to the textual and the particular. For example, in this issue, a close-reading tool authored by students from the Revolutionary Papers Classroom (RP Classroom) translates Urdu poetry and essays from *Savera* (*Dawn*) to discuss literary production as shaped by decolonization and the 1947 Partition. *Savera* was a literary magazine published since 1946 in Lahore, in present-day Pakistan. It was prominently associated with the Progressive Writers' Movement, a South Asian anticolonial writers' collective founded in 1936 by a group of primarily North Indian intellectuals.[27] Areej Akhtar, Javaria Ahmad, and Sana Farrukh Khan discuss how the PWA sought to liberate and modernize Indian literature and championed Marxist-inspired approaches to aesthetics, urging members to ground their art in the material conditions facing a colonized India strapped with the internal oppressions of caste, class, and patriarchal tradition. In particular, the authors chart how progressive intellectuals interpreted the events of the 1947 partition of the subcontinent, the formation of nascent states in India/Pakistan, and the cultural implications of a newly erected international border in South Asia. "Annotations" in their teaching tool sketch in the lives of key literary figures, such as the feminist writer Ismat Chughtai, to situate close readings within the anticolonial movement. Embedded within the translations and archival text presented in the tool, these annotations are design elements that frame crucial historical context and comparative linkages.

The close-reading tool forces intimate engagement with texts that often constitute "sources" routed into the privileged space of academic theorizing but are seldom considered as theoretical texts in and of themselves. In so doing, it hopes to enable a "Global South theory from below" rooted in noncanonical text authored at the margins of state and elite intellectual institutions. In this vein, Thayer Hastings's tool in this issue deploys the close-reading template to spotlight the theoretical and political labor performed by Palestinian *bayanat* (leaflets). The *bayanat* (singular *bayan*) were communiques and pamphlets circulated during the first intifada, a grassroots anticolonial uprising between 1987 and 1993 that challenged the Israeli occupation and oppressive regime in the West Bank and the Gaza Strip. More than half a million Palestinians participated in civil disobedience, general strikes, boycotts, and advocacy in an environment of brutal state repression and violence. The *bayanat* were authored and circulated by the United National Leadership of the Intifada (UNLI), a broad coalition established during the uprising to coordinate Palestinian resistance.[28] Hastings presents translations and archival reproductions of selected *bayanat* to teach readers about the forms, aesthetics, and political practices deployed by Palestinian anticolonial resistance. The leaflets were often slipped under doorsteps, deposited at bus stops, and distributed by night under curfew, working to connect an underground leadership with the mass and serving as an organizing tool for the first intifada.

The third template for teaching tools is the "table." The table model takes its name and concept from a literal tabletop, recreating the visual spread of documents laid out on a desk in a library. Inspired by the visual experience of exploring documents in an archive, the table model curates selected political and cultural documents produced by movements. The tool's interactive digital design allows readers to enlarge, reorder, and map clusters of documents arranged according to themes suggested by the tool author. The table template is most directly tailored as an archival engagement, offering a repository for preserving and contextualizing print ephemera associated with movements. Thus table teaching tools built around oppositional publications can help contemporary struggles and political educators construct syllabi and alternative archives. They can also counter the enclosure of revolutionary print by elite institutions and official archives, and combat the state-led erasure of alternative histories in authoritarian Global South contexts. For example, in this issue, Sara Marzagora and Rafeef Ziadah's table tool on *Lotus* presents a curriculum for teaching and engaging anticolonialism (fig. 3). *Lotus* was a literary journal published by the Afro-Asian Writers Association from Cairo and Beirut between the 1960s and 1980s. It featured poetry, short stories, and essays in translation, drawing contributions from a wide range of Third World contexts and connecting newly decolonized populations with those still fighting for liberation. The tool is clustered around pedagogical resources and provides historical background and archival access to the magazine. It is based on a collaborative project at King's College London that explored student-led pedagogy rooted in the anticolonial archive in conversation with contemporary politics and student experiences. Marzagora and Ziadah argue that the multilingual and multigeneric form of *Lotus* offers productive

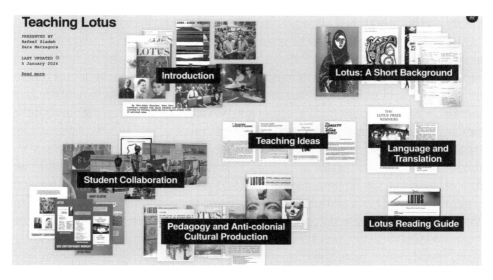

Figure 3. The table tool "Teaching *Lotus*" maps a syllabus built around the iconic Afro-Asian literary magazine.

entry points for a more inclusive, collective, and creative pedagogy, as the magazine pushes disciplinary bounds and academic form to prompt reflection on racialized and uneven structures that persist within the university and beyond. The table tool emphasizes the visual and aesthetic practices of anticolonial, left, and oppositional movements through the minimal use of text and commentary in its design. Marzagora and Ziadah deploy this visual focus to exhibit classroom engagement with multilingual literary and visual production. They discuss how it helped develop a nuanced understanding of colonialism in ethnically and linguistically diverse classrooms and how a creative and collaborative approach to assignments encouraged students to connect reportage on Martin Luther King's assassination with Black Lives Matter. The tool presents a blueprint for similar pedagogical initiatives to be replicated in other contexts with other periodicals.

Another table-format tool in this issue, Pablo Álvarez and Francisco Rodriguez's study of *APSI* magazine presents a snapshot of Chilean resistance to the military dictatorship during the 1970s and 1980s. *APSI* (Information Services Advertising Agency) was born in the early years of Augusto Pinochet's dictatorship, an era marked by a brutal crackdown on left forces in Chile. Álvarez and Rodriguez present archival covers, articles, and illustrations from the magazine, which styled itself as a fortnightly "international news bulletin" to dodge state censorship. As the authors detail, the ban on publishing on Chilean politics and internal affairs compelled an internationalism that came to form the core of *APSI*'s journalistic and political practice. Their teaching tool maps the development of a dissident Global South publication under extraordinary conditions of political repression and silencing, outlining the strategic aesthetic and editorial choices made by journalists to keep democratic cultures alive under authoritarian conditions. *APSI* improvised a range of formal and rhetorical strategies to sustain anti-dictatorship political critique in Chile, as the magazine's deliberately nondescript name, its use of humor, and its ventrilo-quism of Chilean politics through coverage of socialist and anticolonial struggles elsewhere enabled its survival. The tool also unearths the alternative political insti-tutions and revolutionary networks that supported and were in turn sustained by *APSI*. It discusses the intersection between Catholicism and anti-dictatorship poli-tics in 1970s Chile through the role played by the Vicaría de la Solidaridad (Vicariate of Solidarity) and the support of left-wing Chilean exiles based in Italy. The teaching tool presents *APSI* as a platform for coordinating popular and left-wing critique of Pinochet's dictatorship and teaches us about the connections between Chilean resis-tance and similar struggles across the Global South.

As a teaching aid, the three teaching tool templates offer an eclectic and interactive form that seeks to democratize learning about Global South revolution-ary cultures. As such, the tools are a direct engagement with contemporary calls to "decolonize the curriculum" as they excavate and interpret noncanonical, anticolo-nial, and left production archived in revolutionary periodicals. In the following sec-tion, I expand on this engagement by discussing how these digital teaching tools attempt a project of "learning from anticolonialism" by sharing reflections from the RP Classroom.[29]

Revolutionary Papers in the Classroom: On "Decolonizing" the Curriculum

The ongoing struggle to decolonize universities emerged out of the "Rhodes Must Fall" movement in South Africa. The Must Fall movement was sparked by the resis-tance of primarily Black students at the University of Cape Town against restricted access to quality higher education, racial representation at the university, and a white-washed curriculum.[30] The mobilizations spread to campuses in the UK and other global north locations and have brought the demand for decolonization to bear on sanitized conversations around "diversity" and "multiculturalism." Protesting the egregious absence of nonwhite voices and non-European thought in the curriculum, students have called for overhauling the colonial university and structures of white supremacy that govern teaching and scholarship. While the question of "decoloniz-ing the mind" was raised decades ago by the likes of Ngũgĩ Wa Thiong'o in contexts of anticolonial struggle, its revival and belated engagement by global north publics is a welcome development in metropolitan reckoning with the legacies of empire. At the same time, however, decolonization has swiftly been appropriated by university administrations as a "buzzword" and "shorthand for reforms."[31] As Eve Tuck and K. Wayne Yang rightly point out, decolonization is not a metaphor, and the "cultiva-tion of critical consciousness" cannot be allowed to stand in for "the more uncom-fortable task of relinquishing stolen land."[32] These concerns echo Frantz Fanon and

Ngũgĩ Wa Thiong'o, who insisted that decolonizing the mind is only the first step toward overthrowing empire, and that the task of liberating knowledge must go hand in hand with that of organizing political resistance. Without a doubt, the "cultivation of critical consciousness" is no substitute for political action, however, that does not render futile the pursuit of critical knowledge around imperialism's past and present. One way to guard against the fetishization and metaphorization of "decolonization" is to shift emphasis toward anticolonialism—defined, "in this specific context of intellectual labour and knowledge generation as the practice of thought and action towards the goals of decolonisation . . . 'anti'-colonial *practice* [thus] invokes a critical and radical spirit of enquiry and action rather than a singular state to be feasibly arrived at" (emphasis mine).[33] The Revolutionary Papers teaching tools seek to participate in the movement to decolonize the curriculum by "learning from anticolonialism"[34] by archiving, analyzing, and connecting the contexts in which it emerged. They are an experiment in anticolonial pedagogy today, an attempt to excavate earlier imaginaries of decolonization that can shape present resistance to neocolonial knowledge. The tools combine scholarship centered on the Global South, engaging the terrain of anticolonial, Marxist, and antiracist movements as debated, organized, and documented in oppositional periodicals. This focus on the archive of noncanonical print is also a response to calls across disciplines to overcome dominant frameworks for studying colonialism. Centering revolutionary papers in scholarship and pedagogy can challenge the postcolonial theoretical emphasis on the bordered nation, the canonical status of anglophone writing, and the privileging of a small group of male anticolonial figures like Nehru or Mandela. Thus, through digital tools that are interactive, conversant with the contemporary, and focused on movement archives, we hope to emphasize anticolonialism as *practice* and *process* over a "postcolonial" that signals the formal end of empire even as it studies its afterlives, or a "decolonial" that threatens to become a homogenizing precolonial nativist "state" to be arrived at.

The RP Classroom emerged out of this pedagogical experiment. The initiative convened a semester-long undergraduate course and workshop at LUMS University in Lahore, Pakistan. The course drew on revolutionary periodicals as a syllabus for teaching a comparative history of anticolonial, Third World, and left movements. Digital teaching tools were used extensively as a teaching aid for class discussions and background reading in the course, which ran from January to June 2023. In the course, undergraduate students studied periodicals published by a range of anticolonial and left movements across geographical contexts, including the bulletin of the Black Panther Party and *Publica(c)tion*, a 2017 Black, student-driven publication printed in South Africa to extend the work of the Must Fall movement.[35] In the end, students worked on a collaborative final project in which they created their own teaching tools presenting anti-authoritarian and dissident magazines from Pakistan sourced from the Punjab Public Library and the South Asia Research and

Resource Centre (SARRC), an independent archive that houses Pakistan's anti-dictatorship and left histories.[36] One of these student projects, presented by Areej Akhtar, Javaria Ahmad, and Sana Farrukh Khan, is featured in this issue.

After the course concluded, I met the students to reflect collectively on the process of learning from and teaching with revolutionary print in the classroom. We discussed how even though the course was offered under the aegis of a comparative literature and culture studies program, the focus on the nonacademic and multigeneric form of the revolutionary periodical enabled engagement that subverted disciplinary boundaries. Students described how the focus on periodicals as curriculum pushed their learning in an interdisciplinary and collaborative direction. For instance, for history students, the cross-border and internationalist linkages explored in teaching tools like "The Social Lives of the *Namibian Review*" challenged the methodological nationalism of dominant historiography that tends to rely on territorially bounded, state-centric archives. Similarly, for students of comparative literature and English, an emphasis on the Global South literary magazine as form helped "destabilize the [Eurocentric] canon" and unsettle hierarchies of literary merit that privilege genres like the anglophone novel.[37] For students across the board, the process of visiting archives, interviewing activists, compiling periodical artwork, and translating excerpts from Pakistani periodicals became an "immersive" dive into alternative histories of their own context.[38] Thus, engaging teaching tools on related contexts and authoring their own tools on Pakistan enabled students to become interlocutors and creators for alternative knowledge on their region. Moreover, students described periodicals studied in their teaching tools as powerful counters to the state-mandated Pakistan Studies curriculum, a compulsory component of undergraduate education in Pakistan that was imposed by the 1980s military regime of General Zia ul Haq to cement the "patriotic" Sunni Muslim citizen-subject.[39]

For some students, the classroom engagement with revolutionary periodicals and teaching tools opened up possibilities for unearthing buried political pasts. Given the colonial conditions governing languages in Pakistan, almost every student reported that they required language-related assistance in engaging Urdu and Punjabi periodicals studied in the course. With no formal language support available at the university, an elite institution offering instruction almost exclusively in English, students naturally turned to family and community members—uncles, mothers, grandparents—as guides and collaborators to read with. In part, this was enabled by the nonacademic and popular form of these periodicals, which included publications that family and community members were already familiar with. This facilitated an intergenerational conversation about political resistance and alternative histories of Pakistan, an engagement eased by community familiarity with the Urdu magazine form.[40] In contrast, assigned academic articles in English, which supplemented the syllabus, could not create this kind of dialogue.

For one student in the class, engaging with and researching *Tulu* (*Rise*), a Soviet-funded Pakistani socialist propaganda magazine, became a means to discover and document the entanglements of print culture and political organizing with family histories. Noor said that she had "always known that her father and uncles had been involved in student politics" back in the day, but she had never found the opportunity to talk to them about their political activities in any detail.[41] It was when she sought her father's help with reading the original Urdu articles published in *Tulu* that she discovered more. Her father was deeply familiar with the publication and had received a stipend from the Soviet Union embassy for distributing copies of *Tulu* to students and intellectuals associated with the National College of Arts in Lahore in the 1980s. Noor ended up interviewing her uncle who had also been involved in socialist student politics and *Tulu*. Thus Noor's engagement with revolutionary papers in the classroom enabled her to link family pasts with histories of political resistance in Pakistan. Scholarship and community memory could be synergized through the *Tulu* archive, revealing connections between political movements and the practices and subjectivities of ordinary people. Moreover, student engagement with periodicals as living archives rather than textual objects compelled them to take the lead in sketching the ecologies surrounding these print forms. The interdisciplinary methodology of the digital tools prompted students to go beyond engaging movement archives to contributing and generating materials through interviews and translations of content. By incorporating political biography, subalternized oral narratives, and ethnographic insight into community memory, students worked toward an expansive view of revolutionary print. As Miller-Likhethe eloquently argues in an essay in this issue, this analytical move is necessary for scholarship on print culture "from below," which must go beyond textual study to address the "processes of political education and practices of collective readership" that defined ordinary people's relationship with print culture.[42]

For Sohaib,[43] another student in the course, reading revolutionary periodicals enabled both an excavation and a critical reflection on community history. Reading about the Baloch insurgency in Pakistan alongside Marxist-Leninist militancy against the sultan in Muscat triggered a critical discussion in the classroom on the dangers of romanticizing community memory and the erasures and elisions that can exist therein. Students studied Mahvish Ahmad and Mir Muhammad Ali Talpur's teaching tool, which presents a detailed, linear account of the Baloch liberation struggle, focusing on the Balochistan People's Liberation Front's (BPLF) battle against the occupation of Baloch lands in Pakistan.[44] As the only Baloch student in the classroom, Sohaib possessed a deep familiarity and unique insight into the context surrounding *Jabal*, the underground organ of the BPLF. However, when the syllabus turned from *Jabal* to Marral Shamshiri-Fard's teaching tool on the PFLOAG, Sohaib saw a gap in the same Baloch oral history that had transmitted to his generation the memory of the BPLF's struggle. In 1970s Oman, scores of

Baloch mercenaries fought the PFLOAG revolutionaries at the behest of the sultanate in Muscat, and Sohaib described how he had heard elders relay how many of
them had fought "terrorists" in Oman at the behest of the sultan during the
1970s. He thoughtfully addressed the erasure of the PFLOAG's struggle within
community memory, commenting on the conflation of Omani liberation struggle
with terrorism in the same Baloch oral history that extolled the BPLF's anticolonialism. Thus, in the classroom and beyond, close engagement with revolutionary
papers can encourage a comparative, connective perspective that can nuance histories of anticolonial communities and Third World solidarities.

Conclusion: Reflections on "Decolonial" Scholarship, Politics, and Digital Pedagogies

As this essay has suggested, centering the archive of revolutionary papers drawn
from anticolonial, left, and Third World struggles in scholarship and pedagogy can
deepen ongoing attempts to answer the question: what does a decolonized curriculum look like? One possible answer lies in a focus on print cultures of revolutionary
movements, which can ground decolonization in the terrain of struggle. Anticolonial
and left struggles of the Global South were embedded in particular, regional contexts and literary-linguistic cultures and therefore furnish a productive site for excavating situated knowledges. Such perspectives are often marginalized in the colonial
archive and by academic production that privileges canonical, single-author anticolonial texts authored in dominant languages like English. Through a comparative
focus on revolutionary papers, we can unearth and internationalize situated knowledges emanating from distinct geographies to anchor extant understandings of key
anticolonial concepts like freedom, solidarity, and critique. Further, privileging the
intellectual production, political practices, and communities of Global South print
as a site for theorization can expand understandings of decolonization and anticolonialism beyond the circumscribed logics of the nation-state. For example, alongside
others featured in this issue, periodicals like *Sawt al-Thawra* and *Lotus* subverted
the boundaries that govern language, genre, and national geography to present historically located theorizations of concepts like socialism, Afro-Asianism, and Third
Worldism. Moreover, by inhabiting the messy, shifting terrain of ongoing movements,
these publications often directly engaged, or at the very least reflected, contradictions
within anticolonialism and decolonization. Therefore revolutionary papers can serve
as a teaching tool to sharpen and complicate understandings of decolonization by
pushing existing postcolonialist theorizations that often only offer a reductive
"choice between stark oppositions of colonizer and colonized societies, on the one
hand," and "notions of hybridity" with little room for resistance outside that allowed
by the colonizing power, on the other."[45]

In doing so, revolutionary papers can guard against what Tuck and Yang
decry as the "vague equating of colonialisms."[46] They can bring into analysis

injustices *internal* to colonized societies by highlighting how movements debated and contested the oppressions of native elites and postcolonial states alongside the ravages wrought by empire. This remains a pressing concern, for example, Kalpana Wilson, Giti Chandra, and Lata Narayanaswamy point out how in India, far-right Hindutva ideologues are "gaining legitimacy by adopting decolonial language," propagating an Islamophobic, upper-caste imaginary of an Indian past in which "'Hinduism' is produced as a singular, decolonial and monolithic narrative."[47] Thus, in a contemporary climate in which responses to decolonization range from misinformed hue and cry about the wholesale "cutting of white men from university reading lists"[48] to blanket "epistemic deference"[49] to any and all knowledges rooted in "non-Western" contexts, a focus on revolutionary papers can emphasize the political and pedagogical practice of decolonization as an engagement with anticapitalist and anti-imperialist visions oriented toward social justice.

That said, it is important to acknowledge the limitations presented by digital humanities interventions for radical archiving and movement history. While the tools are a conscious step away from the political economy of academic publishing and toward an alternative curriculum that can connect anticolonial knowledges with political struggle, there is much to be done to collectivize their form. For one, their online digital availability increases their accessibility and ensures a home to movement documents that might otherwise be neglected in state and institutional archives. However, in contexts with limited digital and functional literacy, web-based archival engagements like the teaching tools in this issue may remain an alienating and exclusionary medium. Especially among working and rural classes in areas like Pakistan, computers and mobile devices are not readily available or affordable, and access to the internet can be limited. Even a few of my mostly urban, elite-educated university students struggled to access and navigate the teaching tools and needed to be guided through the design and digital functionality of the tools before they could engage with them independently.

Thus, at the very least, digital tools require a community setting, with facilitators familiar with the technology involved. Only then can they function as an aid for pedagogy and political education. Moreover, communities and movement intellectuals should be engaged as coauthors and interlocutors in an attempt to push the tools' digital form in more inclusive and collective directions. For example, the teaching tool on the *Voice of the Children / Die Kinderstem / Izwi Labantwana* presented by Mishca Peters and Children's Movement organizer Marcus Solomon facilitated an intergenerational reflection between anti-apartheid activists and the Must Fall–aligned Interim People's Library collective, who were both present at the Community House in Cape Town at the 2022 Revolutionary Papers workshop.[50] In this way, teaching tools on revolutionary periodicals can embed digital humanities scholarship in community settings to aid collective remembering and people's archiving. However, only a few tools on the Revolutionary Papers website were authored and disseminated with direct community and activist engagement. These include "The Social Lives of the *Namibian Review*" (Benson, Gamedze, and Mush-aandja) and "Regimes and Resistance: Kenya's Resistance History through Underground and Alternative Publications" (Wamai and Waweru), which are featured in this special issue and emerge out of the Know Your Continent popular education series and the archival activism of the Ukombozi Library.

Moreover, digital tools also stand to gain from community and activist involvement at the design level, that is, through co-creative processes that engage movement voices in shaping not just the content and circulation of the tool but its very form and function. For example, Ahmad and Talpur's tool on *Jabal* was also created, like *Voice of the Children*, through close collaboration and discussion with movement intellectuals. The *Jabal* teaching tool was widely circulated in Baloch political circles and discussed at length in an online seminar. Many who had been part of the 1970s Baloch insurgency were present, and the teaching tool sparked reflection and remembering around a history facing erasure, censorship, and controversy in Pakistan. Although for most of their lives, BPLF members remained reluctant to disclose details of their political activities due to ongoing state repression and fragmentation within the Left, *Jabal*'s excavation encouraged renewed engagement with the history of left-wing militancy in Pakistan. In fact, editors and readers of the 1970s magazine volunteered their personal copies for digitization so that the teaching tool could function as a complete archive of the BPLF's political and intellectual history. It became apparent that the design and function of the teaching tool would have to be stretched to accommodate the community's needs, who wish to deploy its digital technology for archiving and documenting, alongside analyzing and narrating insurgent Baloch pasts.

Thus digital humanities projects must also work to undo hierarchical paradigms for design and technology in which specialists like archival scholars determine the aesthetic and form in which movement histories are presented. Any Freirean approach to pedagogy must extend to embrace design practices, and constitutively engage with the ways in which communities instrumentalize and relate to technology and digital infrastructures. Sasha Costanza-Chock points out how "everyone designs, but only certain kinds of design work are acknowledged, valorized, remunerated, and credited," calling attention to the ways in which "the political economy of design" can often deter community control of design processes and practices.[51] Given the recent turn toward the digital humanities, shifting methodologies of archival research and literary studies threaten to fetishize and enforce the enclosure of movement documents in elite academic and state institutions. Thus, going forward, the digital pedagogical experiment presented in this issue must interrogate the relationship between design, power, and social justice alongside a critical engagement with the archive and canon. Although we are not there yet, as a collective, Revolutionary Papers is striving to resist the framing of revolutionary print and its communities as fetishized objects or research subjects, and to engage movements as co-researchers and co-designers. The teaching tools in this issue hope to reflect and share for wider discussion this ongoing process, an effort and as yet unfinished project to document and understand through anticolonial periodicals "the ever shifting spaces and moments in which collective resistance and dreams for justice are made and remade."[52]

Sara Kazmi is assistant professor of English at the University of Pennsylvania. She is currently working on a monograph tentatively titled *Literary Dissent and Popular Tradition in India/Pakistan*.

Notes

I would like to thank Mahvish Ahmad, Koni Benson, and Chana Morgenstern for their comments on an earlier draft of this essay, which emerges out of our work together on the Revolutionary Papers project. I am also deeply indebted to my students, whose engagement has inspired and clarified the insights in this piece. Thanks is also owed to the Department of Humanities and Social Sciences at LUMS University for supporting and facilitating the Revolutionary Papers Classroom initiative through a research grant.

1. See, respectively, Nieftagodien, *"Congress Militant"*; Katzeman and Broderick, "'Ka Aina No Ka Poe o Hawaii.'"
2. Ahmad, "Movement Texts."
3. Ngũgĩ Wa Thiong'o, *Decolonising the Mind*, 9.
4. Revolutionary Papers, "Teaching Tools," https://revolutionarypapers.org/teaching-tool/.
5. Seligmann, "Literary Infrastructure."
6. Seligmann, "Literary Infrastructure," 2.
7. For a detailed analysis of colonial language policy in Panjab, India, see Mir, "Imperial Policy, Provincial Practices"; for more on colonial and postcolonial language politics in the region, see Rahman, *Language and Politics in Pakistan*.
8. Mir, "Imperial Policy, Provincial Practices," 412.
9. Ngũgĩ Wa Thiong'o, *Decolonising the Mind*, 4. See Bulson, *Little Magazine*.
10. Bulson, *Little Magazine*, 195.
11. Halim, *"Lotus,"* 563; Chandan, "A Capital Gain."
12. Elam, *World Literature*, xiv.
13. Elam, *World Literature*, 7.
14. Freire, *Pedagogy*, 54.
15. Nieftagodien, "Congress Militant," conference paper.
16. Nieftagodien, *"Congress Militant."*
17. Freire, *Pedagogy*, 71.
18. Lenin, "Declaration of the Editorial Board of *Iskra*."
19. Longford, *"Dawn."*
20. Longford, *"Dawn."*
21. Miller-Likhethe, "Black Internationalism."
22. Waweru and Wamai, "Ukombozi."
23. Flinn and Alexander, "Humanizing an Inevitability," 331, 332–33.
24. Lizzie Malcolm, in conversation with the author, December 12, 2023, online.
25. Morgenstern, "Archive of Literary Reconstruction."
26. Bsheer, *Archive Wars*, 32; Zaman, "Pedagogy."

27. For more on the Progressive Writers' Movement, see Gopal, *Literary Radicalism in India*; and Jalil, *Liking Progress*.
28. Hastings, "Manasheer al-Intifada."
29. Gopal, "On Decolonisation and the University," 887.
30. Chantiluka, Kwoba, and Nkopo, *Rhodes Must Fall*, 24.
31. Gopal, "On Decolonisation and the University," 882.
32. Tuck and Yang, "Decolonization," 19.
33. Gopal, "On Decolonisation and the University," 889 (emphasis added).
34. Gopal, "On Decolonisation and the University," 887.
35. Naidoo, "Publica[c]tion."
36. To hear Ahmad Salim introduce his archive and his work, see his talk delivered at the event "Dissident Histories of Pakistan," November 1, 2021, LSE Sociology, cohosted by SARRC, Revolutionary Papers, and Archives of the Disappeared, YouTube video, 13:37, https://www.youtube.com/watch?v=MMRwkMDFx_I&t=172s. For other teaching tools based on SARRC's collection, see Kazmi, "Mazdoor Kissan Party Circular"; and Ahmad and Talpur, "*Jabal*."
37. Areej Akhtar, in conversation with the author, December 10, 2023, online.
38. Munema Zahid, in conversation with the author, December 10, 2023, online.
39. For a detailed account of the complex development of ideas of citizenship and identity in Pakistan, see Qasmi, *Qaum, Mulk, Sultanat*.
40. For more on the history of print culture in modern South Asia, see Robb, *Print and the Urdu Public*.
41. Noor Us Sahar, in conversation with the author, December 10, 2023, online.
42. Miller-Likhethe, "Black Internationalism."
43. The student's name has been changed to protect their identity.
44. Ahmad and Talpur, "*Jabal*."
45. Loomba, "Overworlding the 'Third World,'" 172.
46. Tuck and Yang, "Decolonization," 19.
47. Wilson, Chandra, and Narayanaswamy, "Contested Development Imaginaries."
48. Gopal, "On Decolonisation and the University," 874.
49. Wilson, Chandra, and Narayanaswamy, "Contested Development Imaginaries."
50. Peters, "Voice of the Children."
51. Costanza-Chock, *Design Justice*, 14.
52. Nagar and Arasu, "Holding Movements."

References

Ahmad, Mahvish. "Movement Texts as Anti-colonial Theory." *Sociology* 57, no. 1 (2023): 54–71. https://doi.org/10.1177/00380385221098516.

Ahmad, Mahvish, and Mir Muhammad Ali Talpur. "*Jabal*, the Voice of Balochistan." Revolutionary Papers, updated October 21, 2021. https://revolutionarypapers.org/teaching-tool/jabal-the-voice-of-balochistan/.

Benson, Koni, Nashilongweshipwe Mushaandja, and Asher Gamedze. "Mapping the Social Lives of the *Namibian Review*." Revolutionary Papers, updated April 27, 2022. https://revolutionarypapers.org/teaching-tool/the-namibian-review/.

Bsheer, Rosie. *Archive Wars: The Politics of History in Saudi Arabia*. Stanford, CA: Stanford University Press, 2020.

Bulson, Eric Jon. *Little Magazine, World Form*. New York: Columbia University Press, 2016.

Chandan, Amarjit. "A Capital Gain in Last 100 Years: Marx in Punjabi." *Indian Express,* November 22, 2022.

Chantiluka, Roseanne, Brian Kwoba, and Athinangamso Nkopo, eds. *Rhodes Must Fall: The Struggle to Decolonise the Racist Heart of Empire.* London: Zed Books, 2018.

Costanza-Chock, Sasha. *Design Justice: Community-Led Practices to Build the Worlds We Need.* Cambridge, MA: MIT Press, 2020.

Elam, Daniel J. *World Literature for the Wretched of the Earth: Anticolonial Aesthetics, Postcolonial Politics.* New York: Fordham University Press, 2020.

Flinn, Andrew, and Ben Alexander. "'Humanizing an Inevitability Political Craft': Introduction to the Special Issue on Archiving Activism and Activist Archiving." *Archival Science* 15, no. 4 (2015): 329–35. https://doi.org/10.1007/s10502-015-9260-6.

Freire, Paulo. *Pedagogy of the Oppressed.* Thirtieth anniversary edition. New York: Continuum, 2005.

Gopal, Priyamvada. *Literary Radicalism in India: Gender, Nation, and the Transition to Independence.* London: Routledge, 2005.

Gopal, Priyamvada. "On Decolonisation and the University." *Textual Practice* 35, no. 6 (2021): 873–99. https://doi.org/10.1080/0950236X.2021.1929561.

Halim, Hala. "*Lotus*, the Afro-Asian Nexus, and Global South Comparatism." *Comparative Studies of South Asia, Africa, and the Middle East* 32, no. 3 (2012): 563–83. https://doi.org/10.1215/1089201X-1891570.

Hastings, Thayer. "Manasheer al-Intifada: Bayan no.1 (UNLI), Palestine." *Radical History Review*, no. 150 (2024): 229–32.

Jalil, Rakhshanda. *Liking Progress, Loving Change: A Literary History of the Progressive Writers' Movement in Urdu.* New Delhi: Oxford University Press, 2014.

Kazmi, Sara. "Mazdoor Kissan Party Circular." Revolutionary Papers, updated October 21, 2021. https://revolutionarypapers.org/teaching-tool/mazdoor-kissan-party-circular/.

Lenin, Vladimir Ilyich. "Declaration of the Editorial Board of *Iskra*." September 1900. Marxists Internet Archive. https://www.marxists.org/archive/lenin/works/1900/sep/iskra.htm (accessed January 7, 2024).

Longford, Sam. "*Dawn*: Sites of Struggle, Contested Historical Narratives and the Making of the Disciplined Cadre." Revolutionary Papers, updated April 24, 2022. https://revolutionary papers.org/teaching-tool/dawn/.

Loomba, Ania. "Overworlding the 'Third World.'" *Oxford Literary Review* 13, no. 1 (1991): 170–91.

Miller-Likhethe, Mae A. "Black Internationalism, Print Culture, and Political Education in Claude McKay's *Banjo*." *Radical History Review*, no. 150 (2024): 53–79.

Mir, Farina. "Imperial Policy, Provincial Practices: Colonial Language Policy in Nineteenth-Century India." *Indian Economic and Social History Review* 43, no. 4 (2006): 395–428.

Morgenstern, Hana. "An Archive of Literary Reconstruction in *al-Jadid*." Revolutionary Papers, updated February 21, 2021. https://revolutionarypapers.org/teaching-tool/an-archive-of -literary-reconstruction-in-al-jadid/.

Nagar, Richa, and Ponni Arasu. "Holding Movements, Agitating Epistemes: Introducing a Multipart Series on Remembering, Retelling, and Dreaming for Justice." *Agitate Journal*, https://agitatejournal.org/holding-movements-agitating-epistemes-introducing-a-multipart -series-on-remembering-retelling-and-dreaming-for-justice-convened-by-richa-nagar-and -ponni-arasu/ (accessed January 21, 2024).

Naidoo, Leigh-Ann. "Publica[c]tion: Publishing an Alternative and the Creative Process of Critique." Paper presented at the conference "Revolutionary Papers: Counter-institutions, -Politics, and -Culture in Periodicals of the Global South," April 30, 2022, Cape Town, South Africa.

Ngũgĩ Wa Thiong'o. *Decolonising the Mind: The Politics of Language in African Literature.* Oxford: James Currey, 1986.

Nieftagodien, Noor. "Congress Militant: the paper as a revolutionary organizer," paper presented at the conference "Revolutionary Papers: Counter-institutions, -Politics, and -Culture in Periodicals of the Global South," April 30, 2022, Cape Town, South Africa.

Nieftagodien, Noor. "*Congress Militant*: Revolutionary Paper as Political Organizer." *Radical History Review*, no. 150 (2024): 103–124.

Peters, Mishca. "Voice of the Children." Revolutionary Papers, updated April 24, 2022. https://revolutionarypapers.org/teaching-tool/voice-of-the-children/.

Qasmi, Ali Usman. *Qaum, Mulk, Sultanat: Citizenship and National Belonging in Pakistan.* Stanford, CA: Stanford University Press, 2023.

Rahman, Tariq. *Language and Politics in Pakistan.* Karachi: Oxford University Press, 1997.

Robb, Megan Eaton. *Print and the Urdu Public: Muslims, Newspapers, and Urban Life in Colonial India.* New York: Oxford University Press, 2020.

Seligmann, Katerina Gonzalez. "The Void, the Distance, Elsewhere: Literary Infrastructure and Empire in the Caribbean." *Small Axe: A Caribbean Journal of Criticism* 24, no. 2 (2020): 1–16. https://doi.org/10.1215/07990537-8604442.

Shamshiri-Fard, Marral. "*Sawt al-Thawra*." Revolutionary Papers, updated April 21, 2022. https://revolutionarypapers.org/teaching-tool/sawt-al-thawra/.

Tuck, Eve, and K. Wayne Yang. "Decolonization Is Not a Metaphor." *Decolonization: Indigeneity, Education, and Society* 1, no. 1 (2012): 1–40.

Wilson, Kalpana, Giti Chandra, and Lata Narayanaswamy. "Contested Development Imaginaries: Hindutva and the Co-optation of Decolonisation." *Debating Development Research*, August 4, 2023. https://www.developmentresearch.eu/?p=1596.

Zaman, Taymiya. "Pedagogy: Why I Won't Teach the Modern Middle East." https://taymiya zaman.com/pedagogy/ (accessed May 16, 2024).

Mapping the Social Lives of *The Namibian Review*

Koni Benson, Asher Gamedze,
and Nashilongweshipwe Mushaandja

*T*he Namibian Review: *A Journal of Contemporary South West African Affairs* was produced in Stockholm and then Windhoek between 1976 and 1987, a decade in which the independence struggle in South West Africa was intensifying. The magazine agitated for an end to the South African occupation, based on the will of the Namibian people. Each edition aimed to publish articles from a broad political, economic, cultural, social, and literary spectrum (fig. 1). Contents included updates from the front lines, analysis of the latest international negotiations, articles, letters, and replies from fronts and civic organizations. *The Namibian Review* aimed to facilitate "continuous political dialogue between Namibians of varying points of view who [were] bold enough to confront the fundamental problems." It exposed tensions within the liberation movement by featuring debates about strategic direction, contradictions and accountability, and opening its pages to dissenting voices. For its editors, this democratic commitment provided a forum for debate and an arena for "the establishment of the broadest possible united front against foreign domination," laying the groundwork for life in a democratic society.[1]

Two of the founding members of *The Namibian Review* were Kenneth Abrahams, a medical doctor, and Ottilie Abrahams, a committed teacher, principal, and feminist activist. Throughout their lives they were involved in the formation of anticolonial liberation political parties, underground movements, study groups, schools,

Radical History Review
Issue 150 (October 2024)   DOI 10.1215/01636545-11257473
© 2024 by MARHO: The Radical Historians' Organization, Inc.

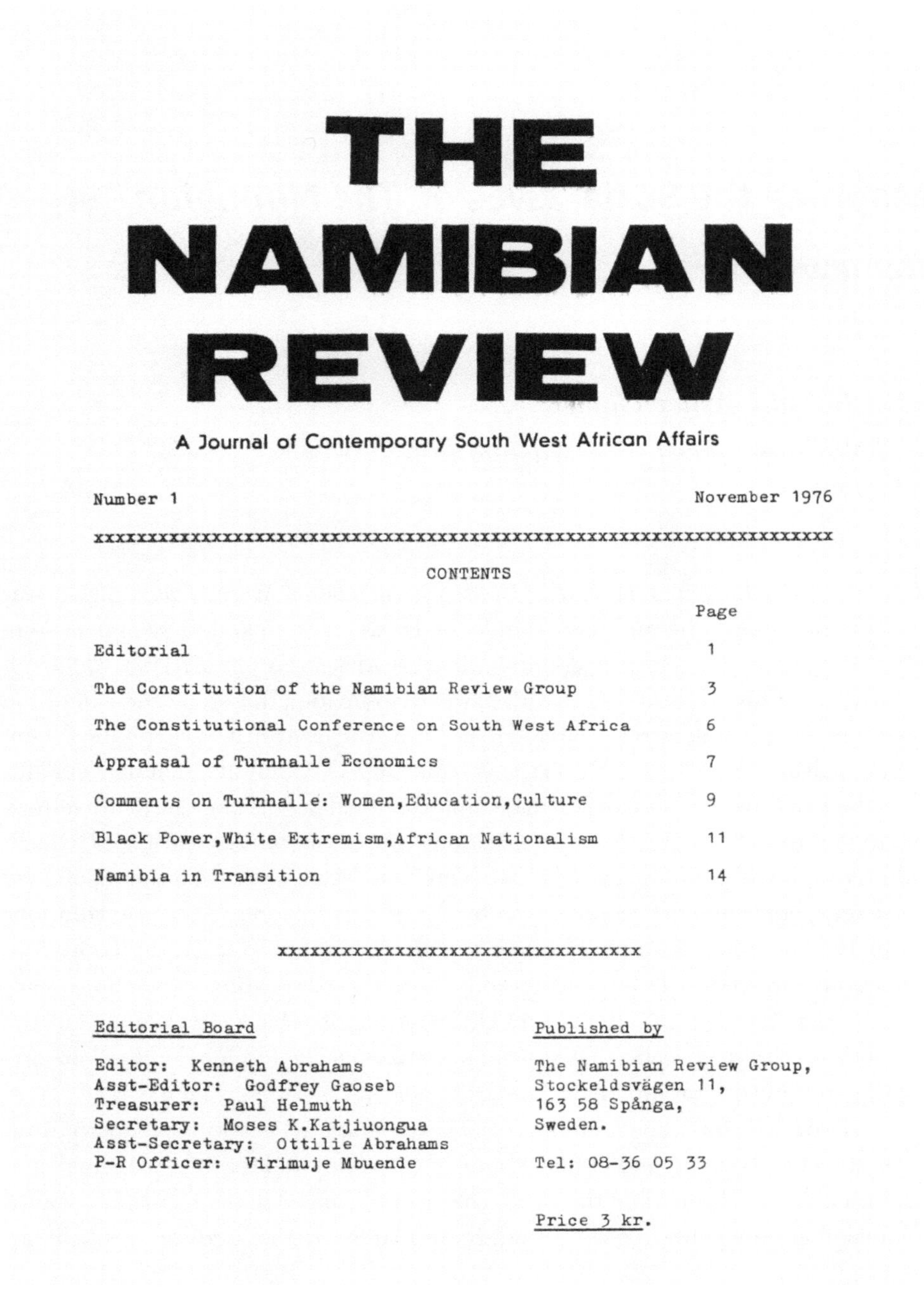

THE NAMIBIAN REVIEW

A Journal of Contemporary South West African Affairs

Number 1   November 1976

xxxxxxxxxxxxxxxxxxxxxxxxxxxxxxxxxxxxxxxxxxxxxxxxxxxxxxxxxxxxxxxxxxxxxxxxx

CONTENTS

xxxxxxxxxxxxxxxxxxxxxxxxxxxxxxxxxxxxxx

Editorial Board   Published by

Editor: Kenneth Abrahams   The Namibian Review Group,
Asst-Editor: Godfrey Gaoseb   Stockeldsvägen 11,
Treasurer: Paul Helmuth   163 58 Spånga,
Secretary: Moses K.Katjiuongua   Sweden.
Asst-Secretary: Ottilie Abrahams
P-R Officer: Virimuje Mbuende   Tel: 08-36 05 33

                                         Price 3 kr.

Figure 1. *Namibian Review*, no. 1 (1976).

movement publications, and more. *The Namibian Review* was just one piece in a much larger puzzle of labors, movements, and debates about Southern African liberation; this is reflected in our approach to piecing together and engaging the sociopolitical history of this journal.

As a publication within contemporary Namibian consciousness and in the emerging academic field of Namibian studies, *The Namibian Review* is practically unstudied—either unknown or ignored. We only stumbled across it, and later became fascinated with it, through our work as educators and activists in African history and political education. Our digital teaching tool highlights how we locate and draw on the journal in this context. In the tool, we share interactive African history education and research materials that we produced as part of the ongoing social lives of this critical journal.

The Namibian Review was one of many publications written by African intellectuals directly involved in the liberation struggle. It was a space to imagine and advocate for Namibia's transition to independence.[2] These writings emphasized nonpartisan politics, placing liberation above any party or nationalism. This was unique and in part why *The Namibian Review* can be read as history, political theory, intervention, and invention. In a 1980 editorial that "reviewed" *The Namibian Review*, the editors wrote: "we hope that Namibians will realise just how necessary it is for us to 'invent' i.e. analyse, suggest, and propose, ways and means to solve our problems, settle the independence dispute and create a better life for us and our children."[3] This creative and analytical disposition informed the journal's political orientation to the national question and to the questions of nonsectarianism, national fronts, sole authenticity, representation, leadership, and education, all of which have huge implications for the current narrowing of political options and the nationalist party's domination of the state and liberation struggle narratives today. We revisit this publication both for the history contained in its pages and also for its production, networks, and politics as one way to resurrect critical pedagogy and anticolonial imaginaries. Our teaching tool highlights our interest in locating it and studying it, together, as both an education in history and organizing and as a method of producing radical thought within the movement.

Our teaching tool outlines what we call a post-border praxis, collective work that combines study, imagination, and creation for building cultures of resistance through organizing and education work with historians, educators, activists, students, and artists across different spaces and borders of southern Africa.[4] As educators, scholars, and activists, our work with *The Namibian Review* and our study of its wider social and political lives has been integral to our unfolding creative approach to African history research and political education across the region. This approach has included facilitating popular education programs such as the Know Your Continent (KYC) workshop series, where we create spaces to collectively and creatively study African history as a way to reflect on contemporary politics in the interests of changing them. As a response to our critique of the inadequacies of mainstream history education being rooted in Eurocentrism, patriarchy, and colonialism, part of the KYC approach is to generate new materials and practice alternative ways of building relationships through radical history education. The intention is to reimagine and reshape both the normative content of African history education and the dominant modes in which it is researched and taught in South African education institutions.[5]

To that end, drawing on the KYC approach, the tool presents a few examples of interactive experimental African history educational materials connected to the history of *The Namibian Review*. The first example is "Radical Histories I: SACHED and Some Others," which was initially published in *Pathways to Free Education*, an independent journal produced by student activists. The piece approached the terrain of education as a site of struggle under apartheid by tracing conservative moves in education policy and radical counter movements, experiments, and alternatives in South Africa.[6] To support an interactive engagement with this historical timeline, the tool also includes a game called Radical History Bingo, with introductory notes, general instructions, and the materials needed to play the game for both the facilitators and the participants. Another piece included in the tool is "Radical Histories II: Ottilie Abrahams Speaks" which traces the political life journey of Ottilie Abrahams through the various organizations in which she was involved. Her remarkable life included: militant underground reading groups in Cape Town; education work in guerrilla training camps in Tanzania; expulsion from the South West African People's Organisation; exile, organizing, teaching, and study in Zambia and later, Sweden; participation in the establishment of the Namibian Women's Association; and work in food security and alternative education in independent Namibia.[7] The game is an interactive mapping activity, a history, a curriculum, and a work in progress that includes playing cards for each participant to contribute toward piecing together Abrahams's political life journey (fig. 2). The game puts her lifework in the context of the Herero and Nama genocide, German colonialism and land dispossession, apartheid forced removals, student movements, political movements, radical education initiatives, women's organizations, and more.

Our work learns from the extremely disciplined antidisciplinary approach of the freedom fighters involved in the creation and writing of *The Namibian Review*. The journal was one part of the broad and expansive political lives of Ottilie and Kenneth Abrahams, and, with regards to Ottilie in particular, it forms a rare archive of her writing. She and her comrades refused to divide education from scholarship or from political and organizational work. They also refused the apartheid–post-apartheid divide and remained involved in radical, popular, and political education in the independence period. We take their example and focus on the radical possibilities for the region by documenting and inserting the critical movements and materials which they produced into education spaces today. In this way we are connected to, part of,

Figure 2. "Mapping the Life Journey of Ottilie Abrahams: Revolutionary, Teacher, Feminist."

and extending "the social lives of *The Namibian Review*." In the effort to extend its social lives, our curriculum materials are inspired by what Paulo Freire calls the creative practice of reading; rather than merely depositing information, they intentionally make space for more to be written and heard in the process of education.

Unfinished and ongoing, our research on the history of *The Namibian Review* thus flows into curriculum and political work. The journal was part of a constellation of publications connected to independent organizations that produced novel analyses and conversations between liberation movements across southern Africa. As a platform and as a political aspiration, *The Namibian Review* teaches us about some of the most important and unfinished debates of the liberation struggle. In interactively mapping the wider and ongoing social life of the magazine, we are able to connect across and reject colonial boundaries of time and place and practice, "daring," as Thomas Sankara would say, "to invent the future."[8]

Koni Benson is a historian, organizer, and educator. She is a senior lecturer in the Department of Historical Studies at the University of the Western Cape, working with social movement archives and with student, activist, and cultural collectives across southern Africa. She is a co-convener of the Revolutionary Papers Project and author of *Crossroads: I Live Where I Like* (illustrated by the Trantraal Brothers and Ashley Marais, foreword by Robin D. G. Kelley, 2021). Contact: kbenson@uwc.ac.za.

Asher Gamedze is a cultural worker based in Cape Town.

Nashilongweshipwe Mushaandja is a cultural worker, educator, and writer based in Windhoek, Namibia, with practice/research interests in African performance practices, sono-somatic archives, and public cultures of social movements. He obtained a PhD in performance studies from the University of Cape Town. He is a member of the Owela Live Arts Collective Trust.

Notes

1. Abrahams, "Editorial."
2. Prior to its publication there was the *South West News* (published from 1959 to 1960 by the African Publishing Company of the Old Location, Windhoek). Two other texts to be read in relation to the review include Mburumba, *Namibia: The Making of a Nation*; and Katjavivi, *History of Resistance in Namibia*.
3. *Namibian Review*, no. 17 (1980).
4. For more on post-border praxis, see Benson and Gamedze, "Beyond a Classroom."
5. For more on Know Your Continent, see Benson, Gamedze, and Koranteng, "African History in Context."
6. Benson and Gamedze, "Radical Histories I."
7. Benson, Gamedze, and Mushaandja, "Radical Histories II."
8. Sankara, *Thomas Sankara Speaks*.

References

Abrahams, Kenneth. "Editorial: Introducing the Namibian Review." *Namibian Review*, no. 1 (1976): 2–3.

Benson, Koni, and Asher Gamedze. "Beyond a Classroom: Experiments in a Post-border Praxis for the Future." In *Critical Methods for the Study of World Politics: Creativity and Transformation*, edited by Shine Choi, Anna Selmeczi, and Erzsébet Strausz, 121–35. London: Routledge, 2020.

Benson, Koni, and Asher Gamedze. "Radical Histories I: SACHED and Some Others." *Pathways to Free Education* 3 (2017): 48–62, 184–86.

Benson, Koni, Asher Gamedze, and Akosua Koranteng. "African History in Context: Toward a Praxis of Radical Education." In *Reflections on Knowledge, Learning, and Social Movements: History's Schools*, edited by Aziz Choudry and Salim Vally, 104–17. London: Routledge, 2017.

Benson, Koni, Asher Gamedze, and Nashilongweshipwe Mushaandja. "Radical Histories II: Ottilie Abrahams Speaks." *Owela: The Future of Work* (Windhoek: Kaleni Kollektive) (2019): 40–49 and map insert.

Katjavivi, Peter. *A History of Resistance in Namibia*. Oxford: James Currey, 1988.

Mburumba, Kerina. *Namibia: The Making of a Nation*. New York: Books in Focus, 1981.

Sankara, Thomas. *Thomas Sankara Speaks: The Burkina Faso Revolution 1983–87*. Translated by Samantha Anderson. New York: Pathfinder, 1988.

"Critical Realisms" in *Savera*

Mapping an Evolution of Progressive Urdu Literature in Post-partition India

Areej Akhtar, Javaria Ahmad, and Sana Farrukh Khan

The epistemic boundaries that determine the various social and intellectual inquiries through which we theorize about our world are delineated almost exclusively by Euro-American systems of knowledge. Therefore, the Global South is rendered a blank epistemological canvas that passively receives and co-opts Euro-American formulations of the world but is inherently incapable of producing its own political idioms, visions, and theories. Excavating the region's intellectual traditions unveils a vast array of anticolonial, nationalist, socialist, secularist, and Marxist theorizations that are not merely native derivations of Euro-American concepts but alternative ways of thinking about the individual and community.[1] The primary aim of this teaching tool is therefore to curate an archive of the Global South's indigenous political vocabulary that destabilizes hierarchies of colonial epistemology.

The tool's regional focus on the anticolonial politics of India invites readers to think about the Global South as not just a theorized but a theorizing space. India's long-standing history of colonial incursions spans over four centuries, with the period of the British Raj from 1858 to 1947 witnessing various imaginations of decolonization, nationalism, secularism, and socialism, among others, that form the region's vast repertoire of resistance visions. These visions particularly flourished in the years leading up to and following what is called the 1947 partition of India. This refers to the geographical division of the subcontinent into the sovereign states of India and

Radical History Review
Issue 150 (October 2024)   DOI 10.1215/01636545-11257486
© 2024 by MARHO: The Radical Historians' Organization, Inc.

Pakistan, with Hindu and Sikh areas assigned to the former and Muslim-majority provinces to the latter. The prelude to partition consisted of mounting nationalist and anticolonial fervor in India, as demonstrated by the founding of two competing political parties, the Indian National Congress led by Hindus and the All-India Muslim League for Muslims, both of which eventually formed the political governance of nascent India and Pakistan, respectively.[2]

This period in Indian colonial history was also characterized by an unprecedented literary fecundity through which diverse political idioms of nationhood, progressivism, language, gender, class, and ethnicity were discursively constituted and debated to facilitate communal rebuilding in the postcolonial context. The inauguration of the Progressive Writers' Association (PWA) in 1936 in Lucknow, India, by a group of writers committed to mining literature's revolutionary potential for social transformation is a crucial signifier of the subcontinent's diverse history of revolutionary politics.[3] This radical literary movement sought to critique and expose the inequities structurally built into native systems of class, gender, ethnicity, language, and nationality in Indian society through critical literary interventions. Writing primarily in Urdu, one of the native languages of India, progressive writers experimented with various literary techniques and forms; the mimesis of social realities that is at the heart of realism was no longer adequate since a critique and potential reformation of these realities was also aimed for. Therefore, India's encounter with the empire and the unique sociohistorical circumstances it produced in its wake birthed a new literary genre, critical realism, which can be seen as the cultural by-product of a society undergoing a colossal transformation—from colonial subordination to postcolonial rebuilding.

Coined by Ahmed Ali, one of the founding members of the PWA, "critical realism" can be seen as a politico-literary category that was occupied not just with the criticism of the colonial "other" but first and foremost with the criticism, interrogation, and finally, reformation of the native Indian "self."[4] Critical realist literature was therefore self-reflexive literature that compelled its readers to look "inward" at natal institutions of class, gender, language, ethnicity, and religion that contributed to social inequalities rather than simply looking "outward" at colonial wrongdoings. While the PWA introduced a new form of literary realism that located the self as a subject of both criticism and reformation, critical realism has not been recruited or studied in contemporary literary theory as canonized by the Euro-American academy.

The teaching tool seeks to rectify this lacuna by mapping the genealogy of this obscure yet revolutionary Indian literary tradition. To that end, the tool relies on the 1948 issue of *Savera* (*Dawn*), a left-wing Urdu literary magazine published by Naya Idara Publications under the editorship of three chief PWA members, Ahmed Nadeem Qasmi, Zaheer Kashmiri, and Arif Mateen (fig. 1). By providing English translations of selected pieces from the magazine and supplementing them with a

Figure 1. *Savera* cover, 1966. The image was obtained from Rekhta Urdu archive and is in the public domain.

comparative literary analysis, the tool becomes a literary archive through which an anticolonial Indian history can be accessed and read in a manner that departs from the normative teleological structures of studying history. For example, a short story published in the magazine, "A Letter from a Prostitute," centers around two Hindu and Muslim girls who end up in a dilapidated brothel in Bombay through a series of abductions in the wake of the sectarian violence of 1947. The translated excerpts and thematic contextualization of the story presented in the tool open new methods for examining and uncovering the neglected violent histories of Indian and Pakistani gendered nationalisms. Similarly, poems from the magazine are translated and analyzed to reconstruct the peripheral history of the refugees produced in the wake of the migration between India and Pakistan. The tool is therefore a way of reading into and reading through literature alternative histories of colonial India that depart from state-sanctioned or imperial narratives of national histories.

Despite *Savera*'s centrality to experiments in critical realism across the genres of poetry, prose, and drama, the near absence of scholarship on it that we witnessed during the compilation of this tool demonstrates not just the academic reluctance to mine Global Southern intellectual histories for political theorization but also the systemic denigration of certain sources or forms of knowledge in favor of others. Existing knowledge of the partition of India, its political idioms, or anticolonial cultural productions is studied through standardized sources which are often researched, reviewed, published, and disseminated within and by the Euro-American academy itself. What constitutes an academic source is therefore predetermined by an epistemological hierarchy that is subverted through this tool's use of an unorthodox academic source—the magazine. The tool aims to create a decolonial literary pedagogy that catapults to the forefront a hidden curriculum of India's revolutionary print culture. In doing so, it reveals the possibility of uncovering new political concepts in the intellectual history of the Global South that may enrich and expand the study of humanities in the contemporary academy.

Areej Akhtar is a senior at the Lahore University of Management Sciences (LUMS) majoring in English literature and minoring in religion. Her undergraduate thesis centers on the genre of harem literature, focusing particularly on the construction of the Muslim women's sensuality through the spatial and gendered category of the "Orient." She is currently a research assistant at the Speculative Literature Foundation, Chicago.

Javaria Ahmad is an anthropology/sociology graduate and a qualitative researcher with a minor in education from LUMS. Currently serving as an instructional design partner, Javaria is interested in researching and reforming classroom pedagogy; her other research interests include subaltern and postcolonial studies and the experiences of marginalized communities, especially women and religious minorities in South Asia.

Sana Farrukh currently resides in Lahore, Pakistan. They graduated from Lahore University of Management Sciences with a bachelor's degree in political science and plan to pursue a career in Pakistan civil services. They took part in the Revolutionary Papers issue on critical realism in the subcontinent as a part of their print cultures course final project.

Notes

1. Menon, *Changing Theory*, 7.
2. Khan, *Great Partition*, 26.
3. Gopal, *Literary Radicalism in India*, 17.
4. Gopal, *Literary Radicalism in India*, 14.

References

Gopal, Priyamvada. *Literary Radicalism in India: Gender, Nation, and the Transition to Independence*. London: Routledge, 2013.

Khan, Yasmin. *The Great Partition: The Making of India and Pakistan*. New Haven, CT: Yale University Press, 2017.

Menon, Dilip M., ed. *Changing Theory: Concepts from the Global South*. Johannesburg: Wits University Press, 2022.

APSI

Studying the Underground Critiques
of an Overground Magazine

Pablo Álvarez and Francisco Rodriguez

Between 1973 and 1990, the military dictatorship in Chile became one of the most ferocious regimes during the "hot" Cold War in the Southern Cone. Spaces of criticism and resistance were heavily restricted because of censorship and crackdown by Pinochet. In 1975 this led to the shutdown of human rights organizations like Comité Pro Paz. By the end of the 1970s and the beginning of the 1980s, however, increased international pressure forced the Pinochet regime to open up some space, albeit limited. Former journalists and members of the Comité who had experienced exile and repression at the hands of the junta joined forces to found *APSI*, or Agencia Publicitaria de Servicios Informativos. With the help of a small international grant, *APSI* was initially given permission to publish international news and became one of a handful of magazines allowed to circulate. In this teaching tool, we show how this permission to operate in the open was deployed to surreptitiously circulate subversive criticism of the Pinochet regime. The teaching tool offers us a route into studying the concept of "underground" criticism in a magazine otherwise overground.

The legal status offered by the junta to magazines like *APSI* served to camouflage the regime's authoritarian practices. Yet *APSI* was constantly harassed by the military government and for some periods even shut down. *APSI* used this constant shift between being legal and illegal to articulate resistance. It used the legal consent provided by the junta to construct a dissident narrative against the regime. As a

Radical History Review

Issue 150 (October 2024)   DOI 10.1215/01636545-11257499

© 2024 by MARHO: The Radical Historians' Organization, Inc.

result, *APSI* was able to produce sensitive and critical material against the dictatorship by skillfully deploying the legal status provided by that very same junta as shown in figure 1.

One of the key ways it did this was by initially sticking to reporting on international affairs, which was its initial purpose and original remit. Critical news about the world became a means through which the magazine fostered transnational, counterinstitutional networks in different regions like Africa, the Middle East, Asia, and other corners of Latin America. News about Argentina, South Africa, Palestine, and Vietnam became a prominent feature on the pages of *APSI*. *APSI*'s writing, however, reflected a politics of international solidarity with other sites of "hot" Cold Wars and anticolonial and anti-authoritarian politics across the globe. Critical articles on apartheid in South Africa and voices in *APSI* condemning the Israeli occupation of Palestine were a constant feature, earning it its reputation as an international magazine. This concern for the Third World and the nonaligned movement reflected progressive thinking in Latin America and was widely considered part of a broader anti-dictatorship politics.

A close look at *APSI* shows us how an overground, anti-authoritarian publishing organization framed global news to shape critical ideas about authoritarianism and oppression at a time when such topics were banned in local political conversations within the country. *APSI* can contribute to understanding the main issues that constituted Chile's anti-dictatorship politics through tracking the conversations it tried to open up using news on international events. *APSI*'s trajectory and content can help unpack how anti-dictatorial publishing groups operated in Chile and how they ensured the circulation of content otherwise considered incendiary. Over time, this focus on international issues gave way to a focus on local issues as *APSI* started touching on topics like the economy, local politics, and popular culture. These topics merged creatively and unexpectedly on the magazine's pages as part of *APSI*'s broader anti-dictatorial politics.

The present teaching tool can help unpack key concerns central to the formation of anti-dictatorial publishing groups across Chile. Through three thematic sections—focusing on censorship, critiques of neoliberalism, and internationalism—the tool allows users to navigate how *APSI* presented left critiques and ideas through sarcasm and mockery of Pinochet's self-representation. Humor was one of the ways in which *APSI* circumvented Pinochet's censorship machinery. Following the controversial approval of the new constitution in 1980, when the regime doubled down on its authoritarian practices, Pinochet sat at the helm of the presidency of Chile and cultivated an image of statesmanship. A cult of personality emerged around Pinochet, painting him as a selfless statesman rising above the political fray. Of course, mocking him through humor was risky, becoming a severe offense that chanced censorship and persecution. *APSI* remained undeterred, introducing humorous sections after the first days of massive protests in 1983. The first cartoonists joined *APSI* in 1979, and Juan

Figure 1. *APSI*, no. 136 (1984). This cover shows how much potential a researcher can obtain by analyzing *APSI* magazine. It shows the courage to expose a subject vetoed by the dictatorship in a time of great turmoil.

Guillermo Tejeda began to depict influential politicians worldwide. In this environment, caricature of Pinochet became a poignant form of expression that reflected the anti-dictatorship politics of *APSI*. A notable example is issue 171 of 1986, which shows Pinochet as a dancer, playfully undermining his supposed solemnity.

The role of humor as a tool against the dictatorship has often been overlooked in Chilean historiography. While historians and academics have underscored the significance of popular culture and the various forms of entertainment as one of the mechanisms employed by the dictatorship to divert attention, they have paid less attention to the potential of humor to undermine the regime's censorship.

The founders of *APSI* were young individuals who experienced the end of Allende's socialist dream. Their early opposition to the dictatorship's neoliberalism exemplifies their commitment to the ideals of democratization and socialist renewal.

As we illustrate, *APSI* reported on events in the country and the world, making visible ideas considered subversive by the dictatorship. Intellectuals, politicians, and journalists had a space in *APSI* to write ideas that allowed them to counteract the regime's policies.

A study of this magazine is a starting point to unpack the effects of anti-dictatorial voices during the dictatorship in Chile. *APSI*'s history challenges a simplistic binary between the legal and illegal in the history of anti-dictatorial journalism in Latin America. The dialectical relationship between the "legal" status of *APSI* and the critical voices against the junta that emerged from its weekly publications offer us a new approach to understand how "underground" voices emerged on the pages of a heavily censored overground publication, made possible as a result of international pressure on the military dictatorship. *APSI* was a collective project of men and women who experienced the violence of the military dictatorship from day one. Its transformation from an international affairs magazine into an anti-dictatorial publishing house expresses the path that the Chilean Left walked as a part of a broader anti-dictatorial movement in Chile.

Pablo Álvarez has a PhD in social sciences from the University of Chile. Currently he is researcher and professor at Universidad Diego Portales in Santiago de Chile. His main topic of interest is international relations and contemporary history, with a focus on the political history of the twentieth-century nonaligned movement.

Francisco Rodriguez is a PhD student in history at the State University of New York, currently researching the cultural and social relations between the communities of the Arab diaspora in Latin America, with a focus on the conformation of cultural and political identity during the twentieth century.

Teaching International Solidarity through *Lotus: Afro-Asian Writings*

Sara Marzagora and Rafeef Ziadah

Lotus was the trilingual (Arabic, English, and French) journal published by the Afro-Asian Writers Association from 1968 to 1991 (fig. 1). Initially headquartered in Cairo, but with the French and English editions printed out of East Germany, the journal relocated to Beirut in 1973 following Anwar Sadat's peace treaty with Israel and the consequent Arab boycott of Egypt, and again to Tunis in 1982 following the Israeli invasion of Lebanon. Issues of the magazine ranged between 80 and 150 pages and were richly illustrated throughout. *Lotus* provided the means for cultural producers across anticolonial struggles to share knowledge, theorize, and build relations. In the pages of *Lotus*, artists and writers from all over Africa and Asia promoted anticolonial militancy through poetry, short stories, visual arts, and essays. Crucially, they attempted to build connections among newly decolonized peoples and those still struggling for independence. *Lotus* is therefore a project of intellectual, political, and aesthetic internationalism, which promoted solidarity as an editorial praxis, debated it theoretically, and textualized it as genre and form.

From this point of view, *Lotus* offers students and educators a vast archive to analyze the relationship between anticolonial scholarship, anticolonial creativity, and anticolonial militancy.[1] Rather than a top-down study of the period of decolonization through the prism of the Cold War, military alliances, diplomatic treaties, and international legislation, *Lotus* offers more bottom-up histories and a different entry point, through literature and art, to understand how Afro-Asian solidarity was

Radical History Review

Issue 150 (October 2024)   DOI 10.1215/01636545-11257512

© 2024 by MARHO: The Radical Historians' Organization, Inc.

conjured up and produced in practice.[2] The magazine testifies to a socialist vision of global transformation that entailed a commitment to learning each other's languages, sustaining cooperation across vast and often fraught geographies, and finding words and arguments for each other's struggles. Contributors argued explicitly that the structural nature of racist and colonial oppression requires us to think and write comparatively. For this reason, Hala Halim argued that *Lotus* provides an "alternative . . . line of descent" for the field of comparative literature, one that sees the discipline emerging out of the anticolonial, anti-Eurocentric movements in the Global South.[3] As part of its structural analysis, *Lotus* also articulated powerful literary and artistic critiques of development and underdevelopment, which alert international development students to the political economy of race and racialization, and to the relationship between global capitalism and (neo)colonialism. In this sense, *Lotus* lends itself to advancing a more critical pedagogy in both of our disciplines: comparative literature and international development.

As a teaching device, *Lotus* itself urges its readers to look outside the classroom, and students can find in *Lotus* a template to think about the continuity of colonial and racist power configurations, on the one hand, and of the connected struggles against them, on the other.[4] Our students, for example, immediately situated the 2020–21 Black Lives Matter movement and the Palestinian solidarity protests in the UK as part of the political lineage of the time of *Lotus*. The contradictions, tensions, and potential limitations of the *Lotus* project are, of course, part of the legacy of the journal,[5] and they provide a framework for researchers and students to critically appraise the unfinished character of the project of anticolonial solidarity.

In its centering of anticolonial resistance and countering of Eurocentric historiography, *Lotus* pedagogically advances the efforts to decolonize the university and university curricula, while also providing some of the tools needed to oppose their institutional co-optation. A "decolonization" of knowledge production entails questioning the material processes through which history and memory are produced, destroyed, and silenced; *Lotus* bore witness to some of these processes. The *Lotus* archive today is scattered and incomplete, partly as a result of those same colonial geographies that the magazine set out to oppose and that forced its operations to relocate twice. Nearly every issue of *Lotus* centered Palestinian liberation as an urgent Afro-Asian demand, but studying the history of this solidarity comes up against the 1982 Israeli destruction and looting of the PLO archive in Beirut.[6] More of that destruction is being wrought as we write this piece, as the son of Muin Bseiso, the Palestinian poet who edited the Arabic version of *Lotus* in its Beirut years, is trying to save his father's papers from the bombs and displacement of Israel's attack on Gaza.[7]

Finally, not only does *Lotus* teach how to *think* solidarity, but it also interpellates its readers on the necessity to *do* solidarity. The printed words in *Lotus* keep referring the readers back to the sociohistorical context beyond the page, and the

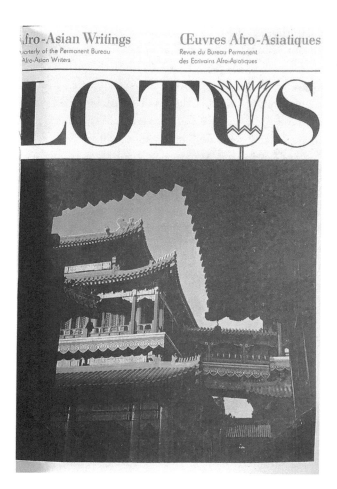

Figure 1. Cover of one of the French and English issues of *Lotus*.

intentional sociohistorical embeddedness of the journal comes with a call to act toward social transformation. And just as this literary internationalism was the product of extensive collective work, *Lotus* can prompt researchers and students to work collaboratively in the present, including across languages. The praxis of solidarity that the *Lotus* contributors incite is accessible to present-day students, and the questions that students would need to articulate if asked to replicate the *Lotus* editorial experience in the present—about the political and intellectual basis of working *with* others and *for* others—are themselves already part of that praxis.

Our teaching tool is the outcome of a collaborative project at King's College London, involving the Department of Languages, Literatures and Cultures and the Department of International Development.[8] *Lotus* had, at its core, an educational thrust, and our choice to work on this journal comes from recognizing that this educational thrust has not run out of salience in the present. Together with students, we examined how we can effectively use the literary and artistic archives of Afro-Asian solidarity to challenge historical and present colonial structures and racial discrimination. The images throughout our online teaching tool are from the exhibition created by the students as part of this project. Students worked directly with graphic designer Toka Alhamzawey to select pages and texts from *Lotus*, group them under thematic rubrics, and organize them visually for public display. The teaching tool offers background information on *Lotus* and the history of the Afro-Asian Writers' Association, with a reading guide featuring existing scholarly publications related to the magazine, and sets out the key findings of our project. We were particularly keen to document how the students established extensive connections between the anticolonial struggles of the time of *Lotus* and contemporary social justice movements. Based on our experience, we then advance some general considerations on the pedagogical importance of anticolonial archives and provide some initial suggestions of specific ways *Lotus* may be used in the classroom. Through the teaching tool, we aim to facilitate conversations, in academia and beyond, about the enduring legacies of colonialism and racism, while also shedding light on how movements for justice have envisioned and strived to build a better world through militant words, images, and actions.

Sara Marzagora is senior lecturer in comparative literature at King's College, London. She specializes in global intellectual history and the history of political thought, with a particular focus on Ethiopia and the Horn of Africa.

Rafeef Ziadah is senior lecturer in politics and public policy at King's College, London. She specializes in political economy, gender, and race, with a particular focus on the Middle East and East Africa.

Notes

1. We have both published pedagogical reflections on *Lotus*; see Desai and Ziadah, "*Lotus* and Its Afterlives"; and Abdelkhalek and Marzagora, "Afro-Asian Solidarity in the Classroom."
2. For the need to move away from the high diplomacy of, for example, the 1955 Bandung Conference toward more bottom-up perspectives on the Cold War, see Lewis and Stolte, "Other Bandungs."
3. Halim, "*Lotus*, the Afro-Asian Nexus."
4. Hope, "This Tree Needs Water!"
5. Fatima, "Institutionalizing Afro-Asianism."
6. Sleiman, "The Paper Trail of a Liberation Movement."
7. Elhalaby, "Our Siege Is Long."
8. For a report on the project, see Marzagora and Ziadah, "Inclusive Pedagogy."

References

Abdelkhalek, Malak, and Sara Marzagora. "Afro-Asian Solidarity in the Classroom: Internationalist Pedagogy and the Journal *Lotus*." In *Handbook of Transnational Periodical Studies*, edited by Marianne Van Remoortel and Fionnuala Dillane. London: Brill (forthcoming).

Desai, Chandni, and Rafeef Ziadah. "*Lotus* and Its Afterlives: Memory, Pedagogy, and Anticolonial Solidarity." *Curriculum Inquiry* 52, no. 3 (2022): 289–301.

Elhalaby, Esmat. "Our Siege Is Long." *Public Books*, October 27, 2023. https://www.publicbooks
.org/our-siege-is-long/.

Fatima, Maryam. "Institutionalizing Afro-Asianism: *Lotus* and the (Dis)contents of Soviet–
Third World Cultural Politics." *Comparative Literature Studies* 59, no. 3 (2022): 447–67.

Halim, Hala. "*Lotus*, the Afro-Asian Nexus, and Global South Comparatism." *Comparative
Studies of South Asia, Africa and the Middle East* 32, no. 3 (2012): 563–83.

Hope, Jeanelle K. "This Tree Needs Water! A Case Study on the Radical Potential of Afro-Asian
Solidarity in the Era of Black Lives Matter." *Amerasia Journal* 45, no. 2 (2019): 222–37.

Lewis, Su Lin, and Carolien Stolte. "Other Bandungs: Afro-Asian Internationalisms in the Early
Cold War." *Journal of World History* 30, nos. 1–2 (2019): 1–19.

Marzagora, Sara, and Rafeef Ziadah. "Inclusive Pedagogy: Integrating Cultural Production
and Anti-colonial Archives." King's Research Portal, 2022. https://kclpure.kcl.ac.uk/ws
/portalfiles/portal/184662511/Final_Lotus_toolkit.pdf.

Sleiman, Hana. "The Paper Trail of a Liberation Movement." *Arab Studies Journal* 24, no. 1
(2016): 42–67.

Revolutionary Print Culture in the Arabian Peninsula

Introduction to the *Sawt al-Thawra* Teaching Tool

Marral Shamshiri

Education will either contribute to the complex dynamics of the reproduction
of imperialism, as it has often done, or be a powerful force in creating a new
world free from exploitation, oppression and destruction.
—Sara Carpenter and Shahrzad Mojab, *Revolutionary Learning*

In April 2022 I presented a teaching tool on the periodical *Sawt al-Thawra* (*Voice of the Revolution*) at the Revolutionary Papers conference in Cape Town, South Africa. *Sawt al-Thawra* was a weekly bulletin published in the 1970s by the anticolonial liberation movement in Dhufar, Oman, led by the Popular Front for the Liberation of Oman and the Arabian Gulf (PFLOAG), or Jabhah al-Shaʿbīyah li-Taḥrīr ʿUmān wa-al-Khalīj al-ʿArabī in Arabic. When I first found this periodical while doing my PhD research, I was amazed at how a little-known revolutionary movement in the Gulf was deeply connected to left-wing currents across the world. *Sawt al-Thawra* articulated the PFLOAG's revolutionary conception of the world and placed the Dhufar Revolution in conversation with the global constellation of revolutionary Third World, leftist, and anticolonial networks.

One of the obscured chapters in Britain's imperial past is its colonial policies in Oman during the nineteenth and twentieth centuries, and in particular, the British role in crushing the anticolonial revolutionary movement in Dhufar between

Radical History Review
Issue 150 (October 2024)   DOI 10.1215/01636545-11257525
© 2024 by MARHO: The Radical Historians' Organization, Inc.

1965 and 1976.[1] In the era of formal decolonization and the declining power of the British Empire, an eleven-year guerrilla war sought to liberate Dhufar from British-backed sultanic rule, marking the region as the epicenter of the anticolonial and left-wing revolutionary movement in the Arabian Peninsula. However, a British-led colonial counterinsurgency eventually defeated the revolutionary movement in Dhufar with the assistance of regional and mercenary forces including Iran and Jordan. In the face of this military defeat, *Sawt al-Thawra* is an important archival source that presents an abundance of information, detail, and documentary evidence on both the colonial counterinsurgency and the PFLOAG's activities and international connections; forming a rich and complex counternarrative to the largely concealed British account.

The British-led counterinsurgency in Oman is most frequently found in specialized British military history and Cold War syllabi, which typically focus on the practice, strategies, and success of the counterinsurgency from the British perspective. In 2013, Abdel Razzaq Takriti's trailblazing monograph *Monsoon Revolution* read the history of the Dhufar Revolution against the grain of colonial archives and used primary and secondary sources produced by the revolutionary movement. Takriti recovered the history of the most significant revolutionary movement in the Arabian Peninsula from the binds of British small wars and counterinsurgency historiography, placing Dhufar within a global history of British imperialism, revolutionary movements in the Arab world, and the South-South revolutionary transnationalism of the 1960s. In the historiography of the modern Middle East, this study opened the path for the history of left-wing movements in the Arabian Peninsula, and more widely, the history of decolonization and revolution in and beyond the Middle East in the global 1960s and 1970s. Yet these historical approaches remain marginalized in relation to the dominant frameworks used to study the Middle East today, such as authoritarianism, Islamism, sectarianism, and oil.

In an academic setting, the *Sawt al-Thawra* teaching tool aims to aid the existing literature on the Dhufar Revolution and the histories of the Left, anticolonialism, and the global 1960s and 1970s. It allows users of the tool to read selected content from the revolutionary periodical *Sawt al-Thawra* and to crucially understand the periodical in its social and historical context. *Sawt al-Thawra*'s pages (fig. 1) were filled with news items, articles, reports, and interviews concerning not only the revolution, military operations, and the counterinsurgency and its collaborators, but also connections with and mentions of global revolutionary movements and socialist states across the world. By presenting the transnational and transregional networks and conversations that the periodical was a part of, the tool breaks away from disciplinary silos, taking histories of the Middle East out of an "area studies" framework and toward a global history framework. It also attempts to bridge linguistic barriers by presenting Arabic-language sources with translated excerpts. In this way, the tool is of interest not only to those interested in Middle Eastern history but

Figure 1. *Sawt al-Thawra*, no. 84, December 29, 1973. Courtesy of Special Collections, University of Exeter.

also to students, movements, and activists interested in how anticolonial and Third Worldist movements, international solidarity networks, and the question of women's liberation took shape in the Arabian Peninsula.

The *Sawt al-Thawra* teaching tool builds on existing historical research to present primary source material from the revolutionary movement in Dhufar and connected movements in a digital form. This format allows anyone with stable internet access to see the material. As Lara Putnam has argued, digitization has "transformed historians' practice in ways that facilitate border-crossing research."[2] While these primary sources are typically available to the public, many barriers still exist in terms of who gets to engage in "border-crossing research"; those without a formal affiliation or with constraints on funding or international travel cannot easily access these archives, and the bulk of historical research remains behind paywalls in journal articles and expensive academic books. The digital format of the tool, along with the pedagogical initiative of the Revolutionary Papers project more broadly, goes some way toward democratizing access to British, Omani, and global history archives. It challenges how the conservative discipline of history has traditionally gatekept and suppressed archives, sources, and narratives of the past and maintained what Mojab and Carpenter refer to as the reproduction of imperial power.[3]

By focusing on the revolutionary paper as a central thread and historical object, the teaching tool ties in a number of visual materials—photocopied pamphlets, posters, images, and other sources gathered from various archives. Some of these materials, namely *Sawt al-Thawra*, have been used in existing historical research, while other sources are newly unearthed in the research detailed in the tool. All of the primary source material presented in the tool is published in a visual format for the first time—a form that disrupts the traditional text-based approach to learning and allows contextualized global history to be taught in a dynamic and lively way. For example, the tool describes the organized global network of committees in solidarity with the revolution in Dhufar and the Gulf, and highlights the covers and contents pages of issues of *Gulf Solidarity*, a periodical published by a support committee in California, USA, which reprinted excerpts from *Sawt al-Thawra* in English to "encourage active support for the revolution in the Gulf." Visual primary sources such as cover artwork, posters, and photographs are often neglected in political history, which favors the written word in both research output and in the teaching materials used in our syllabi. The tool is instead designed to allow users and educators in particular to teach the history of anticolonial movements with a focus on the visual history of materials produced in the 1970s.

I hope that the *Sawt al-Thawra* teaching tool supplements teaching and learning on the Dhufar Revolution, global history, anticolonialism and decolonization, social and political movements, and revolutionary print culture in the global 1970s—from the perspective of the liberation movements who fought for new worlds from below, and for those who continue to organize and mobilize on various fronts today.

Marral Shamshiri is a PhD candidate in international history at the London School of Economics and Political Science (LSE). She is coeditor of the book *She Who Struggles: Revolutionary Women Who Shaped the World* (2023). Her recent writing and research has been published in *Comparative Studies of South Asia, Africa and the Middle East*; *History Workshop* magazine; *Kohl: A Journal for Body and Gender Research*; Revolutionary Papers; and *Silver Press* blog.

Notes

1. Oman was then known as the "Sultanate of Muscat and Oman," as designated by the British in the mid-nineteenth century, and Dhufar was a dependency of the sultanate. Takriti, *Monsoon Revolution*, 15.
2. Putnam, "The Transnational and the Text-Searchable," 377.
3. Carpenter and Mojab, *Revolutionary Learning*, 126.

References

Carpenter, Sara, and Shahrzad Mojab. *Revolutionary Learning: Marxism, Feminism and Knowledge*. London: Pluto Press, 2017.

Putnam, Lara. "The Transnational and the Text-Searchable: Digitized Sources and the Shadows They Cast." *American Historical Review* 121, no. 2 (2016): 377–402.

Takriti, Abdel Razzaq. *Monsoon Revolution: Republicans, Sultans, and Empires in Oman, 1965–1976*. Oxford: Oxford University Press, 2013.

Manasheer al-Intifada

Bayan no.1 (UNLI), Palestine

Thayer Hastings

How to Read a *Bayan*

The first Intifada, 1987–93, was one of the most heavily documented social movements of the twentieth century. The *bayanat*, or communiqués, of the first Intifada were used to organize the everyday life of what emerged as a mass popular uprising of Palestinians against repressive Israeli military rule. While the *bayan* (sing.) form has a long and broad history in Arabic textual culture and political thought, the Intifada *bayanat* (pl.) were particular to the moment and hence are known in Palestinian discourse as the "Intifada leaflets" or *manasheer al-Intifada* (fig. 1). The *bayanat* were not the only defining media of the Intifada but were one among many vehicles for political communication, such as graffiti and posters, photography and news coverage, and statements from bodies like the Palestine Liberation Organization or the Israeli military government. The *bayanat* were also central to the materiality of the Intifada, which included house demolitions, checkpoints, barricades, and the rocks used by Palestinians to defend their communities from the Israeli military and police. Within that proliferation of media and material, what does analyzing communiqués, and one communiqué in particular, do for an understanding of the Intifada and for revolutionary history? This project poses an answer to this question by detailing the form and content of the *bayan* in relation to the broader uprising. Highlighting a single *bayan* authored by the underground anonymous

Radical History Review
Issue 150 (October 2024)   DOI 10.1215/01636545-11257538
© 2024 by MARHO: The Radical Historians' Organization, Inc.

Palestinian leadership, the United National Leadership of the Intifada (UNLI), the first *bayan* in most chronologies, offers a methodology for engaging with the body of Intifada *bayanat* as a source.

A study of this *bayan* enables an understanding of the materiality of the *bayanat* in general: the paper they were printed on and their destruction as a measure against arrest by the Israeli military. Imprisonment, the punishment for being caught with a *bayan*, meant that most copies of the hundreds of thousands printed were destroyed. The illicit nature of these texts contributes to why they are largely unknown outside the Palestinian context. Nonetheless, the serialized and widely distributed *bayanat* became central documents to and a form of documentation for the uprising. Slogans spray-painted onto walls in cities, villages, and the camps made their way into paper form in the *bayanat*, signed, as the one presented here was, "until the fall of the Occupation." Likewise, linguistic features of the *bayanat*, such as the header that announced itself through repetition: "a call . . . a call . . . a call," became iconic utterances that continue to index the first Intifada and its will to action. Despite the illicit and ephemeral quality of the original *bayanat*, the correlating web pages gesture toward how digital versions of the communiqués circulate among Palestinians. The *bayanat* have shaped the way Palestinians collectively remember and interpret the first Intifada. Attending to the design and social features of the *bayanat* also opens the possibility of comparing paper and digital mediums for political communication and organizing.

The *bayanat* are one starting point for understanding how a popular uprising was lived and how it evolved on an everyday basis. This specific *bayan*, distributed on January 8, 1988, one month into the Intifada, offers insights into uprising tactics like general strikes or road sabotage and into the organizations that were involved, such as the popular committees and strike forces. It deepens understanding of how information circulated, the political ethos of the uprising, its gender dynamics, and the language and rhetoric of the Intifada. The *bayan* indexes a scale at the level of the street: those who could be reached through the physical distribution or posting of paper documents, via word of mouth, or those who would have listened to them read aloud on local radio stations. The result of this local scale was more than the creation of an audience through reception or consumption of information; rather it involved the formation of a participatory, entangled, and cocreated public.

The *bayanat* demonstrate in very practical ways how a public—that is, the rebellious Palestinian public who together forged and sustained the Intifada—was mediated and therefore took shape. Participants in the Intifada created this public in part by circulating, concealing, reading, and implementing calls to action articulated in the *bayanat*. The January 8 *bayan* called for "all sectors of our heroic people everywhere [to] commit to the call for a complete general strike, from the date of 11 January 1988 through the evening of Wednesday 13 January 1988." This three-day general strike was widely upheld across the West Bank and Gaza Strip. It was also

Figure 1. This is a scanned image of a *bayan* (communiqué or leaflet) from the first Intifada. It was distributed on January 8, 1988, in the first days of the popular uprising throughout Palestine.

punished by the Israeli military government through mass arrests, use of force that resulted in dozens of injuries to protesting Palestinians, and comprehensive curfews imposed on fifteen refugee camps as well as parts of the city of Ramallah. In this context, the January 8 *bayan* served as a key medium for coordinating collective action and the cohesion of a rebellious public.

The *bayanat*, then, are public documents in and of themselves—ones that, over the years of the Intifada, could be followed or ignored, imitated or undermined, enforced or rejected. This single-page *bayan* alone gestures toward many directions of social innovation and alternative world making. The collective projects glimpsed in the *bayan* include an ethics of refusing Israeli military rule, and the popular committees that presented alternatives to forms of social reproduction under settler colonialism and capitalism more broadly. The *bayan* also refers to the labor of revolution by describing the leaflet as a "work program" inclusive of all members of Palestinian society. Whether enacted or never fully realized, the collective projects gestured to in the *bayan* are indicative of needs and conversations that grew out of and took form in the Intifada context. Because these documents proliferated widely over multiple years, and Palestinians across social sectors responded to the calls for action contained in them, taken together, the *bayanat* can be read as key political texts of the Intifada era. Studying this particular *bayan* enables an understanding of the transformative early Intifada environment, where new political horizons and realities became possible.

Thayer Hastings is a PhD candidate in the anthropology department at the CUNY Graduate Center in New York City with a focus on political anthropology of the Middle East. His dissertation explores the sensibilities and sensory experiences of documents and evidence inflected by colonial bureaucratic anxieties. It interrogates ideas of mobility, sovereignty, and political ethics from the vantage of Palestinian Jerusalem.

Regimes and Resistance

Kenya's Resistance History through Underground and Alternative Publications

Njoki Wamai and Kimani Waweru

The Revolutionary Papers Teaching Tool "Regimes and Resistance: Kenya's Resistance History through Underground and Alternative Publications" was created to counter the deliberate invisibility of the history of resistance by the Kenyan Left after 1963, when the British colonial occupation ended following a violent liberation struggle led by the Kenya Land and Freedom Army (popularly known as Mau Mau). Alternative movements and the radical publications they produced tell a different story from the dominant narratives advanced by the right-wing authoritarian regimes of Jomo Kenyatta and Daniel Moi. These narratives of the Kenyan Left have been previously ignored, or when they have been made visible, they have been discredited as subversive threats to national security and stability in postcolonial Kenya.

Given the Cold War politics of the 1960s to the 1990s and the coups and wars that engulfed East Africa and the Horn, any dissent against the authoritarian regimes of Kenyatta and Moi was interpreted as a threat not only to national security but also to the global geopolitics of East versus West. The authoritarian regimes of Kenyatta (1963 to 1979) and Moi (1979 to 2002) were firmly on the Right, with benefits such as grants and defense partnerships with Western powers. It is against this background that the alternative movements and individuals represented in this teaching tool resisted the state. Central to these movements were newspapers and

Radical History Review

Issue 150 (October 2024)   DOI 10.1215/01636545-11257551

© 2023 by MARHO: The Radical Historians' Organization, Inc.

pamphlets. The teaching tool is framed around these alternative publications produced during different regimes. It draws on materials housed in Ukombozi Library (Kenya's first public revolutionary and socialist library), which countered the dominant colonial and postcolonial publications.

This tool maps these publications through four time periods that motivated different types of publications. The first section maps the anticolonial resistance publications produced by Africans during the colonial period (1920–63). The colonial period had two types of newspapers: those representing foreign and colonial settler interests, such as the *East African Standard*, the *Daily Nation*, and *Kenya Weekly*;[1] and those representing the interests of native Kenyans, such as *Muigwithania*, *Mumenyereri*, *Ramogi*, *Sauti ya Mwafrika*, and *Mwalimu*, among others. These African publications were mainly Kiswahili and African-language newsletters that sought to provide an update of social and political issues that concerned Africans. As the British occupation intensified, these publications became spaces for resistance writing as Africans wrote about their aspirations for freedom and reclaiming their land, leading to their banning during the 1952 state of emergency.

The second section maps leftist publications during the first postindependence Kenyatta regime between 1963 and 1978. They were produced in the context of a newly independent state, the Cold War, and an increasingly authoritarian Kenyatta regime. Left- and East-leaning politicians such as Jaramogi Odinga, Pio Gama Pinto, and Bildad Kaggia questioned Kenyatta's land policies that privileged distributing land to elites over peasants disenfranchised by the colonizers. This time period produced publications from left-leaning Marxist intellectuals, including politicians, intellectuals, academics, and journalists, against the repressive regime and right-wing politics of the Cold War which the regime supported. Publications produced were initially public documents like the Kenya Peoples Union newsletter, which published *Kenya: Twendapi?* by Abdilatif Abdalla in 1968.[2] After this publication, Abdalla became the first Kenyan to be jailed for sedition in independent Kenya in 1965 for questioning postcolonial elite greed. Other publications at that time were satirical plays by the Kenyan academics Ngũgĩ wa Thiong'o, Micere Mugo, and Ngugi wa Miiri, including *The Trial of Dedan Kimathi*. When the regime started banning publications and jailing intellectuals opposed to the increased authoritarianism these publications went underground. This led to the development of internal movement publications and the emergence of underground movements like the Workers Party and the December Twelve Movement (DTM) (Kinyatti 2008).

The third set of publications that emerged were in resistance to the second authoritarian regime of Daniel Moi (1978 to the 1990s). Publications during this time period were not markedly different from the previous time period in terms of their Marxist ideology. However, this period had a greater diversity of publications and increased distribution as antigovernment sentiment grew, especially after the attempted 1982 coup, which led to arrests and detention of leftists

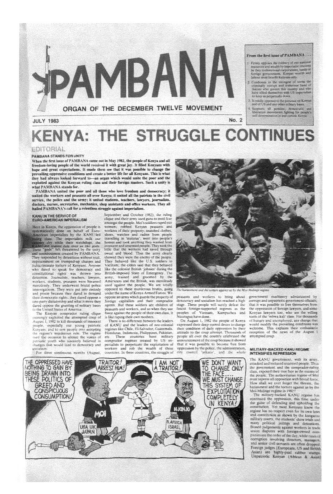

Figure 1. *Pambana: Organ of the December Twelve Movement* (Kenya), no. 2, July 1983.

including academics, journalists, students, and workers. Moi became an authoritarian dictator and his regime was characterized by the worst human rights violations in Kenya's history. It is in this period that several movements and publications emerged more visibly, including the December Twelve Movement (DTM) and *Muungano wa Wazalendo wa Kukomboa Kenya* (Mwakenya; see fig. 2); Ukenya, among Kenyans in diaspora; and Umoja. The different movements produced alternative publications including *Pambana*, an organ of DTM (fig. 1). Cheche, another publication, was also produced by DTM.[3]

On May 18, 1982, the journalist Wang'ondu wa Kariuki was arrested along with others and charged with possession of *Pambana*, becoming the first victim of Daniel Moi's sedition charges and jailing. The court had relied on decree by Moi the dictator that those found in possession of "underground papers like *Pambana*" should be convicted.[4] According to the editorial in the first issue, "*Pambana* was a

Figure 2. The Draft Minimum
Programme of Mwakenya,
Muungano wa Wazalendo wa
Kukomboa Kenya (Union of Patriots
for the Liberation of Kenya),
September 1987.

turning point in Kenya's history as a people's newspaper compared to the foreign-owned press that misrepresented Kenyan reality."[5] The editors argued that "all efforts to found a liberal press had been discouraged and thus the people's press was an underground press speaking to the majority poor, dispossessed Kenyans who have hitherto been so fully ignored" by the mainstream press such as the *Nation*, the *Standard*, and *Kenya Weekly*.[6]

Soon after the August 1982 attempted coup by air force officers, hundreds of left-leaning intellectuals and university students were arrested and charged with sedition along with many great Kenyans, and jailed between August 1982 and 1988. Kamoji Wachira, Willy Mutunga, Oduor Ong'wen, Paddy Onyango, Raila Odinga, Maina wa Kinyatti, and Kamonye Manje were among those jailed. The first group of students arrested after the coup attempt were Titus Adungosi (who later died in prison), Paddy Onyango, Joseph Hongo, Maurice Adongo Ogony, Onyango C. A.,

Oginga Ogego, Francis Kinyua, Onyango Oloo, Thomas Mutuse, Johnstone Simiyu, Jeff Mwangi, Ongele Opala, Muga K'Olale and Wahinya Bore. Another group was tortured in the regime's torture chambers in the basement of the Nyayo House before detention or release.[7] Kenyans such as Shiraz Durani, Ngugi wa Thiong'o, Micere Mugo, and Ngugi Mirii, among others, were left for exile.[8]

The fourth set of publications emerged in the 1990s, as external and internal pressure on the Moi authoritarian regime increased for reforms. This period in our teaching tool is titled "Dangerous Reading, the End of Authoritarian Rule and Democratic Reform (1990s)." Having detained and tortured most of the movement members and banned their publications, underground publications were scarcely available. Leftist journalists within mainstream organizations continued providing the much-needed space for expression despite the repressive circumstances through columns and magazines such as the *Beyond Magazine* by the National Council of Churches of Kenya, *Society Magazine*, *Viva Magazine*, *Finance*, *Nairobi Law Monthly*, and the *People Weekly Newspaper*. Once the authorities realized that neutral titles focusing on law, finance, fashion, and church matters were merely to camouflage the articles on resistance, they arrested and forced into exile most of the editors and writers involved in these magazines, including Bedan Mbugua, Mugo Theuri, Salim Lone, Njuguna Mutonya, Wahome Mutahi, Njuguna Mutahi, and Gitobu Imanyara, among others.

Ukombozi Library has grown from a physical library space hosting revolutionary material to also include a physical meeting place for social justice activists and a publishing house for socialist and leftist literature in Kenya. Social justice activists have owned the Ukombozi Library and transformed it into a revolutionary space for political education. Through the political education sessions at Ukombozi Library, a split-off library at the Mathare Social Justice Centre has been established, and publications have emerged as reflections from the reading group inspired by the Italian leftist Antonio Gramsci, now known as the Organic Intellectuals Network. Through the reading and reviewing of important books that reflect on class struggles and the quest for justice for the workers and proletariat in postcolonial Kenya, the Organic Intellectuals' Network has produced three publications.[9] In conclusion, Kenya's underground publications provide the history of Kenya's resistance against various forces including racism, colonialism, fascism, and imperialism.

Njoki Wamai, PhD, is a scholar-activist serving on the Ukombozi Library management committee and assistant professor in politics and international studies at the USIU-A, Kenya.

Kimani Waweru is the coordinator of Ukombozi Library.

Notes

1. The *Standard* (established in 1902) and the *Nation* (established in 1952) are still in existence to date. The *Standard* is the oldest newspaper; it was established as the *African*

Standard by Alibhai Mulla Jeevanjee, who later sold the paper to a British businessman in 1905, who then renamed it the *East African Standard*. These papers supported the British colonial government and were written in English, which was not commonly spoken by Africans and Asians in Kenya before the 1960s.

2. Kresse, "*Kenya: Twendapi?*"
3. Durrani, *People's Resistance to Colonialism and Imperialism in Kenya.*
4. "Kenya's 'Seditious' Paper *Pambana*."
5. "Kenya's 'Seditious' Paper *Pambana*."
6. "Kenya's 'Seditious' Paper *Pambana*."
7. For a full list of those victims arrested, confined, tortured, jailed, and deceased, see *We Lived to Tell: The Nyayo House Story*, 70–74. Publicly available at https://library.fes.de/pdf-files/bueros/kenia/01828.pdf.
8. For a full list of those victims exiled, see *We Lived to Tell: The Nyayo House Story*, 70–74. Publicly available at https://library.fes.de/pdf-files/bueros/kenia/01828.pdf.
9. Mathare Social Justice Centre, "Organic Intellectuals."

References

Durrani, Shiraz. *People's Resistance to Colonialism and Imperialism in Kenya.* Nairobi: Vita Books, 2018.

"Kenya's 'Seditious' Paper *Pambana*." *Index on Censorship* 11, no. 6 (1982): 34.

Kresse, Kai. "*Kenya: Twendapi?* Re-reading Abdilatif Abdalla's Pamphlet Fifty Years after Independence." *Africa* 86, no. 1 (2016): 1–32. https://doi.org/10.1017/S0001972015000996.

Mathare Social Justice Centre. "Organic Intellectuals." *Africa Is a Country*, November 18, 2021. https://africasacountry.com/2021/11/organic-intellectuals.

Theuri, Mugo, and Njuguna Mutahi. *We Lived to Tell: The Nyayo House Story.* Nairobi: FES, 2003. https://library.fes.de/pdf-files/bueros/kenia/01828.pdf.

Errata for Desiree Valadares, "Uneven Mobilities: Infrastructural Imaginaries on the Hope–Princeton Highway," *Radical History Review* 147 (2023): 158–85. https://doi.org/10.1215/01636545-10637232

Desiree Valadares did not acknowledge her use of Ben Bradley's book *British Columbia by the Road: Car Culture and the Making of a Modern Landscape* (Vancouver: University of British Columbia Press, 2017). She sincerely regrets this error and makes the following corrections to her article:

p. 162 The sentence following the subheading *Staging the Scenic* should read: "Ben Bradley's history of the Hope–Princeton Highway reveals that when it first opened to the public in 1949, it was considered "neither intrinsically scenic nor particularly interesting." Endnote: Bradley, *British Columbia by the Road*, 39.

p. 162 An endnote should follow the sentence, "To make this route more interesting to motorists, pullouts and overlooks were carved into the mountains." Endnote: Bradley, *British Columbia by the Road*, 39, 76–85.

p. 162 The sentence, "These two provincial agencies worked together to manage landscape experiences for motoring tourists along BC highways." should read: "As shown by Bradley, these two provincial agencies worked together to manage landscape experiences for motoring tourists along BC highways."

p. 162 An endnote should follow the sentence, "The agencies collectively proposed the creation of E. C. Manning Park, a provincial park along the Hope–Princeton route, as a backdrop that would provide both scenic vistas and recreational opportunities." Endnote: Bradley, *British Columbia by the Road*, 19–64; and Bradley, "Behind the Scenery."

p. 163 In the sentence that begins, "This 1950s brochure, published by the Daily Province . . . ," the date should be 1966, not the 1950s.

Radical History Review
Issue 150 (October 2024)   DOI 10.1215/01636545-11538317
© 2024 by MARHO: The Radical Historians' Organization, Inc.

p. 164 The caption for Figure 3 should read: "*History on the Highways*, published by BCGTB in 1966 and was created by artist Lewis Saw." The caption should have the following note: This image was reproduced from Ben Bradley's Flickr album and appears as an illustration in his book, *British Columbia by the Road*, 208. An original copy of *History on the Highways* is available at the Royal British Columbia Museum Archives.

p. 165 The caption for Figure 4 should read: "Print ads from the late 1940s by BCGTB touting 'Old mysteries in a new world,' 'Visit Alluring British Columbia Canada,' and 'British Columbia, Canada: The Vacation-Land That Has Everything.' Author's private collection."

p. 165 The first line of the third paragraph should read: "As Bradley argues, 'Motoring was a radically new way' of exploring the interior of the province of BC, and driving made motorists feel like 'active explorers' of the vast landscapes that surrounded them, rather than 'passive consumers.'" Endnote: Bradley, *British Columbia by the Road*, 3.

p. 165 An endnote should follow the sentence, "The promotion of automobile tourism in BC should be located within the larger Keynesian expansion and industrial production of roads and automobiles that occurred in the postwar period in Canada." Endnote: Dawson, *Selling British Columbia*; Bradley, *British Columbia by the Road*.

p. 166 An endnote should follow the sentence, "The creation and expansion of provincial parks and public history campaigns, such as the Stop of Interest signs program, were intimately tied to highway beautification efforts and tourism promotion along provincial roads. " Endnote: Bradley offers the first comprehensive scholarly history of the BC Stop of Interest signs, which were introduced in 1958 as a British Columbia Centennial Project. Also see earlier work by Michael Kluckner, *Vanishing British Columbia*, on "roadside memory," and BC Stop of Interest signs for the Ghost of Walhachin.

p. 168 The sentence, "The Canadian government also looked to road and railway camps for the Doukhobor people (pacifist populations of Ukrainian descent from the Austro-Hungarian empire), who were interned during World War I and whose forced labor helped to build the infrastructure around Banff National Park in Alberta." should read: "The Canadian government previously interned people of Ukrainian descent from the Austro-Hungarian empire during World War I under the War Measures Act. While interned at Castle Mountain Internment Camp, their forced labor helped to build the road infrastructure around Banff National Park in Alberta."

pp. 181–85 The following references should be added to the reference list:

Bradley, Ben. "Behind the Scenery: Manning Park and the Aesthetics of Automobile Accessibility in 1950s British Columbia." *BC Studies*, no. 170 (2011): 41–65.

Kluckner, Michael. *Vanishing British Columbia*. Vancouver: University of British Columbia Press, 2011.

Keep up to date on new scholarship

Issue alerts are a great way to stay current on all the cutting-edge scholarship from your favorite Duke University Press journals. This free service delivers tables of contents directly to your inbox, informing you of the latest groundbreaking work as soon as it is published.

To sign up for issue alerts:

1. Visit **dukeu.press/register** and register for an account. You do not need to provide a customer number.

2. After registering, visit **dukeu.press/alerts**.

3. Go to "Latest Issue Alerts" and click on "Add Alerts."

4. Select as many publications as you would like from the pop-up window and click "Add Alerts."

read.dukeupress.edu/journals